Judges in Contemporary Democracy

Judges in Contemporary Democracy

An International Conversation

Edited by
Robert Badinter *and* **Stephen Breyer**

WITH THE PARTICIPATION OF

Robert Badinter
Former President, Constitutional Council of France

Stephen Breyer
Justice, United State Supreme Court

Antonio Cassese
Former President, International Criminal Court for Former Yugoslavia

Ronald Dworkin
Professor, New York University School of Law

Dieter Grimm
Former Vice President, Constitutional Court of Germany

Gil Carlos Rodriguez Iglesias
Former President, Court of Justice of the European Communities

New York University Press • *New York and London*

NEW YORK UNIVERSITY PRESS
New York and London
www.nyupress.org

Library of Congress Cataloging-in-Publication Data
Judges in contemporary democracy : an international conversation /
edited by Robert Badinter and Stephen Breyer.
p. cm.
Includes bibliographical references and index.
ISBN 0–8147–9926–4 (cloth : alk. paper)
1. Judges.   2. Judgments.   3. Judicial process.
4. Political questions and judicial power.
I. Badinter, Robert.   II. Breyer, Stephen G., 1938–
K2146.J83   2004
347'.014—dc22   2004002925

New York University Press books are printed on acid-free paper,
and their binding materials are chosen for strength and durability.

Manufactured in the United States of America

10 9 8 7 6 5 4 3 2 1

[L]earning is not a race in which the competitors jockey for the best place, it is not even an argument or a symposium; it is a conversation. . . . [E]ach study appear[s] as a voice whose tone is neither tyrannous nor plangent, but humble and conversable. [Its effect] is not superimposed but springs from the quality of the voices which speak, and its value lies in the relics it leaves behind in the minds of those who participate.

—Michael Oakeshott, *"The Idea of a University"*

Contents

Acknowledgments

Robert Badinter and Stephen Breyer would like to thank the following for their time and assistance: Dominique Remy-Granger, Deborah Gershenowitz, Lael Yudain, Maritza Okata, Norman Dorsen, Jennifer Yoon. We also thank the Librairie Arthème Fayard–Publications de la Sorbonne, which published the French edition of this book under the title *Les Entretiens de Provence: Le juge dans la société contemporaine*. Both English and French were spoken at meetings. Dominque Remy-Granger translated the English portions into French. Stephen Breyer translated the French portions into English.

Preface

We present for the interested reader a work that does not fall within any traditional category of published material. It is neither a joint essay nor a collection of academic articles. Rather, it is the record of an organized conversation. Perhaps the closest parallel is the published account of discussions about democratic institutions conducted by former University of Chicago President Robert M. Hutchins during the 1950s and 1960s.[1]

I

The project arose through a chance meeting of friends in Paris in the spring of 1999. There we had the idea of bringing together a small group of experienced jurists to discuss the growth of judicial authority and the enhanced role of the judge in many modern Western democracies. Given the pervasive nature of the phenomenon, we thought that an exchange of views would prove fruitful, particularly if the group's members were of different nationalities and possessed experience reflecting different judicial cultures.

We drew up a list of judicial colleagues who we hoped would be able to join us the following summer. We hoped to meet in calm and pleasant surroundings. We intended our conversation, while focusing upon a subject of common interest, to seek neither finality nor shared conclusions. Rather, the conversation would find its purpose in the discussion itself—in the free exchange of thought, the interplay of ideas, the opportunities for clarification, the creation of new insights, and the excitement that accompanies intellectual stimulation and growth.

II

New York University encouraged us. We found a former farmhouse, now a small hotel, in Bonnieux, France, amidst the great scenic beauty, art, and music of Provence. And we organized our group: Antonio Cassese (Italy), former president of the International Criminal Tribunal of the former Yugoslavia; Ronald Dworkin (United States and Great Britain), professor at the New York University School of Law and professor emeritus, Oxford University; Dieter Grimm (Germany), former vice-president of the Federal Constitutional Court of Germany; Carlos Rodriguez Iglesias (Spain), President of the Court of Justice of the European Union; along with the two organizers, one a former French Minister of Justice and former President of France's Conseil Constitutionnel, the other a member of the Supreme Court of the United States.

We divided the general topic of the role of judges in contemporary democracy into six sub-topics. In an effort to stimulate discussion, each of us prepared a paper on one designated topic and circulated it to the other participants in advance of the meeting. In August 2000 we met in Bonnieux. We discussed each topic for three to four hours. Our discussions were recorded, transcribed, and edited by Dominique Remy-Granger.

III

Our basic topic—the expansion of judicial power, authority, and prestige—inevitably led us to consider ways in which the judicial system has reacted (and how perceptions of that system have changed) in response to contemporary social and political changes over the past half-century. The following are illustrative: First, consider, for example, the judge's role within the democratic political process. Long ago, Alexis de Tocqueville noted that American judges, unlike their European counterparts, were "vested with an immense political power," the "cause" of which "is in this sole fact: Americans have recognized in judges the right to found their rulings on the *Constitution* rather than on the *laws*. In other words they have permitted them not to apply laws that might appear to them unconstitutional."[2]

Today almost all Western democracies have come to believe that independent judiciaries can help to protect fundamental human rights through judicial interpretation and application of written documents containing guarantees of individual freedom. European nations have given both national and trans-national judges authority to do so, as well as to apply such "governing" documents as those that constitute the European Union. Hence, to a degree, we are all "constitutional" judges now. Do we all then necessarily play what de Tocqueville called a "political" role? Do any, or all, of us exercise a "political" authority?

More precisely, what does it mean to be a "constitutional" judge? How should a constitutional judge act? What are the proper criteria for constitutional decision-making? How do the answers vary across different societies? How do those societies consequently perceive the powers, duties, and authority of today's judge—whether or not that judge is cloaked with "constitutional" authority?

Second, consider the moral authority that a judicial decision tends to carry. One might argue that this authority has grown, whether or not deservedly so, just as the prestige and moral authority of other institutions, including religious institutions and democratically elected legislatures, has declined. If that is so, are there connections? What are the causes? What are the effects? To what extent, for example, does any such increase in the moral authority of courts reflect the fact that courts present forums open to reasoned argument, the fact that judges are anonymous, or the fact that constitutional decision-making may intermingle morality and law?

Third, consider the relationship between the judiciary and institutions that shape the public's political perceptions, particularly the media. To what extent do the media depend upon the judiciary for protection of their own necessary freedom? To what extent is the media responsible for the public's perception of the judiciary as honest, non-political, and fair? To what extent are these two circumstances linked? To what extent does, or should, favorable reporting matter to the judiciary as a special kind of governmental institution?

These general questions have a direct impact upon the judge's role in a modern democracy, a democracy that seeks to protect and to reconcile individual liberty and majoritarian decision-making. To stimulate a conversation that might shed light on these, and related, general questions, we created six subtopics, each the subject of a preparatory paper and separate discussion:

1. Judicial Activism. What is it? How does "activism" vary from one society to another? What is the relationship of an "activist" interpretation of a constitution to a "purposive" interpretation? Is the term "activist" inevitably pejorative? Can "activism" be reduced to a simple judicial desire always to increase the power or authority of the judiciary? To what extent does any such "territorial imperative" explain judicial decision-making?

2. The Secular Papacy. Has the judiciary become the twenty-first-century equivalent of the twelfth-century papacy? Do ordinary citizens look to judicial decisions as sources of moral authority? What is the relationship between political morality and constitutional law? To what extent is the legal soundness of the latter grounded in social fairness or other aspects of morality? Are the determinations of international judicial institutions, for example, international criminal courts, closely linked to moral determinations, involving, for example, necessity, torture, or rape? To what extent are court decisions influenced by current moral views of only a portion of society in respect, for example, to homosexuality?

3. Judicial Intervention into the Political Process. To what extent do courts influence the outcome of elections, or help to guarantee fair elections, through, for example, supervision of the drawing of proper election district boundaries, supervision of campaign finance regulations, or supervision of other campaign practices? How do courts in our several nations reconcile limitations on campaign expenditures with guarantees of free expression? To what extent can judges or prosecutors, through their power to enforce ethics-in-government or other criminal laws, influence political outcomes? Is the status quo in this respect a stable one?

4. International Criminal Justice. What is the source of legitimacy of the newly created human rights courts, such as the court at Strasbourg, the Rome Treaty's international criminal court, or the International Criminal Court for the former Yugoslavia and Rwanda? Since national judicial systems may already punish serious crimes, and since such judicial systems might be given extra-national jurisdiction, why is there a demand for interna-

tional criminal courts? Can those courts be made effective? How? To what extent should they criminalize acts, such as rape, which are already crimes under ordinary law? How do they reconcile different national views about human rights, for example, the "expression-related" right to engage in "hate" speech?

5. The Judiciary and the Media. Does judicial enforcement of human rights law inevitably protect the media from legal sanctions? How is press freedom to be reconciled with interests in personal privacy, the harms caused by hate speech, or the need in a democracy for a fair political playing field? To what extent does media respect for the judiciary reflect the media's own desire to "protect their protectors?" To what extent does judicial independence depend on that respect? Can judges or prosecutors resist the media lure of "star-power"? Can they remain objective and anonymous in the face of such temptation? What are the potential consequences for the judiciary of greater media involvement in the judicial process, for example, television in the courtroom?

6. Judges Consider Their Own Roles. What are the basic ethical rules that govern the judge's decision-making? How do we determine when a judge has departed from the necessary fairness and objectivity, perhaps substituting a personal ideology for the law? How are we to reconcile judicial independence with the judge's governmental role—a role that leaves room for political influence in respect to appointment or promotion? How can we reconcile that independence with the need for judicial discipline in order to assure personal honesty and competency in judicial decision-making? Can we avoid the competing risks of political interference on the one hand and the self-interested nature of judicial "corporatism" on the other?

Although we found few answers to these questions, we found the discussion fruitful. Why? For one thing, because the legal systems and underlying social circumstances within both Europe and the United States have grown ever more similar. Thus a discussion of campaign finance laws, and their relation to free expression, sheds light on constitutional problems that judges of different courts will likely face. Questions such as "Why did you decide that way? What about this resulting problem?" will provoke answers that will inform, though they will not necessarily determine, the resolution of similar problems faced by judges of another court.

For another thing, the discussion proved fruitful because our legal systems and our experiences remain different enough for a single phrase or question to have produced quite different reactions. The word "activism" may call to one judge's mind a German court decision protecting citizens against the risks of nuclear power, while, for a different judge, it brings to mind quite different European Court decisions about Sunday closing laws or the powers of the European Parliament. The ability of a single word to have different connotations with different implications for different listeners drove the discussion forward, through argument.

IV

We present here an edited version of our discussions. We list two minor caveats. The Anglo-American reader must remain aware of the fact that a prosecutor in the continental systems of law is a judge. That is not simply a matter of translation. In principle, a *juge d'instruction* or a *juge du parquet,* while much like an American prosecutor, has been trained as a judge, instructed to act not as an advocate but as an investigator impartially searching for the truth. That reader should also keep in mind the fact that continental judges, normally sitting without juries, may see themselves in part as investigators, maintaining a more active control of tribunal proceedings than do many of their Anglo-American counterparts (who are more likely to see themselves as referees of proceedings controlled to a much greater extent by the advocates). Nonetheless, judicial roles are similar enough to have made our discussions interesting and, we hope, useful.

At the very least, this discussion remains a kind of artifact, a first-hand account of how several judges and law professors from different nations experienced, at the beginning of the twenty-first century, what is commonly referred to as the "globalization" of constitutional law. We hope that the reader will profit from an examination of this artifact and that it will stimulate thought and further exploration of the important subjects that were addressed. We only regret that the reader cannot also enjoy, except through the exercise of imagination, the pleasant atmosphere, and the resulting friendships that grew out of the open, collegial daytime discussion and the evenings filled with music "'neath the starry skies" of Provence.

> March 2003
> Robert Badinter
> Stephen Breyer

NOTES

1. See, *e.g.*, William O. Douglas, The Rule of Law in World Affairs (Center for the Study of Democratic Institutions 1961); R. Hutchins, Two Faces of Federalism (Center for the Study of Democratic Institutions 1961).

2. Alexis de Tocqueville, Democracy in America 96–97 (Mansfield & Winthrop ed. 2000).

Introductory Remarks

Robert BADINTER: I shall discuss a phenomenon that has appeared in every Western democracy. (I speak of "democracies" because other forms of government are simply too different.) That phenomenon consists of the augmentation of the power of the judge. That growth, in one form or another, has taken place everywhere. It long has characterized American society. In Europe, it has been particularly noticeable, at least to men of my age, since the end of World War II. In France, taking as a point of departure the period just after the Occupation and the Liberation, and comparing the importance of the judicial authority with that of the political authorities, I find considerable change. That change encompasses what we all know and recognize: the augmented authority of constitutional law and related legal bodies (a phenomenon that comes from America despite the fact that Hans Kelsen, in Europe, undertook the basic conceptual work) and the rising prominence of international legal entities. This latter phenomenon, in my view, is even more important and more original than the former, given its implications for national sovereignty and, beyond that, for the power of those who represent Nations before the international entities. And by now, the end of the century, it has proceeded to what is, theoretically speaking, the most interesting point of all: the birth of an international penal jurisprudence, which operates within certain limits, and which we shall undoubtedly discuss.

This is where we are today. At the same time, we witness a parallel, yet odder, phenomenon. We see an increase in the judge's power and influence along with a simultaneous decline in the authority of what I might call "models." Every society creates models—in the form both of individuals and of social categories. In some societies, the priest is revered; in others, the military officer is revered; in yet others, the property owner is revered, the administrator is revered, the artist is revered, or the great charismatic political leader is revered. But today we see a world in which the "models" that we have inherited little by little have lost their glamour and their ability to generate values, as if they were veiled lanterns or lighthouse beacons that gradually have lost their brightness. No one admires generals any longer, except perhaps in the United States. Nor is anyone in Europe any longer interested in military glory. That is because today the professional armed forces are simply super–police forces. I do not need to remind you how discredited politicians are today. Today, the public regards professional politicians as generally suspect, as sometimes ridiculous, and as perhaps necessary in the way that technicians are necessary, but nonetheless untrustworthy. In any case, politicians certainly are not sources of moral inspiration. Today's politicians are not the great leaders of yore. The political world is cast in the light of generalized public suspicion.

The same is true of the Church. In certain of our Nations, ecclesiastical officials continue to have a moral role to play. I sometimes have the impression that, in the United States, religious leaders still play a political role. I have had the feeling that, in Germany, such men as the President of the Federation of Reformed Churches play a spiritual role—though more limited in its scope than in times past. I do not need to remind you of what the Catholic Church once was in Spain. Its mistaken past alliances weigh heavily upon the present. In Italy, there is, of course, the Pope. And the Pope does play a very important role, for he is a world personality. But I am less certain of the influence of his message. Consider, for instance, the topic of family values. Everyone listens to the Pope's message, but no one actually follows what he says: "No premarital sex. Do not use birth control." But everyone uses it. The Pope is a great artist. He is one of the few who can bring together a huge crowd of the kind that only the greatest rock stars can attract. But I am not certain that the Pope's message goes very far. And, in any event, his is a model that few can easily imitate—unless one wishes to become a priest. The model is gradually losing its strength through lack of recruitment.

In my own view, we are also witnessing a diminution of the prestige of academia. I am not certain that even the German public, which held the great academicians in the highest regard, still holds university professors in that same respect. The German public respects the learning, certainly, but it does not grant university professors the same kind of social status. Among us here in France, the regard accorded the academic world differs markedly today from what it once was. There remains in France the special standing of "intellectuals." The intellectuals remain a distinctive group whose influence is now linked with today's true superpower: the media. In France today, the intellectual plays a public role, not so much as a result of his academic work or the books that he writes, but as a result of his "media" work. In reality, it is the realm of the media that continues to give the intellectual a certain measure of influence.

In contrast to all of this, the judge continues to see his influence grow. The public listens to him and is impassioned by his decisions, which are published and commented upon. And, in my view, it is his function as judge, not his individual personality—this is the important point—which cloaks him with a charisma that his own personality often does not merit.

This conclusion is driven by two factors. First, we live in societies that, at one and the same time, are ever more characterized by rules and codes and are ever more subject to conflict. Second, informal, traditional methods of resolving conflicts have disappeared. It used to be that the local lawyer, the village priest, the school teacher, the mayor, and the head of the family, among others, would mediate serious conflicts. But they no longer have the moral authority necessary to stop conflict at its source. Today, we turn to the judge, who, in carrying out his function of saying what the law is, says what is just. Justice is an essential value in our time. And in a world in which divine justice remains imaginary, the public demands justice here on earth.

People aspire, above all, to a just society. People hope that justice, as they conceive of it, will be done. That aspiration, as applied both to personal problems and to those of society, is a constant. And who, looking at the matter from the point of view of social mechanics or structure, has sworn to tell us what is just or to find the just solution? The judge! Of course, in doing so, he will be subject to criticism. After all, virtually by definition, a judgment is not a source of general pleasure. Not everyone welcomes a judgment with satisfaction—not the parties, not public opinion. Nonetheless, intrinsically, the judge is the source of justice. The judge will tell us what the law is and at the same time create the law. And when a judge, particularly one of a higher court, creates law, the judge will inevitably codify contemporaneous values. That is why I have referred to the judiciary as the "secular papacy."

I have wanted us to meet and to consider this new phenomenon—the judge's role and its function in contemporary society—whether or not it is openly acknowledged. I have spoken at length about this to Stephen Breyer, and he shares my opinion. We come from societies that, in respect to legal background and philosophical culture, resemble each other, but are not identical. We are here, not as an exercise in comparative law, but to confront and discuss our own experiences. We intend to set forth our own opinions about the different aspects of a problem that I have described as the augmentation, in contemporary society, of the judge's power, and the consequences of that augmentation. We shall focus upon the phenomenon, analyze it, attempt to explain it, and consider where it will take us in tomorrow's society. Specifically, we will consider what role judges will be asked to play.

In my country, many have spoken (usually with a shudder) of the "government of judges." That is not the issue here. We consider here a somewhat different phenomenon: a "judicial republic" in which the judge has the final word. The judge is the "great pontiff." The judge holds a position that is unique, and one that has the power to transform the role and status of other authorities in society.

On this subject, each of us has his own views and experiences. How will we clarify the subject? How will we provide enlightenment? The questions we ask will, in my opinion, prove as important as the answers that we provide.

Stephen BREYER: What is a judge? A judge is not a rich man, a scientist, or a media star. Nor is a judge someone whom young people particularly admire. (The young do idolize basketball players, perhaps those who are rich, and certainly media stars.) Still, judges share a certain point of view and certain ideals.

Robert BADINTER: Even so, Stephen, I had the feeling that in the United States the judge was king. When I read about your decisions on the first page of the Herald Tribune, I say to myself that the Supreme Court—here the incarnation of a supreme pontiff—enjoys supreme social recognition. Is that not so? American society would recognize no greater place than that held by the judges. When we watch movies or television, are we not left with the same impression? The judge is inevitably there. Justice is the pillar of American society. And the master of justice is the judge. Have I simply been under the influence of a Hollywood illusion?

Ronald DWORKIN: My impression is that we should distinguish a basketball star—that is, the fame and the inspiration—from the people who count, and the people who are important in the community. And I think that if you ask people what they want to be when they grow up, they say very rich, or famous in sport. But if you say to them, who is powerful in this country, then I think you get the Supreme Court Justices—no lower court judge, but Supreme Court Justices—almost immediately. I am more taken, if I understood it, with your idea.

Stephen BREYER: Certainly the media writes more about Supreme Court Justices than it writes about other judges. But it is important not to exaggerate the judge's importance. I am uncertain of the extent to which the public—outside the bar—takes a regular interest even in media reporting about the Supreme Court.

Gil Carlos RODRIGUEZ IGLESIAS: I agree precisely with Ronald DWORKIN. I believe that we must distinguish a judge's power, on the one hand, from a judge's social prestige, on the other hand. The two do not necessarily go together. Certainly, in Europe, judges in general do not enjoy any great social prestige despite the fact that the public believes that the criminal law judge is important and recognizes that judges exercise more and more power. But, at the same time, we can put this fact together with some of your observations about those groups whose authority has increased and those whose authority has diminished. Take university professors, for example. Their comparative importance differs in different countries. It is my impression that, in the United States, the professional judge in general enjoys greater prestige than does a professor. In Germany, on the other hand, the social and professional prestige of professors is considerably greater than that of judges (with the exception of the German Constitutional Court, which is special and highly professorial).

Ronald DWORKIN: Is the prestige of the professors greater than that of the judge?

Stephen BREYER: In the United States, in general, no.

Dieter GRIMM: In Germany, certainly, with the exception of the judges of the Constitutional Court.

Ronald DWORKIN: In some countries, the judge is part of a civil service profession, which includes people who have just begun their careers. In England and the United States, by contrast, a judge is someone who is often already distinguished or already had certain political success and then is appointed to be a judge. There is a difference in the personnel and background. But I think that if you concentrate on the office of the judge, rather than on the fame of a particular judge—going back to the question—they do think judges have power! In all our questions, it will be important to separate the constitutional court judge from the basic judge, a figure in black robes who is also acting as a magistrate or fixing parking tickets and so forth. If one goes back to the question, who has more prestige in Germany? Say, not Jürgen Habermas but an ordinary professor, or a member of the Constitutional Court?

Dieter GRIMM: One really has to differentiate between constitutional courts and the traditional judiciary. And if someone is a judge and a professor, people would address him as "Herr Professor," and not as "Herr Richter" (*i.e.,* judge), because this is, in general, conceived of as being more important.

Antonio CASSESE: Do you not think that, at least in Europe, one should make the distinction between judges and prosecutors? In most European countries, the prosecutors belong to the judiciary and prosecutors often are among its most prestigious members. They are the *vedettes* (*i.e.,* the stars), they are the ones who make the headlines of the newspapers.

Gil Carlos RODRIGUEZ IGLESIAS: In Spain, the functions that are carried out in Italy by the prosecutor (*pubblico ministero*) are functions of the judge, as in France (*juge d'instruction*).

Antonio CASSESE: In some European countries, judges of the constitutional courts are more prestigious than most other members of the judiciary. Nevertheless, the most famous and prestigious are those members of the judiciary who lead the public action against crimes, particularly crimes involving corruption by politicians.

Robert BADINTER: If I may, I should like to point out a line of demarcation that we have drawn in our thinking between power and glory, and between power and fame. With respect to a judge's work, there are two different aspects of the rise in power. At the outset, there is a factual matter regarding the degree of power that the judge exercises. Even the most anonymous judge working at an inferior level in the judiciary finds that society is trying to transfer to him ever greater power. I can give you many French examples showing this transfer of power to the entire judicial institution, which, in effect, means a transfer of power to each and every judge. The greater the scope of the judiciary's jurisdictional authority, the greater the power of the individual judge. Of course, of the great mass of judges, only certain judges—an elite—will have considerable power with respect to the entire nation. That is why, in my opinion, we should consider constitutional court judges and international court judges separately. Nonetheless, society ever more frequently sees the judge as a provider of, and asks and expects the judge to provide, both truth and justice. I would say that the growth in the power of the judiciary will occur at every level, from the lowest to the highest. The media problem is a different one, however.

Stephen BREYER: We could clarify by taking a hypothetical opinion poll with three questions. First, we could ask, "Who makes the decisions that affect you the most, the President, the Supreme Court, Wall Street, or the media?" Second, "Whom would you prefer to make those decisions?" The answers to the two questions will be different. Third, we could ask mothers, "What career would you prefer for your children?" They will not answer, "Basketball."

I

Judicial Activism

I.I. Presentation

Professor Dieter Grimm

I

The title "judicial imperialism" chosen by Robert Badinter for the first seminar session could suggest that the growing importance of courts in the last century has its main reason in judicial activism: The judges conquer more and more terrain that was formerly reserved for political decisionmaking or societal self-regulation. Yet, this would not be the complete truth. Before the judiciary can expand into areas previously dominated by other forces, courts must be established and endowed with competencies to decide social and political conflicts. The decision that conflict is better left to the judiciary for resolution is not made primarily in the judicial, but in the political, sphere. Without the willingness of politicians to delegate the settlement of conflicts to courts, judicial activism would lack the institutional basis to otherwise command it.

As a matter of fact, we can observe a constant growth of judicial power in the last century, which has as its roots a number of policy decisions. One reason was the general process of legal regulation of more and more spheres of life, which spanned the whole century and far outpaced the simultaneous process of deregulation in a few other fields. This process may have slowed down toward the end of the century, but it was certainly not stopped, much less reversed. In connection with the rule of law, it contributed to an extension of judicial conflict resolution, as all court statistics prove.

The process of increased legal regulation was, however, not the only source of the growing importance of the judiciary. The other factor was the willingness of the legislature to subject its own decisions to judicial scrutiny. While judicial control of administrative acts was already widely accepted in the nineteenth century, it took more than 150 years to convince societies that the achievement of constitutionalism was of little value without constitutional adjudication. For a long period of time, the United States remained alone in allowing judicial review, whereas in Europe it was regarded as being incompatible first with monarchical, and later with democratic, principles. In most cases, experience with dictatorship and its negation of the separation of powers and disregard for human rights was necessary to make way for constitutional courts with the power to review and nullify even acts of the legislature.

The next step in this development was the internationalization of the judiciary in order to secure the respect of supranationally acknowledged human rights within the states. This was first achieved after World War II by the Council of Europe by way of mutual agreement of the contracting states. But, with the exception of the Nuremberg trials, whose legitimacy remained uncertain, the attempt to prosecute violations of human rights without the prior consent of the state concerned is a novelty of the late twentieth century.

If something like judicial imperialism exists, here are the institutional preconditions without which it could not have developed. Judicial imperialism being the subject of this paper, I shall not inquire more deeply into these external reasons for the growing importance of courts and judicial conflict resolution. My intention is, instead, to analyze the internal reasons for the expansion of court power, *i.e.*, the role that judges themselves have in this development. In order to do so, I rely mainly on the model of constitutional adjudication in Germany, partly because it is the one that I know best, and partly because the German Constitutional Court became a model for a great number of countries institutionally, as well as in terms of its jurisprudence. I shall leave international developments to my commentator Antonio CASSESE, who is much more familiar with that issue than I am.

II

As an empirical basis for answering the question whether or not judicial imperialism exists, I shall give a brief description of what the German Constitutional Court added by way of interpretation to the text of the German Basic Law and (perhaps) to the original intent of its framers.

Like most constitutions, the German Basic Law does not contain one comprehensive recognition of liberty and equality, but a catalogue of enumerated fundamental rights, most of which form the legal answer to past oppression by the government. Consequently, government power is limited by the special protection that the Bill of Rights grants only insofar as these guarantees extend. Since the object of protection is usually described in very broad terms—art, property, the home—the range of constitutional protection must be defined more precisely in the process of application, and this definition can be a narrower or a broader one. But outside the demarcation line, government is not subject to the special constraints imposed on it by the Bill of Rights.

The Constitutional Court not only preferred a broad understanding of the various guarantees (*in dubio pro libertate*). It also decided to close the gap that exists between the various enumerated rights. The basis for this operation was an unusually vague guarantee, namely, article 2, section 1 of the Basic Law, which reads: "Every person shall have the right to free development of his personality. . . ." In an early decision, the Constitutional Court construed this provision as covering any activity not protected by one of the following, more precise basic rights. The consequence is that, in spite of the enumeration of certain rights that are regarded as fundamental, any government act that has a limiting effect on a person's freedom to behave how he or she likes can be reviewed by the Court. Because of its vague wording, article 2, section 1 of the Basic Law became an effective means for extending the protection of human rights to counter menaces to individual freedom unknown at the time that the Constitution was adopted. Where such menaces threatened to affect the health of people, as in many cases of technological innovation, the right to life and physical integrity guaranteed in article 2, section 2 of the Basic Law served as a basis for a broader interpretation, *e.g.*, vis-à-vis the use of atomic energy or genetics, or vis-à-vis the emission of pollutants or noise. Where not life and health, but privacy, reputation, sexual orientation, etc., were concerned, article 2, section 1 of the Basic Law was used to support the broader interpretation.

The most important example is an interpretation of article 2, section 1 of the Basic Law that amounts to the invention of a new fundamental right: the so-called right to informational self-determination that is designed to protect the individual against the menaces of electronic data processing, and which has had a revolutionizing effect on many fields of ordinary law. (However, the creation of a "new" fundamental right is less impressive than the endeavors of the Israeli Supreme Court, which, in the absence of a Bill of Rights, developed an unwritten one, deducing it from the principle of democracy. The Israeli Court thus went further than the European Court of Justice which, in a similar exercise, could at least rely on the European Convention on Human Rights, which was ratified by all member states, and on the member states' Bills of Rights.)

Even more important because of its applicability to all constitutional guarantees for individual liberty was the invention of the principle of proportionality, which today bears the main burden of protecting freedom against government intrusions. The Basic Law starts from the premise that fundamental rights are not absolute rights. Every right may be abused, and every one may collide with the same right of others or with another fundamental right. Therefore, the legislature has the power to limit those rights in the interest of legitimate public purposes or in order to harmonize conflicting fundamental rights. Consequently, most constitutional guarantees contain a limitation clause that, in some cases, is rather detailed, and in others (among them a right as basic as the right to life) is content with requiring a general law. A provision applying to all fundamental rights, article 19, section 2 of the Basic Law, adds that in no case may the statutory limitation affect the essence of the right at stake.

According to this text, the power of the legislature to limit fundamental rights can be extremely far reaching. The Constitutional Court regarded this as not in line with the function and rank of the Bill of Rights and, in order to maintain the priority of fundamental rights over ordinary law, developed the principle of proportionality. The principle means that a law that limits a fundamental right is constitutional only (1) when it is suitable, (2) when it is necessary to achieve its purpose, and (3) when it establishes a reasonable balance between the fundamental right limited by the law, on the one hand, and the good in whose interest the limitation lies, on the other hand. Compared with the text, the barrier against government action is considerably advanced by this interpretation. Correspondingly, the absolute barrier in article 19, section 2 of the Basic Law has lost almost all importance. Today, most civil rights cases are decided under the principle of proportionality and, among these cases, the decisive test is usually stage 3 balancing, which leaves rather wide discretion to the Court.

Everything described up to now lies within the domain of protecting the individual against government intrusion into his or her sphere of freedom—*i.e.*, negative rights. In a 1958 landmark decision, the so-called *Lüth* decision,[1] the Court began to conceive of fundamental rights not only as subjective rights enabling the individual to defend himself or herself against government acts affecting a constitutionally protected freedom. In the Court's view, fundamental rights are at the same time objective principles (or "values," in the earlier terminology) permeating the whole legal order and guiding lawmaking as well as the application of the law.

The immediate effect of *Lüth* was to extend the influence of the Constitution on ordinary law beyond the sphere of lawmaking to law interpretation and application as well. A law whose purpose or effect is to limit the use of a fundamental right has to be interpreted and applied in the spirit of the Constitution. As a result, the administration of justice, particularly the interpretation of the Civil Code, which formerly belonged exclusively to the civil courts, came under the control of the Constitutional Court. The absence of a clear boundary between statutory interpretation of a constitutional dimension and ordinary law has become a constant source of critique of the Constitutional Court— mostly that it went too far, sometimes that it did not go far enough.

The remote effect of *Lüth* consisted of adding another dimension to the concept and functioning of fundamental rights. In the understanding brought forth by *Lüth*, fundamental rights require the government not only to refrain from certain actions, but also to take action in order to establish or to maintain substantial freedom in the segment of social reality in which a fundamental right is to take effect—*i.e.*, positive rights. Freedom, then, is no longer exclusively the freedom of the individual, but also the institutional freedom of the societal framework in which individual freedom is exercised; freedom of the press or of broadcasting, for instance, as distinct from freedom of the individual publisher or journalist. And the guarantee of institutional freedom can well justify limitations of individual liberty.

The most important consequence of the value-oriented interpretation of fundamental rights is the acknowledgment of a duty of the government, and in particular of the legislature, to protect constitutionally guaranteed liberties when they are threatened, not by government, but by third parties or societal forces. This obligation (*Schutzpflicht*) was explicitly developed in the first abortion decision (in 1975),[2] in which the

Constitutional Court declared the abolition of penal law unconstitutional on the ground that article 2, section 2 of the Basic Law obliges the state not only to respect life, but also to defend it against attacks by others. This is different from the approach taken by the Austrian Constitutional Court, which chose an originalist interpretation: that since, at the time of adoption of the Constitution, the basic rights were directed only against the state, and the state did not want to perform abortions itself, but rather allowed others to legally do so, no constitutional question was at stake.

The idea of a duty of the legislature to actively secure constitutionally guaranteed liberties—although developed in a case where an existing legal protection was abolished by the legislature—gained its true importance in the context of legislative abstention from defending a threatened freedom, *e.g.*, against the threats posed by new technological developments, such as atomic energy, genetic manipulation, etc. This obligation can be fulfilled by substantial regulation, for instance, by prescribing certain security standards. But it can also require organizational structures that are suitable to promote the purpose of the constitutional guarantee or procedural rules favorable to freedom-oriented decisions in cases where substantial standards are difficult to formulate.

The obligation to legislate in order to maintain freedom was gradually extended to the preconditions of the exercise of a fundamental right, particularly in areas where the exercise is not just a matter of an individual's will, but rather depends on social or legal prerequisites—for instance, education as a prerequisite to enjoy the free choice of a profession. It may even include financial means to make use of a freedom, *e.g.*, elementary help for the needy, but also a sufficient financial endowment for public broadcasting so that it can fulfill its constitutionally envisaged function in competition with commercial broadcasting.

There remains, however, a difference in range between fundamental rights in their capacity as negative and as positive rights. The obligations that negative rights impose on the state can be fulfilled in one way only: The state has to omit any action that would constitute a violation of the right. Consequently, actions that infringe on such rights may be nullified by the Constitutional Court. Positive rights, by contrast—in particular, the obligation to protect threatened rights by legislation—can be fulfilled in various ways, as long as they are in accord with the Constitution. The Constitution does not prescribe a specific means to fulfill the duty. Therefore, judicial review is limited to the question whether the legislature reacted at all to a menace against a certain freedom and whether the solution that it adopted was adequate to meet the threat. Thus, it happens quite frequently that the Constitutional Court rejects law, not because it went too far in restricting a fundamental right, but because it did too little in order to protect it.

All these interpretations have extended the meaning of the Constitution beyond the original understanding. Restrictive interpretations are rare; in the field of fundamental rights they are almost nonexistent. In sum, the interpretations outweigh in my view the formal amendments to the Basic Law, although these were by no means few in number (46 in 50 years) or of minor importance. In any case, they have narrowed the room for political decisionmaking while, at the same time, the domain of the judiciary has grown.

III

This expansive mode of expounding the Constitution may be analyzed in terms of judicial imperialism. When it comes to the legitimacy of judicial review, it may even be necessary to discuss the development under this perspective. Nevertheless, it would not be appropriate to apply this criterion only. For, it is not sufficiently susceptible to the specific conditions and motives of judicial behavior. Although it would be naive to deny the existence of an institutional self-interest on the part of courts, the judicial setting leaves little room for pursuing this interest.

The judiciary has to decide individual conflicts according to pre-established norms. The cases are brought by parties, and although it is true that courts, in particular supreme courts or constitutional courts, may have the right to select cases for decision, they remain limited to decide problems presented to them by others. With very few exceptions, constitutional courts are not free to concern themselves with problems that they think deserve a legal answer. In addition, the cases rarely present a social or political problem in its full range. Mostly, it is a small portion of a much more complex situation that is submitted for judicial scrutiny. The hetero-determination of courts, both in agenda and the criteria, and the piecemeal character of their work make it difficult to develop a long-term strategy vis-à-vis other actors.

Moreover, courts operate under the premise of finding a just solution for the conflict at hand, whereby the standards of the "just" are pre-determined in abstract and general norms. Not being subject to democratic accountability, judges derive their legitimacy from demonstrating that they apply these norms instead of creating them. In most cases, the norms are in need of interpretation and concretization, and the broader they are formulated and the older they have become, the more room they leave for the volitive elements of norm application. But even then, the courts' understanding of what a constitution is and the legal method that they use to determine its meaning seem to play a more important role than strategic interests in expanding their own terrain.

For the German Constitutional Court, for instance, the experience with Nazi dictatorship and the failure of the first democratic constitution, and the firm intention to make the post-war constitution matter in political and social life, were much more decisive factors in its activism than the endeavor to establish a judicial empire and to curtail the realm of the political actors. The concern with successful constitutionalism corresponded with a methodological approach whose interpretive goal is to give optimal effect to a constitutional norm in a given situation. This understanding of the role of a constitutional judge did not favor the more passive formalistic mode of interpretation predominant in the second half of the nineteenth century and during the Weimar Republic. Neither was it favorable to the likewise more passive method of originalism. Rather, the basic understanding of the court's role made it susceptible to the social context in which constitutional norms take effect and social change which may affect the purpose of the constitutional norm if its meaning is not adapted to the new situation. As a matter of fact, the previously described jurisprudence of the Constitutional Court in the field of fundamental rights can altogether be explained as a reaction to changing conditions for the realization of freedom. They were rooted in legal considerations. For the purposes of our discussion, it is therefore crucial to distinguish between intent and effect. The intent was a normative one; the effect may have been imperialism. Imperialism can, of course, itself become a normative argument leading to judicial self-restraint. But it seems difficult to convince judges not to enforce what they seriously have found to be a requirement of the Constitution.

It is true that its methodological approach helped to immunize the German Constitutional Court from political criticism, since such criticism was perceived as disrespect for the Constitution. It also helped immunize the Court from being reprogrammed by constitutional amendments, for the Constitution cannot regulate its own understanding. But it would be difficult to show that the methodological choice was made in order to achieve the immunizing effect. With regard to *Lüth*, the most important decision by the Constitutional Court, one can even show that the judges were not aware of the far-reaching effects that the decision would have on the balance of power between the Constitutional Court and the legislature.

The fact that the Constitutional Court found much popular support for its general line of expounding the Constitution (not, of course, for every single decision) reassured it in its attempt to interpret the Constitution in a way that gives utmost practical effect to its provisions. One of the reasons for popular support of constitutional courts may be found in the well-known deficiencies of party politics in pluralistic democracies. As the professionalization of politics grows and electoral victory becomes the predominant concern of political actors, counter-vailing powers that operate under a different premise are increasingly welcome. Professionalization of party politics favors short-term orientation and tends to instrumentalize all fields of life that operate under a different logic for political purposes. In light of this development, the role of supreme or constitutional courts seems to change. The emphasis of their function shifts from the protection of individual liberty against governmental intrusion to (1) reminding political actors, when they are ready to sacrifice sacred principles for tiny momentary successes, of their long-term commitments set forth in the Constitution; (2) insisting on equal treatment where political actors tend to privilege their clientele or societal forces that hold veto power; and (3) restoring citizens' confidence in government promises and assurances when the government changes course quickly without taking into account the investment that citizens may have made in reliance on the previous approach. To put it in an exaggerated way: The border guard is being replaced by a soldier.

On the other hand, the shifting function pushes courts to even more activism. In their new role, they do not keep the government within its constitutional boundaries, but require it to act where it is reluctant to do so. This looks like another gain in judicial power. But at the same time, it makes courts more vulnerable. When a court declares a governmental act null and void, the act becomes legally nonexistent. An insubordinate government would have to make the same decision anew in order to impose its will. It seems rather unlikely that this would happen in a well-functioning constitutional system. By contrast, when the court forces the government to take action in order to fulfill a constitutional obligation, resistance does not require a clear act of insubordination. The government can avoid complaints by just remaining passive. It is the specific weakness of constitutional courts that the power is in the hands of those who are affected by their decisions. The institutional self-interest of courts may therefore well set limits to judicial imperialism.

1.2. Judicial Activism

Discussion

Dieter GRIMM: You may have noticed that I had some problems with the expression *impérialisme* because I think that it makes things very clear, but it also has the connotation of usurpation on the part of judges. It gives the impression that the judiciary conquers terrain that formerly was reserved either for political decisionmaking or for societal self-regulation. I admit that this can be so, but before it can happen, the courts must be established and courts must be endowed with competencies. Once this has happened, courts have a basis for expansion. But, of course, they cannot create the basis themselves. Therefore, I think that it is important, first of all, to acknowledge a remarkable willingness of politics to subject political behavior to judicial control in the twentieth century. It started on the national level, effectuated either by ordinary courts or, even more frequently, by constitutional courts. Constitutional adjudication is meanwhile an almost universal achievement. But late in the twentieth century, it began to expand on the international level, and not in the form of arbitration, which has existed for a long time, but in the form of international criminal courts, which act independently of prior consent of the nations that may be subjected to their jurisdiction. I think that it would be extremely interesting to inquire into the reasons why politicians were ready to hand over so much power to courts. If we did, we would learn something about the historical pre-conditions for judicial review, and we would also learn something about the conditions of success or failure of constitutional adjudication, and why in many of the countries where constitutional adjudication was recently established, it may well fail. We do not have very promising news from some of these countries.

But, as I understand it, that is not our subject, because that would be not judicial imperialism, but political self-restriction. I would like instead to stress and emphasize the internal aspect, the way courts and in particular constitutional courts make use of their power. In my presentation, I used the example of the German Constitutional Court, one reason being that I know it best, the other being that it can be considered as a particularly active court. I know of more active courts—the Hungarian Constitutional Court and the Israeli Supreme Court, for instance—but I would count the German Constitutional Court among the active courts that have had considerable influence on a number of other courts. I do not repeat these steps, which I described in a selective manner in my presentation. I could have shown similar approaches, not with regard to fundamental rights, but with regard to the structure and the organizational parts of the constitution. In sum, I think that the decisions of the Constitutional Court changed the German Constitution more deeply than the formal amendments, of which we have had many. The formal amendments to the Constitution changed the text; the court rulings changed its meaning.

The question is: Can we correctly describe what happened in terms of imperialism? When it comes to the question of legitimacy of our courts, it is necessary to discuss it in terms of imperialism because the terrain claimed for judicial review is no longer open for political, and thus democratic, decisionmaking. It is extremely difficult, in my view, for politics to reconquer, so to speak, the terrain once lost to the judiciary. Politics has two options: Either it can try to convince the court to overrule a previous decision or it can reprogram, so to speak, a constitutional court by constitutional amendments, which usually is not very easy. But I do have doubts as to whether imperialism is an adequate means to understand what happens in terms of the expansion of the power of the courts. The reasons for my doubts are that usually, with some exceptions, imperialism is not the motive for the expansion. Imperialism is not sufficiently susceptible to the specific conditions and motives of judicial behavior.

Two considerations lead me to say that. The first one is that, although there is certainly institutional self-interest on the part of courts, there is not much room for courts to pursue their institutional self-interests. The main reason is the hetero-determination of the judiciary, both in agenda and in criteria. I discussed that issue in my presentation and I am not going to comment on it further. More important for me is the second consideration. I think that the main motive for expanding the power of courts and judges is an internal legal one. It is the attempt to find a legally correct solution for problems presented to courts. This happens, of course, in a general cultural context, but this context finds its specific legal reflections. One of them certainly is the general understanding within society, but also the understanding of judges, about what the function of the constitution is and what a constitution is good for. And a very important factor is the way in which judges determine the meaning of the constitution vis-à-vis a specific problem, *i.e.*, the method of the interpretation. Method matters. In my view, methodological choice influences outcome. One can see this very well when one compares decisions involving the same issue before and after a change of methodology. Wonderful examples include the U.S. Supreme Court decisions on wire-tapping and the Fourth Amendment in the 1920s[3] and in the 1960s.[4] But the choice of methods is made for legal purposes. It is not generally made in order to accumulate or to expand power; it is made for legal purposes—in order best to fulfill the special function of courts.

If I were to put it into a theoretical framework, I think that systems theory as originally developed by Talcott Parsons and later perfected and elaborated by Niklas Luhmann is perhaps the best analogy. And it is, at the same time, an explanation of the concept, which I discussed in my presentation, that it is difficult to convince a judge not to decide what he thinks the constitution requires. Of course, we all know that the basic assumption of systems theory is that society is divided into functionally specified systems, which on the one hand depend on each other, but which on the other hand are operatively closed to each other. Each of these systems follows a logic of its own and draws its efficiency from its specialization. It operates, so to speak, under a certain code; it is not determined by the codes of other systems. Within the system, people communicate in that code, success or failure within the system is measured against the code, and signals from outside the system are only received if they are formulated in, or can be translated into, that code.

There are a number of consequences. I will mention two of them. The first one is that behavior within a system is always professional behavior. Only a professionalized agent is able to have success, and professionalization of the system means following the specific code of the system. And, of course, the code of the legal system is "legal/illegal" or "constitutional/unconstitutional." Using codes of other systems—the effect of a decision is too costly, for instance, or it minimizes the export chances of the domestic industry, or it helps certain parties to win the elections—is illegitimate and leads to failure within the system. The code is imperative for the agents in the system, but it can be interpreted in one or another way. The second consequence that I would like to mention is that the system is only interested in its own operations and functions and does not develop sensibility or responsibility for the effect of its own operation on other systems. It develops sensibility only insofar as the system suffers from what happens in other systems in return.

This leads me to insist on the distinction between intent and effect. Generally speaking, the intent of courts is a legal one; the effect of what they do may well be a function of imperialism. That does not mean that the effect cannot be influenced if it is regarded to be detrimental. There are opportunities, of course, for limiting the power of judges. One is redefining what is considered to be legal or illegal, and this politics can do by way of legislation or amendment of the constitution. But there is a considerable difference between the ordinary judiciary and constitutional courts. If the legislature does not like what ordinary courts do with the laws enacted by it, they can easily change the legislation. This is not that easy with regard to constitutional courts and, even more important, the method constitutional courts apply is not subject to regulation because method cannot be regulated.

Another possibility is an internal mechanism, so to speak, within the judicial system. One could argue that the results of the interpretation of one or another constitutional provision affect other constitutional principles—the separation of powers, for instance. On that basis, one may argue that a decision is legally wrong and thereby induce courts to change it and limit their power.

A third opportunity occurs when courts create a situation that, through a very expansive interpretation of the constitution, endangers their own position. When they are faced with the threat of losing support, or when compliance by the legislature is no longer guaranteed, then I think that there is a chance that courts, out of their own interest, will limit their own position.

In sum, I would say that there is an enormous gain of power on the part of judges, but it is enabled in the first place by political decisions to establish courts and to grant them more and more powers. On the other hand, judicial power is also augmented by the judiciary itself. And, in my view, it will expand more and more. The main reason seems to be an intrinsic shortcoming of political and democratic decisionmaking, mainly relating to party politics. Although the legislature is the system that should compensate for the shortsightedness of the other powers, it is itself subject to functional specialization and to putting its own self-interest at the forefront. I think that societies feel that they are more and more in need of having within the political system a countervailing power that does not operate under the same premises as do party politics. Again, I would say that it is not imperialism; it is rather the way functionally different societies develop, and judges and courts are not exempted from this secular trend.

Antonio CASSESE: I am afraid I do not have many topics on which I may take issue with Dieter. I will leave aside the question of whether the expression "judicial imperialism" is appropriate or a misnomer.

Robert BADINTER: I used the more provocative expression. I perhaps should have referred to "judicial activism."

Antonio CASSESE: Or expansion of the judicial role?

Robert BADINTER: That expansion has primarily grown out of the nature of things. But the judges are also partly responsible. They have wanted to increase the size of their dominion. At every opportunity, they have advanced their pawns.

Antonio CASSESE: We all agree, then, that the topic refers to the expansion of the judges' role. I will also leave aside the various legal developments and cases mentioned by Dieter, particularly with regard to the German Constitutional Court.

Dieter makes four main points to explain why there has been recently a huge expansion of the role of the judiciary, and one point specifically with regard to the increasing role of constitutional courts, particularly in Germany—and I would add, for instance, in

Japan and Italy and other countries. I will go through them and try to address them in a critical way.

The first point is what Dieter called the general process of legal regulation of our life and the expansion of lawmaking and of legislation. As Robert BADINTER said earlier, given the lack of informal/traditional means of dispute resolution (*notaires, curés,* and *pères de famille*), one needs to rely primarily on judges and, as a result, we need more laws. So the first point was the expanding role of legislation.

The second point—an issue on which Dieter placed much emphasis—is that politicians are increasingly willing to subject themselves to judicial scrutiny. They are prepared to permit judges to review political acts.

The third point is the internationalization of the judiciary. But Dieter left this topic open for me and others to discuss.

The fourth and probably most interesting point was Dieter's discussion of the shortcomings of party politics in pluralistic democracies—the sort of short-term attitudes taken by politicians and their lack of interest in long-term values. This is a point also made in several of the other presentations: that there is a preference in society for long-term values, and such values are set forth in judgments, particularly in decisions by constitutional courts. By contrast, politicians tend to take a very short-term approach and are more interested in winning elections than in propounding or upholding new values.

But, as far as the constitutional courts are concerned, in Germany—and in other European countries—reaction to past dictatorships pushed constitutional courts to play major roles designed to develop values enshrined in the constitution. Constitutional courts tried to adopt expansive and innovative views in interpreting the constitution.

These four topics serve as a general outline of Dieter's key arguments.

I would like to raise one issue in particular with regard to Dieter's second point, namely, that judges are playing a larger role because politicians have decided to hand over some power to judges. I wonder whether politicians are truly aware of this process. I think that it is not deliberate. In my view, politicians probably unwittingly decided that there was a deadlock and that they could not do anything, and then said, "Let us set up some sort of judicial machinery and maybe one day, judges will settle the issues." Therefore, it is not because politicians are interested in judicial review and in judicial settlement of particular legal problems, but simply because of their impotence or lack of imagination. At least, judging from my own experience in the international arena, it is very clear that politicians and diplomats do not predict the role that judges may one day play, and then they get scared later on when they realize that judges really may play a major role. I would say that what Dieter calls the willingness of politics to subject its decisions to judicial scrutiny is questionable.

A second issue that I would like to raise is whether we should also deal with a problem that crops up in international law, but which may probably also have some impact or some role in national adjudication: namely, to what extent judges in fact do not apply the law, but rather create the law. International courts, under cover of applying or interpreting law, actually set new legal standards, either by proclaiming what the general principles of international law are or through *obiter dictum*. I can give you a lot of examples of *obiter dicta* that, in a matter of ten years, have played a significant role in introducing new concepts. For instance, there was a famous commercial case before the International Court of Justice called the *Barcelona Traction Case* (Belgium v. Spain).[5] Spain seized the assets of a company whose principal shareholders were Canadians. This case arose within the traditional, very old Westphalian model of international law: two sovereign countries clashing because of economic interests. The International Court of Justice had previously made an awful decision in the South-West Africa case;[6] there had been a huge disappointment with the Court. One judge, a Polish judge, Manfred Lachs (he told everybody—so I can tell you—because he prided himself in his having done so) said to the other judges: "Why don't we put in a little *obiter dictum* on the difference between synallagmatic obligations or obligations based on reciprocity or quid pro quo (*e.g.*, commercial treaties providing that I sell you goods and you give me money) and obligations *erga omnes* (for instance, the obligation not to perpetrate genocide or not to engage in racial discrimination)." This *obiter dictum* had nothing to do with the legal questions at issue before the Court. Not one word of the *dictum* was necessary for that particular judgment. These 20 or 30 lines of *dictum* have really been a major breakthrough in international law because of this new notion of obligations *erga omnes*. The notion has an enormous potential; it means that each state in the world has the obligation vis-à-vis all the other states not to engage in genocide, apartheid, racial discrimination, gross violations of human rights, and so on. It means that all the other states can demand that another state stop practicing genocide. This at the time was theoretical. It was only *dictum* and was suggested only for political reasons because Judge Lachs felt that the Court was faring poorly in public opinion. He said, "Let us inject some new ideas into our case law." Thus it is interesting to see the extent to which, through *obiter dictum* or so-called interpretation that actually boils down to the creation of new legal standards, courts can expand their own role and actually replace lawmakers. At least, in my area in international law, lawmakers very often are utterly impotent. Lawmakers often cannot make decisions, and the judges step in and decide, in lieu of lawmakers. This is, I think, a topic that should probably be discussed.

I had another query about one of the points made by Dieter when he stated that judges not subject to democratic accountability derive their legitimacy from demonstrating that they apply these norms instead of making them. Are you sure about that? We have all made judgments. We know that we are prone to manipulation. We manipulate laws, standards, political principles, and principles of interpretation. Very often, particularly in a criminal case, I sense that the defendant is guilty, and common sense leads me to believe that we should come to a particular conclusion. Then I say, "All right, let us now build sound legal reasoning to support that conclusion."

Robert BADINTER: Perhaps it would be best to return to the first point that you raised: the undeniable transfer of power to the judge. Did the political will to do that come about through necessity, through convenience, through lassitude, or through desirable revolution? I open the discussion on that issue. What is the cause of this ever-greater transfer of power to judges?

Dieter GRIMM: I think that very often politicians, when they established or expanded the competencies of courts, did not really know what they were doing. They may have done it in order to solve a short-term problem, but with long-term effects. This may well be true. It may even be true for the former socialist states, which, after the fall of communism, were all convinced that constitutional adjudication was what they needed. Still, they may have not been aware of what it really meant. But the question then is, why do they do that now, and why did not they do it previously? So there must be an answer to the question why nowadays, in the twentieth century, they seek solutions from the judges that they did not before.

Ronald DWORKIN: Could I add that there are some cases where it is dramatically evident that they knew what was coming and that it was quite deliberate. One such case is South Africa, which is an extraordinary case. In South Africa, there was a large majority about to assume power for the first time that nevertheless insisted that the power of the majority be subject to checks by a court. And indeed, the court exercised almost immediately power to thwart the will of the majority, for example, in capital punishment. The debates in the African National Council (ANC) were exactly along these lines: "Do we wish to transfer this kind of power to the judges?"

The second place where it is quite self-conscious is what has happened in the last few years in Great Britain, where this decision has been debated exactly in these terms. So I do not think that we can say in either of those places that there has been any kind of surprise or politicians not understanding what they are doing. It is also a case in which there has been some popular involvement in the decision so that there has been a kind of democratic endorsement.

Robert BADINTER: You say that there are certain historical moments when a transfer of power occurs consciously because, compared to the previous situation, people want to establish a strong judicial power. That certainly was true in Eastern Europe.

RONALD DWORKIN: The classic case on the other side is Israel, where this has not been something that the politicians knew that they were getting into (unless they knew it a lot better than I think they did).

Gil Carlos RODRIGUEZ IGLESIAS: Consider Spain, for instance. We perfectly well understood the significance of creating a constitutional court. I believe that the consensus that surrounded the creation of the Constitution and a constitutional court demonstrated a collective desire shared by all political forces to have a common ground of understanding, despite the ideological differences that we had to preserve. Moreover, it was very clear in Spain that, in the search for a basic compromise, all the parties were aware of the fact that the expression of that compromise would be ambiguous in certain respects. We were not at the point of being able to agree on how to resolve certain issues. It was necessary to leave certain expressions in the Constitution ambiguous. Then, if eventually a decision had to be reached, the Constitutional Court would make it. Hence, we acted with full awareness.

Antonio CASSESE: Do you not think that, in South Africa and in Spain, the creation of a constitutional court was a means of protecting minorities? In South Africa, the white minority needed protection from the black majority. So I agree with you that they were quite aware that this was the only means of safeguarding basic rights. This is the case also in Spain and in other countries because it is the only way of safeguarding the basic fundamental rights of people who are not in power.

Ronald DWORKIN: The ANC pressed just as vigorously as the residual white government led by F. W. de Klerk. I went to some conferences and the pressure for a strong Bill of Rights to protect individual freedom was more from the ANC than it was from the then nationalist government. The nationalist government wanted protection for economic interests, particularly property. But when it came to questions of individual liberty, the strong pressure came from two people: Oliver Tambo, who represented the government in exile, and Nelson Mandela. When the Court announced its first decision, which was unpopular—capital punishment is always an unpopular decision—Mandela took the lead in saying, "It is the law. It has now been decided." It was one of the moments that solidified the power of the court. So I agree with you that the white community had a good reason, but it was this residual sense among people who had been oppressed that was the major impetus. I think that this is quite significant: people who had been oppressed by arbitrary power who somehow felt that the protection against arbitrary power came from creating a strong court. Because they could anticipate that the black community was not going to be homogeneous and there were going to be questions about freedom of the press, for example, under any government, they wanted to be sure that the judges had a role and they gave the judges great power.

Robert BADINTER: Yes. I should like to follow on from what Ronald was saying. At the outset, I would confirm that he is precisely correct in respect to South Africa. But, in respect to more general matters, I should like to make an observation and draw a distinction.

The observation: During the later decades of the twentieth century, each time that totalitarian regimes became democratic, there was a political will to build very strong judicial defenses in order to guarantee individual and public liberties. That is certainly true in countries that emerged from the darkness of dictatorship, such as Germany and Italy. The birth of constitutional courts in Germany and Italy was in part a reaction to the dark years and the totalitarian regimes. It was not just an effort to imitate the model of the victor, the United States. We saw the same thing quite clearly on the Iberian Peninsula—in Spain and in Portugal. I have seen the same thing in all the democracies that have emerged in Eastern Europe. In everyone's eyes, the disappearance of totalitarianism had as an initial consequence the building of a strong constitutional court. We find a remarkable historical correlation in all the democracies between an interest in the defense of liberty and the creation of a strong judicial authority. I bring this matter up again because it reflects a general movement, which nothing in the past fifty years belies.

On the other hand—and this is the distinction that follows my observation—the political forces may determine that, in the new constitution and among the new institutions, there is to be a strong, independent judicial authority. But they are not similarly ready to admit the correctness of the concrete individual judicial decisions that inevitably are made once the judicial authority has been created. In that respect, the sorcerer's apprentice may jump out of the cupboard and hit his master, the politician, on the head with his broom. "You wanted a strong judiciary to protect basic liberty. But you neither wished nor expected a strong judiciary, which, when deciding in liberty's favor, continuously accumulates more power." In South Africa, when both the white minority and the black majority conceived of the constitutional court, they thought about the importance of guaranteeing the Bill of Rights. They did not expect our judicial colleagues there to decide first to abolish the death penalty. That they did not expect.

Dieter GRIMM: When Konrad Adenauer suffered his first defeat in a major case in the Constitutional Court—Adenauer had been the head of the Parliamentary Council that wrote the Constitution—he said: "*So haben wir uns das nicht vorgestellt*," which means, "This was not the way we imagined it!"

Robert BADINTER: I draw your attention to this point: There is the stage of creation and of optimism, when society places emphasis on the constitution and, among its institutions, a strong judiciary, as a sign of a strong modern democracy. Later, it must live with its creation, which grows bigger and bigger and obtains more and more power. That is when another set of circumstances comes into being, circumstances that have long been present in the United States, but which now are everywhere in all our societies. As you have explained and shown concretely, the techniques that judges use in reaching decisions are as much techniques for extending their power. Thus, in respect to our first question, the transfer of power to a judiciary begins with a political will, at the beginning, to do so.

Stephen BREYER: Perhaps, but not in the United States. The Supreme Court's power expanded greatly as a result of the legal effort to end legal segregation in the 1960s. The Court had a strong legal basis for holding segregation unconstitutional. But, given the previous 80 years in which segregation was thought legal, the 1954 decision ending segregation[7] was not necessarily expected. And, in any event, it occurred because the Court and much of the country had come to understand that segregation was intolerable. The expansion did not come about as a result of transfer of power by Congress to the courts.

Ronald DWORKIN: It was Congress that tried to stop it.

Stephen BREYER: The Court's exercise of its power to hold segregation unconstitutional reflected, in a certain sense, not so much activism as literalism. The Fourteenth Amendment said that states could not deny individuals "equal protection of the laws." Segregation denied that protection. Hence segregation was unlawful. A Court that interpreted the Constitution literally in the area of segregation—despite the risk of strong political opposition—might then learn from its experience with segregation that it was possible to apply the Constitution's protections literally in other areas as well, say, to prevent police from extracting confessions through force, or to stop states from inhibiting "free expression." The judges themselves expanded the Court's power in the 1950s through the 1970s, but a major external event helped to provoke that expansion, namely, the country's willingness (and perhaps its determination) to end segregation.

Ronald DWORKIN: I think that was not the first expansion.

Stephen BREYER: No, but it was an important expansion.

Ronald DWORKIN: But the preceding expansion, say, in the 1930s has more relevance in a different aspect for what Dieter was saying because it was not quite against a big ground swell when the Supreme Court tried to oppose Roosevelt's New Deal.

Stephen BREYER: I would add that American legislatures fairly often transfer power to courts by writing vague statutes with each legislator hoping for a favorable interpretation. When Congress forbids "discrimination," does the statute refer only to intentionally discriminatory actions or does that word also include actions with a discriminatory effect? Congress may be unable to decide and it may therefore leave the matter to the courts. The same phenomenon can occur with racial discrimination, with prison reform, and even with certain criminal laws.

Dieter GRIMM: All hot issues!

Stephen BREYER: The statute prohibiting discrimination against the disabled has similar ambiguities. Those interested in the legislation—say, those with disabilities, businesses, trade unions, or government departments, whether represented before Congress directly or through lobbyists—may often argue for ambiguous language, but of a kind that will help produce favorable administrative interpretations by government agencies and that will lead to favorable legal interpretations in courts. The legislative process thereby becomes more complex, with groups fighting over what kind of ambiguous language to introduce. Perhaps this same kind of interaction between the legislature and the courts occurs elsewhere, say, in Germany.

Dieter GRIMM: I think that the main criterion is again the self-interest of politicians in cases where a certain issue has to be solved but is likely to provoke much resentment on the part of the voters. Under these circumstances, politicians tend to leave it to the courts, because this allows them to say, "We would have liked to handle it otherwise, but now we are bound." It is imperative, however, when the matter is in the politicians' self-interest that the room for political decision be kept open. In such cases, they dislike courts taking the question.

Stephen BREYER: A legislator may favor ambiguous statutory language, leaving a major question for courts to answer, in two circumstances. First, he may genuinely want the courts to decide the matter, perhaps because, for political reasons, it is too costly politically for the legislator to embody a clear answer in legislation. If the statute provides no clear answer, the legislator can imply subtly to each opposing group of constituents that he really favors its position, thereby obtaining support from both. Second, the legislator may strongly favor one of the two sides but lack the votes to secure a majority. In that case, he may vote for ambiguous language, which is preferable to a legislative defeat, while he also tries to secure other statutory language that he believes will lead a court to reach a result that favors his side.

In both sets of circumstances, the legislator has asked the courts to substitute for the legislature in performing a function that the legislature could have performed. This is a dangerous practice. Critics refer to it as turning the court-monster loose; it may prove habit forming, it weakens the democratic process, and, by drawing the judges into issues too "hot" even for legislatures easily to handle, it may weaken public support for the judiciary.

Ronald DWORKIN: The further effect that it has is that a great deal then depends on the particular personalities of the judges. There is a whole profession called "court watching," which then creates a feedback loop, because it feeds back into the political process, the public becomes more and more aware of who the conservative judges are, who the liberal judges are, who the eccentric judges are, and so forth. This is part of a larger problem that I imagine will arise again and again in these discussions—the politicization of the judiciary. We tend to speak—and we have already spoken here—as if the deficit in the democratic process means that one takes things out of the democratic process and transfers them to the judges. It actually means, I think, that you change the whole political process, because you create a dilemma of how to get the judges that you want appointed and block the appointment of other judges, and how to bring to the public's attention the importance of who the judges are. So you transform the democratic political process, but you have not simply shut that process out. It continues to play an important role in the ultimate disposition, particularly if you take a long-term view about how these issues are going to be decided.

Stephen BREYER: Indeed, when I was nominated to the Supreme Court, I am sure that lawyers for environmental groups, business groups, labor unions, and others read many of the opinions that I had written in the Court of Appeals to try to understand how I would likely decide cases of interest to those groups. Even if I myself have no idea how I would decide a future case involving an environmental statute or an Interior Department cattle grazing regulation, environmentalists and cattle ranchers would like to have an idea, in advance, of what I might do. And the reading by their lawyers of my earlier opinions might lead those lawyers to ask a Senator to ask questions at my confirmation hearing from which they would try to deduce a likely future attitude. That may surprise you.

Consider then what has occurred. The Supreme Court, having decided a major question of constitutional law with a highly controversial political content—that of segregation—and having decided it correctly according to law, may have led the politicians to take a greater interest in the make-up of the Supreme Court. The consequence, too, may have been a greater tendency for Congress to rely upon the Supreme Court to relieve them of some of the responsibility of deciding difficult statutory questions, *i.e.*, questions that are controversial politically. The more that is so, the more that they will take an interest in who is appointed. The political interest is subtle, by the way. No one argues in favor of a judge whose decisions will be affected by politics. Everyone favors independent judges who will act professionally.

Dieter GRIMM: That would not work in the continental systems, first, because judges are appointed, and second, because, when judges are appointed, you do not know what they have decided before because all decisions are anonymous. So the only ones appointed to the Constitutional Court whom you can perhaps predict, and of whom you can speculate how they would decide this or that case, are professors, because they have pronounced themselves in advance. But for the rest, it is almost impossible.

Antonio CASSESE: You said that there are two ways of deciding the level of legislative process. The first is whether or not to send off a question to the judiciary. The second one, that is, to say that we hope that the judges will produce a wonderful decision that is favorable to us, probably only applies to the United States and probably not to Europe.

First of all, it depends on whether the decision is sent to the Constitutional Court (this court normally is more progressive, because some members normally are elected by the parliament, so they are more sensitive to political considerations), or to, say, the Court of Cassation (Supreme Court), where you normally have judges who are very old, old fashioned, and fuddy-duddies. For example, the Italian Corte Suprema di Cassazione (Supreme Court) recently decided that a woman wearing tight jeans could not be raped.

Therefore, as I say, the only solution in continental Europe is to say, "Let us decide to get rid of this political problem and the judges will decide, whether for better or for worse." You cannot anticipate in order to get good progressive judgments!

Ronald DWORKIN: One of your most interesting points was the suggestion that the expansion in judicial role is the response to the internal dynamic of the whole process of adjudication. Once you have the idea deployed that people have rights and that these rights have to be framed in rather abstract ways, then the judiciary is simply responding to the ordinary requirements of adjudication and has no choice but to follow a logic that leads to a considerable expansion in the traditional roles of judicial power. I agree with that, but I think that there are limits to it. I was struck by the distinction that you explored between the court protecting the rights of individuals against the conceded interests of the majority—what we call the negative freedoms or negative liberties—and the further role of the court in policing the decisions that majoritarian institutions make about the best interests of the majority. And, as an example of the second, I am struck by the case of atomic energy. Of course, all the industrial societies now face a trade-off between the advantages of developing atomic energy commercially and the risks that that imposes. Different people will judge those risks differently, different experts will judge them differently, and political communities will make different decisions. But these decisions are not decisions that seem to me well understood as conflicts between an individual right and a social interest. They are something very different; they are conflicts about the correct characterization of the social interest. If the majority of the community, through its elected representatives, decides that the environmental advantages and the greater use of atomic energy outweigh the increased risks, and the court comes along and says, "We do not dictate exactly what level of security you need, but you need more security than you have provided in this legislation," there is nothing in the internal logic of adjudication from notions about human rights that would justify that decision. Furthermore, there is a very good argument against that decision since I understand democratic theory as containing protections for the individual against majorities' self-interest that might overlook the rights of the individual. But it does not seem to me that in a true democracy questions that really are questions of trade-offs about everyone's self-interest should be characterized as questions about human rights and should be taken away from the normal process in which people make their own assessment about the risks and elect people who make judgments of that kind.

I can see that there might be arguments about giving these decisions to technically qualified bodies, like ministerial agencies, and maybe even arguments supporting giving them to judges. I do not exclude the possibility of such arguments. My main worry is that this is not an expansion of the judicial power that would be justified by any internal logic of adjudication, even once human rights are internalized in the legal framework.

Dieter GRIMM: I do not want to say that this interpretation of the Bill of Rights, which the German Constitutional Court adopted gradually, is the logical outcome of internal legal development. It can be different, and we have courts that do not reach this end or that even explicitly exclude it because of other legal reasons like the democratic principle. So I do not want to say that this is the necessary outcome of legal reasoning. What I want to say is rather that, when courts reach this end, they do it by reasoning in a legal way. They start from a notion of fundamental rights that may be different from yours, but it is their interpretation of what fundamental rights in the constitution are, and they draw consequences from that notion. It is a legal process. We can, of course, discuss the question whether this legal process is a good one or a bad one. And I think that this is basically your point. If you want to say that it is impossible to legally reach this conclusion, then I would not agree. When we discuss the problem, whether it is good or not good, I am quite open. But, in my view, a rather narrow conception of fundamental rights underlies your argument. My idea would, first of all, be that fundamental rights furnish a protection not only vis-à-vis the government, but they furnish a protection against threats to the possibility of exercising a fundamental right, regardless of the side from which they come. There are preconditions for exercising fundamental rights and, when they are not guaranteed, the existence of the individual right is not worth very much. However, the Court never claimed the power to answer those questions, which you rightly put as questions of a general balancing between risk and gain. But what the Court really does is put these questions on the agenda when it perceives a considerable risk to the preconditions for the exercise of fundamental rights. It is the legislator who has to decide, but the legislator is not free to avoid the decision. What the Court does is put the issue on the political agenda so that it is binding for the legislator.

Stephen BREYER: How does the Court do that?

Dieter GRIMM: It rules that the Bundestag (the German legislative body) is obliged to make a law or amend an existing law within a certain period. The question is what happens if the legislature does not comply with the decision. This experience we have not really had yet.

Ronald DWORKIN: Remember the abortion legislation? When the old law was kept in force, but it was going to run out. There was some complicated situation.

Dieter GRIMM: There was, indeed, a complicated situation on very few occasions. As a matter of fact, on four occasions during 50 years, the Court itself enacted a transitory law. It ruled that the law had to be amended within a certain period of time, but, in the interim, there cannot be no law in place. In such a situation, the Court has two options. When the absence of any regulation in a particular case would be more detrimental to fundamental rights than the transitory existence of the law that was found to be unconstitutional, the Court declares the old law applicable during the transitory period. If this seems completely unbearable, the Court is free to enact a transitory regulation. But, as I said, this is rare. I remember one case concerning marriage. We had a rule in the Civil Code that when two persons who want to get married cannot agree on a family name, the name of the husband prevails. This was found not to be in accordance with equal protection of men and women, and so the legislature was obliged to amend the law. Yet, had there been no law at all in the meantime, people could not have gotten married. So the Court enacted itself a transitory solution, which avoided the unconstitutional law but did not oblige the legislature to adopt the same rule.

Ronald DWORKIN: There are two distinctions that I think we have to make at this point. One is a distinction that you made, which I think is not what we are pertinently discussing, and that is the distinction between threats to individual rights that come from the government and threats that come from other sources that the government may be obliged to protect against. That is very important. It is certainly not my view that, because assault is the crime of one person against another, the government has no obligation to protect you from assault. That is not my view. That is one distinction that is very important.

The second distinction is the distinction between the court striking down legislation and itself creating legislation. And again, that seems to me not the question that I meant to raise. There are cases in which willy-nilly a court must set in place some regime. If the court says that confessions obtained under certain circumstances will not be admissible in court, then it might be a very good idea for the court to set forth, at least until modified by the legislature, what the police must do. And this could turn out to be quite a complicated code. Again, I am not calling that into question.

What I am questioning is a different line, and that is the line between individual rights to define, in what you say is a narrow way, an individual right and to define in a broader way, so broadly as to make the question of what is the correct trade-off between risk and economic gain a question of human rights or a question of individual rights. I am suggesting that it is a bad idea to describe or identify individual rights so broadly. If you say, for example, that every individual has a right to circumstances in which to develop his or her personality, or circumstances in which his dignity would be protected, then you agree that, of course, a sound economy is necessary in order to allow individuals that right. Then you have in that way turned taxation, economic policy, the interest rate, and whether there should be an international currency into questions of individual human rights. The end of that process will be a dilution of the idea of individual human rights, I believe. In any case, I am suggesting that it is very unwise for judges to interpret these broad human rights in a way that has that consequence.

Antonio CASSESE: I agree with Ronald that, in a way, this new activity is not justified by the internal logic of judicial action. Do you not think, however, that it is more proper and democratic to entrust judges with choices about general issues because they are in a way not under pressure from economic groups, lobbying groups, and so on? In a way, they may lack the expertise that some administrators may have, but they can actually acquire expertise by asking people to give affidavits and to produce documents or materials of that sort. They are not making choices or options on the basis of strong pressure from political parties, economic groups, and so on. From the viewpoint of democracy, I agree with you. It is not a human rights issue. It is a question of whether it is more democratic for judges or for the political majority to decide this issue. I would say that it should be a matter for the judges.

Gil Carlos RODRIGUEZ IGLESIAS: I have a completely different opinion. In my view, society's great problems (such as the use of nuclear energy) must in principle be decided by democratically elected representatives. That is because there are different ways to appraise matters. And the judge will do so from the perspective of one who holds a supervisory position within a framework that is constitutional in nature.

At this point I should like to turn to a legal problem that you emphasized in your presentation. I think that you have illustrated the importance that the principle of proportionality has taken on in the German Constitutional Court's jurisprudence. I have asked myself the following question: Has the proportionality principle become an instrument of judicial imperialism? It leads the judge systematically to substitute his own judgment for that of the legislature. The judge will reconsider the balance that the legislature struck between the public interest and the protection of individual rights. Our Court uses the principle of proportionality often. Yet German critics still systematically claim that, in doing so, we leave to the legislature too much discretion. We will not go as far as German courts—both constitutional and administrative—would in supervising the political authorities' determinations in respect to the balancing of interests.

Stephen BREYER: I have noticed a certain difference between Anglo-Saxon and continental systems on this precise point. I would say that continental systems often have better ways to resolve technical problems, such as those of science and engineering. Such problems often are found in administrative cases resolved by quasi-expert administrative judges or in cases decided by judges who have the authority to summon impartial experts. In the United States, it is often difficult for judges to have as open access to impartial experts. When Antonio CASSESE says, "Just turn it over to the judge," he should realize that, in the United States, the judge cannot easily obtain the necessary technical information. In tort cases, the lawyers find the experts who will testify to a jury about the underlying expert matters. And the tort lawyers sometimes produce "experts" who have very little expertise. In a system such as ours, with serious problems involving a judge's access to relevant technical advice, courts might well hesitate to decide public policy questions that have a technical dimension. In countries where technical questions present less serious problems for the courts, perhaps courts are less hesitant to decide related public policy questions.

Still, I wonder why the German Constitutional Court decided to make questions that turn upon highly technical matters, such as those of atomic power, questions of human rights. After all, it is ordinary German courts, not the Constitutional Court, which may have special ability to deal with such technical matters.

Dieter GRIMM: I can give a historical answer to this question. Although Germany has had constitutions since the beginning of the nineteenth century, the German judiciary was not accustomed to taking constitutional law into account. Civil rights did not matter in the interpretation of ordinary law, for reasons that I could explain. So civil courts applied only civil law, criminal courts only criminal law, and so on. But they did not feel obliged or even permitted to also apply constitutional law. And a constitutional court did not yet exist. Jurisdictions without a specialized court system, and with a general supreme court on top that is entitled to also decide questions of constitutional law, would not necessarily experience that problem. Consider, too, jurisdictions like the Austrian one, where the Constitutional Court is only allowed to review laws but nothing else. We can observe that fundamental rights, when they really matter in criminal law, in civil law, and in administrative law, do not play any role because the Constitutional Court can only review laws, not court decisions and therefore not the interpretation of laws.

This attitude was still more or less the norm when the Basic Law was enacted in 1949. The Constitutional Court wanted to change this, and the way to do it was to say that fundamental rights are not only subjective rights protecting the individual against direct intrusions by the state, but also the most sacred principles for the organization of society as a whole. This is the dogmatic bridge for all the rest that follows. I, myself, find that convincing, and I would like to mention one example that has always struck me. Both the American and the German Constitution guarantee the freedom of broadcasting. In the United States, it is covered by the First Amendment; in Germany it is an explicit right. When you read the decisions of the American Supreme Court and the German Bundesverfassungsgericht (the Federal Constitutional Court of Germany) on the freedom of broadcasting, you would think that they copied from each other, although it is quite clear that nobody knew at that time about the construction of this fundamental right in the other jurisdiction. They both said that this is a right different from the other rights. It does not primarily exist in the interest of the owner of a broadcasting station or of the journalists. It is a right that exists primarily in the interest of the general public, which must be put in a position to decide on its own affairs. In other words, it is indispensable for democracy. Broadcasting renders a public service. So far, the two courts agree. The conclusions drawn from this principle differ. The American Supreme Court concludes that Congress *may* regulate broadcasting, while the German Court says Congress *must* regulate broadcasting, though it must do so in the interest of free communication. This is the basic difference, I think.

Robert BADINTER: We are now discussing a very specific point and one I think very important in respect to judicial activism or imperialism. Here it is: The court says to the lawmaker, "You must act and I shall tell you how!" The court gives the legislature hints. "If you follow that route, it will be constitutional." The court is more or less showing the way: "This is the direction. Go!" This is an extraordinarily important move in terms of power, for it is the judges who say to the representatives of the people, "This is how you should act." And, in my own view, if there is a typical example of judicial imperialism, here it is: when the judge says to the legislature, "You must do this."

Dieter GRIMM: My question is: Why would the legislature do it?

Ronald DWORKIN: Because the public opinion follows! And it is not case by case. There is a sense that the stability of a modern democracy requires that judges be obeyed even when they are wrong.

Robert BADINTER: It is not a stranger. It is the legislature, and the legislature represents the people.

Ronald DWORKIN: But the sense that has been developed that the legislature must stand down—and this is such a widely disseminated view now—is a remarkable development in political theory.

Robert BADINTER: Ronald, you say that it is a remarkable event, one not noticed commonly, and one that is extraordinarily important in terms of political theory.

Ronald DWORKIN: I think that it is noticed, but perhaps I am wrong. I mean, for example, that in the debates in Britain over the last few years, the Labour Party has been remarkably reluctant to take even the rather guarded step of enacting or bringing the Bill of Rights into domestic legislation. And the debate has been exactly about the sovereignty of the people. Once you take this step, it is almost as bad as taking the picture of the Queen off the currency, which the British, I think, will not do for a long time.

Robert BADINTER: The Euro and the Queen!

Gil Carlos RODRIGUEZ IGLESIAS: I should like to emphasize how a judge's power to suggest to a legislator what kinds of laws to write relate to another method of judicial domination, namely, the way in which certain constitutional decisions enjoy an immunity from legislative revision. Those decisions that rest upon certain constitutional interpretations cannot be questioned by legislators. The U.S. Supreme Court decision in the *Dickerson* case[8]—which Stephen BREYER distributed—is particularly interesting in this respect. In that decision, the Supreme Court reaffirmed its decision in the *Miranda* case.[9] It held that the requirements set forth in that earlier case necessary to guarantee the rights of an accused (the "*Miranda* requirements") flow from the Constitution itself. The legislature cannot set them aside even if it were to provide other, alternative ways to guarantee the rights of a defendant. You know that Justice Scalia, in his dissenting opinion, characterized the majority's decision as an obvious manifestation of judicial arrogance.

Stephen BREYER: Our Court was once described in this respect as a "nine-headed Caesar."

Gil Carlos RODRIGUEZ IGLESIAS: It is truly remarkable that a court can not only find fault with the legislator, but also forbid him to secure a constitutional guarantee through a legislative method that differs, not from the Constitution's provisions, but from certain secondary conclusions that the court itself reached through its interpretation of the Constitution. Seen in this light, the court's power is indeed exceptional.

Antonio CASSESE: I will add just one small footnote relating to the discussion about human rights between Ronald DWORKIN and Dieter GRIMM about whether to approach the whole issue of the power of judges from the new point of view of human rights. If I am correct, I understand you to mean that, in Germany and probably in continental Europe, human rights are not only legal entitlements granted to individuals against the state, but even a sort of goal embodying political principles and the purposes of the whole state apparatus. If this is so, I can understand your point much better. I can see why you can weigh the interests of the public as a whole, because, in your view, the constitution does not only say that all the individuals or citizens have a right to freedom, privacy, and so on, but rather that the whole state must function along these broad lines. It is very interesting.

Ronald DWORKIN: I think again that one more distinction is needed. I think that it is right to say that the constitution embodies not just individual rights but collective aspirations of various kinds, one of which and the most fundamental of which is democracy. When Dieter says that you must understand free speech and power, I would not say exclusively, but you must understand the right of broadcasting in part as protecting democracies where there are the rights of individual speakers. I think that is quite right and, in my view, is therefore part of the logic of protecting the constitution and the right interpretation to give judges this power. But I want to distinguish that from questions about the right balance between two aspirations that have themselves constitutional status. One is security and the other is prosperity, efficiency, and the state of the environment. What I resist is taking all the values that a decent society should permit and giving them a status of constitutional aspiration equivalent to democracy. There is no doubt—it is something that I will discuss further in my presentation—that judges must make up their minds among the competing conceptions of democracy. There is no way out. People disagree about what democracy is. It is not the case that you say "democracy" and everyone says, "Oh yes, we know what that is." There is a debate and judges must, like other individuals, make up their minds. But I do not believe that it follows that they must make up their minds about the correct balance between security and efficiency or environmental amenities. You have made an argument that would lead to the opposite conclusion. And I think that we have to discuss that argument further because I think it is in the background of all these discussions. The argument concerns, to put it succinctly, the failure of the democratic process. That is, we might say that, ideally, a democracy should decide questions about atomic energy, risks and gains, and so forth. But you say that the democracy that we have to recognize is in many ways flawed. There are lobbyists, there are single-issue politicians who will garner support—even if it is minority opinion—to win the day, and there is money. In my view, the biggest problem that democracy now faces in the United States is the role of money. Each time that the Supreme Court has had a chance to help, it has forfeited that chance. We could make a long list of the failures of democracy and the reasons why. Therefore, it is tempting to say in the face of not the ideal democracy, but democracy as we find it, that judges should take more and more power or administrative agencies should be given more and more power. But we have to realize that when we are taking that step, we are saying that democracy no longer works.

So it is an undemocratic alternative, and an extremely unfortunate basis on which to rest the increase of judicial power. We would do better, in my view, to seek ways supported by the judiciary to improve democracy. The judges would do better to devote their energies to improving the democratic process rather than filling the gaps left by the shortcomings.

Dieter GRIMM: I agree with that, but I believe that there is the possibility of reconciling the two points of view. I still think that you overestimate what the court does. It does not balance, let us say, security and gain. Never does the question appear in such broad terms. The court does not engage in such balancing. The normal situation is that there is a development, likely a development caused by scientific and technological progress, that creates considerable risks to interests protected by fundamental rights. The government does not do anything about it, although this might not be a deliberate decision. In such cases, the constitutional court does not itself engage in the balancing, but it forces the legislature to tackle the question and to make the policy judgment.

Stephen BREYER: But that argument does not work. Our courts often have said to administrative agencies just what you say to legislatures: "Just reconsider the matter. Look hard at the issues. We will review what you do with some margin of deference." This kind of judicial review, engaged in by the courts of appeals, killed atomic energy in the United States. All the courts said to the agencies was, "Do a better job. Try to balance more carefully." The courts always denied that they themselves engaged in any balancing or any policy judgments. But because they said this often, thereby deferring construction of an atomic plant, the atomic plants could not be built and, eventually, the energy companies gave up trying to build them. I do not know if the result was good or bad. Perhaps the world will be a less dangerous place, but perhaps we will simply use other forms of energy that are more destructive or kill far more people. Nor do I know whether a minor economic recession or genetically modified foods will lead to more deaths. But I do know that—whatever the right answers are—administrators, with greater access to technical information, are far more likely to find those answers than are judges. In order to reach the right answers, is it better in general for constitutional judges to do what you say they should do—police the outer limits of technically based decisions—or is it better to keep constitutional judges entirely out of these areas? I tend to believe the latter.

Robert BADINTER: At this point, is it fair to say that we have sufficient proof coming from both sides of the aisle that, in the past 25 years, there have been remarkable advances in judicial activism, whether or not the judges hide what they are doing and whether their intentions are good or bad? Everywhere we see a movement toward the judge determining the limits. The judge says, "You can go up to here, but no further. You can fill in the gaps, but I mark the outer limits. You build within them." Does that seem to you to be, as

I believe it is, the contemporary dynamic? Whether environmental groups with a specific agenda or other groups facilitate this dynamic is beside the point. I put that to the side. The question is whether there is a general movement in that direction. I think there is. I think that judges take advantage of every occasion to extend their empire. The judge does not turn down whatever opportunity presents itself.

Gil Carlos RODRIGUEZ IGLESIAS: In principle I agree with you. But on the other hand, sometimes a judicial dynamic will require judges to rule on problems that they would prefer not to deal with because they know that they should not be the ones deciding that question. I shall give you an example from our European Court, which has a reputation of being activist. The example arises in the context of the free circulation of goods. Our Court has a broad view of the free circulation of goods and particularly of the phrase "measures with an effect equivalent to quantitative restrictions." That phrase makes it possible to consider virtually every national regulatory measure as if it were a restriction on the free circulation of goods. And the Court consequently has had to consider the legitimacy of all sorts of different regulations. It is easy to see that virtually every regulation can have some restrictive effect upon commerce. At the same time, the EEC (European Economic Community) Treaty has expressly provided some justifications for restricting the free circulation of goods. These include public health concerns, protecting intellectual property, and so forth. A reading of the text of the Treaty makes clear that it is up to the Court to strike the balance.

In 1974, in the *Dassonville* case,[10] the Court broadened the definition of the "measures" that could have an "effect" on the free circulation of goods by defining those measures as including "every national regulation or other national measure capable of interfering with intra-community commerce, directly or indirectly, actually or potentially." This expansion of the concept of "effect" led the Court itself subsequently (in the 1979 case of *Cassis de Dijon*)[11] to recognize possible justifications other than those set forth expressly in the Treaty. The French have called this possibility *exigences imperatives* (imperative demands), badly translated into English as "mandatory requirements" and more often translated as "reasons of general interest." They provide potential justifications for limiting the free circulation of goods. And, by finding that the Treaty implicitly includes them, the Court itself has extended the scope of its decisionmaking with respect to the free circulation of goods.

In any case, the Court at a certain point recognized that this approach required it to pass upon whether legislative determinations were or were not justified—a task that did not arise naturally out of the Court's judicial role. The "Sunday trading" case is a good example.[12] Many municipalities in the United Kingdom required shops to remain closed on Sunday. A group of intelligent lawyers claimed that this requirement amounted to a limitation upon the free circulation of goods in the European Union (EU), for it prevented the sale of goods imported from other EU countries on Sunday, the very day that the public is most likely to do its shopping. We at the Court consequently had to face the question that the English judges had posed: whether this rule forbidding Sunday shopping was compatible with the free circulation of goods.

Initially, the Court took a very strict position regarding the relationship between its own functions and those of national courts. It said that it was up to the national courts to examine in a specific case the proportionality of such measures. The potential "public interest" justifications could be alleged (for example, the preservation of a certain model of social life, preserving a traditional Sunday, meeting certain cultural objectives, etc.). The national court would then examine these objectives (which, in our Court's view, were perfectly legitimate), and the national court would then determine whether they justified the likely minimal interference with the free circulation of goods. The consequence of our cases that set forth this judicial approach was that different British judges reached different conclusions.

At a later stage, our Court itself was led to consider the proportionality of a particular national regulation. Because both law and society require certainty, it was not acceptable for one judge to say, "The measure is disproportionate and, hence, incompatible with European Community law," while another said, "The measure is proportionate and, hence, compatible with Community law." That would not work. Thus the Court itself examined the proportionality of the measure, it affirmed that the effect upon the free circulation of goods was minimal, and it held that there was no incompatibility with Community law.

What interests me about this complicated series of events is that it ended up with the proportionality of laws regulating Sunday trading being determined in a judicial enclosure in Luxembourg. The Court there ultimately decided whether the policy forbidding Sunday trading—a matter that opposing interests had strongly contested—was a "good" or a "bad" policy (though I overstate the matter for purposes of illustration).

Nor has this kind of concern been without influence upon the development of the Court's "free circulation of goods" jurisprudence since the *Keck & Mithouard* decision.[13] In that case, the Court was asked to consider the compatibility of French law forbidding below-cost sales with the Treaty's guarantees of the free circulation of goods. It was argued that a prohibition against below-cost sales prevented firms from using particularly valuable methods for introducing imported goods into a market. The Court held that this kind of regulation of the methods of sale was not a method of regulating the exchange of goods among states. The Court thereby limited the extent to which judicial power would control national policy choice.

Antonio CASSESE: But you limited yourselves.

Gil Carlos RODRIGUEZ IGLESIAS: Yes, we did limit ourselves. Thus, returning to the question that Robert BADINTER raised, I would say that this example of how the Court's jurisprudence evolved shows that the judiciary does not always have the tendency to enlarge its own powers.

Stephen BREYER: There is a certain connection between the Sunday trading problem and the nuclear energy problem. In each instance, judges are interpreting a document (a treaty or a constitution) written with highly general language. The language was probably written with other circumstances in mind. But, given its generality, the language arguably also covers quite different circumstances (with different, but important, political consequences). What shall the judges do? Shall they: (1) create exemptions for certain categories of cases where other authorities (*e.g.*, British judges or administrative agencies) shall have the last word? (2) create special rules of decision for certain categories of cases where it is important that other institutions decide the matter (*e.g.*, national security problems or giving special deference to the agency or Executive Branch decisionmaker)? (3) find a general judicial concept that will allow the court to reach different results in such different cases (*e.g.*, by employing the principle of proportionality)? (Note that the below-cost sale is a different kind of example, for it raises a question of ordinary competition law.)

Robert BADINTER: I would agree about that. I would also note that the principle of proportionality is the most wide-reaching and the most convenient tool that judges have invented anywhere.

Stephen BREYER: But it is not used in the United States, which is a pity. I have cited the European Court of Human Rights' decision in *Bowman*[14] in part to encourage the use of that principle.

Dieter GRIMM: I find it very awkward.

Robert BADINTER: It is an instrument of longstanding usefulness in my country. The Conseil d'Etat (the highest administrative court in France) has used it for a long time. It helps the judge to decide. The judge can choose in the name of proportionality.

Antonio CASSESE: There is another problem. If any constitutional court starts using the notion of "reasonableness," it may prove difficult to establish whether something is "reasonable."

Ronald DWORKIN: Reasonableness is all over the place.

Antonio CASSESE: I draw your attention to an international case concerning a major issue: whether the threat of use of nuclear weapons is illegal. The case was brought before the International Court of Justice by the United Nations General Assembly, which requested an advisory opinion. Quite a number of countries appeared before the Court: Australia, New Zealand, Russia, France, the United States, the United Kingdom, and a number of others. The Court ended up with a "non liquet." They decided by a vote of 7 to 7, with the President casting a vote. The Court's ruling was that it is not clear whether international law bans resort to nuclear weapons in cases of extreme self-defense, when the self-preservation of a country is in peril. In my view, the decision is totally absurd, but I think that it was very good for certain countries, governments, and NGOs to go to the General Assembly and say, "This is a crucial question." But then, the British, the American, and the French governments said, "You judges cannot decide this matter. This is a matter relating to the *politique de dissuasion*. It is a question of foreign policy. Our whole foreign policy is based on deterrence. This has nothing to do with judges." So the judges got terribly scared. They decided by a vote of 7 to 7.

Ronald DWORKIN: Seven judges did not get scared. That is very interesting. All it takes is one more.

Antonio CASSESE: I think that the crucial question is also how judges are appointed and whether they wish to be reappointed. I gather— or rather there are rumors—that some of those judges who were scared wanted to be re-elected by the General Assembly and the Security Council, and they needed the support of the major powers. It is alleged that, for this purpose, they had to vote in a particular way (of course, this is mere speculation, which, as such, may not affect the integrity of international judges).

Ronald DWORKIN: So it is important that the judges not be eligible for re-election, either because they serve for life or because they cannot be re-elected.

Antonio CASSESE: I think that, in Germany and in Italy, members of the Constitutional Court may serve only one term and are not eligible for re-election. Perhaps in France too.

Dieter GRIMM: I think that the term limit is no problem. Re-election or the possibility of renewal is the problem—a huge problem.

Antonio CASSESE: A judge may want to please the government.

Ronald DWORKIN: I once was asked—because I am in favor of limiting the terms of judges to one long term—what judges will be able to do afterwards. There is only one answer: They have to teach at law schools. They cannot get a job in industry.

Stephen BREYER: Why not?

Ronald DWORKIN: The reason judges have to teach at universities is because they are incompetent! The reason they cannot go to industry is that we worry about their decisions in the few years before they leave the bench and go into the industry. So there is only one thing to do: send them off to law school.

Gil Carlos RODRIGUEZ IGLESIAS: On this point, I would like to say that the existence or not of a dissenting opinion is important. In my Court, we are normally more insulated in this respect, for there are no dissenting opinions.

Robert BADINTER: True, there are no dissenting opinions in your Court. But what about cases in which a judge might refuse to decide, saying that the matter is not his affair and that he should not become involved in it? In France, we have decided that the Conseil Constitutionnel (France's Constitutional Court) should not be regarded as having the same powers as the legislature. It is not up to that Court to make the law. If that Court disapproves of a proposed statute, it is up to the legislature to decide what to do about it. The Conseil need not abstain to the same extent in interpreting laws or indicating what might be constitutional. But we have always acknowledged the existence of a certain line that the constitutional judge must not cross because the separation of powers forbids him to do so. Hence, Ronald, we have answered your question affirmatively.

Ronald DWORKIN: But are there no cases in which if you say that it is unconstitutional and therefore void, then there is no law?

Robert BADINTER: Remember that we rule before the publication of the law. We do not rule on laws in existence. We simply render laws aborted; we annul.

Stephen BREYER: In a civil law system, a judge must fill a "void" in a code provision. Hence, a judge will normally feel bound to decide a case that asks the judge to fill that void. In the common law system, a judge is not "filling in the law." In deciding a dispute between two parties, the judge is deciding a case. It is not surprising then that judge-made rules tell the judges both how, and when, to decide the relevant dispute. There used to be rules that kept judges away from deciding cases that would involve the judge in political matters. Some of those rules still exist, particularly in respect to foreign affairs. I doubt that the civil law has a special rule that says to the judge, "Do not decide a matter that involves foreign affairs," but we do have such rules.

Dieter GRIMM: If a case is duly brought—there are some conditions: whether the person or the institution that brought the claim could rightly do so or not—then the only available course is to declare the relevant act constitutional or unconstitutional.

Stephen BREYER: We have instances in which cases are properly brought, issues are properly presented, but we do not decide simply because of the nature of the legal issue, because it involves, say, political affairs or foreign affairs. A case might involve the CIA or certain administrative statutes, and the Court might interpret the statute as showing an intent by Congress that courts stay out of the matter. In such an instance, the courts will not decide the legal issue, leaving the legal matter as they found it.

Ronald DWORKIN: In France, is there no way to challenge on constitutional grounds a legal regime that has been in force for ten years?

Robert BADINTER: No, except if it is rewritten in a new law that is being challenged. If no one sends it to the Conseil, then the purportedly unconstitutional law still remains in existence.

Ronald DWORKIN: So if there is a new law that you declare unconstitutional because it is discriminatory, and then people say, "There are many other laws that are discriminatory in exactly the same way," then there is nothing you can do about those other laws? They are exactly the same, but they were passed a few years ago.

Robert BADINTER: For discrimination, then you would go to Strasbourg (*i.e.*, the European Court of Human Rights).

Stephen BREYER: What about Luxembourg (*i.e.*, the Court of Justice of the European Communities)?

Robert BADINTER: Eventually, in the realm of the EEC Treaty.

Ronald DWORKIN: If the litigant can go to Strasbourg and say, the Constitutional Court of France has declared this kind of thing unconstitutional, but it has not applied it in this case. For instance, the Court has declared an act unconstitutional in the case of school teachers because there was a new law dealing with school teachers. But the same discrimination has been exercised, say, in the military, but the Court has not applied the same reasoning in that case. Then you go to Strasbourg and Strasbourg says, "By your own declarations, this kind of thing is unconstitutional."

Robert BADINTER: They would not say "by your own declaration" because they would refer to ordinary standards. They will, however, use it in the argument.

Ronald DWORKIN: In the argument, they are likely to point to the fact that you actually agreed with it?

Stephen BREYER: Why do you not simplify the rules?

Robert BADINTER: It is not so simple.

Dieter GRIMM: It is not a question of practice, but rather a statutory matter.

Antonio CASSESE: Why go to Strasbourg? Why not go to the Cour de Cassation (France's Supreme Court)?

Robert BADINTER: The question can be raised in the Cour de Cassation.

Stephen BREYER: Would the exact same argument be raised in the Cour de Cassation as at Strasbourg?

Robert BADINTER: Yes. But if the Cour de Cassation says no, then the lawyers will go to Strasbourg.

Antonio CASSESE: No. But, in France, treaties trump statutes because of article 55 of the Constitution. And the Cour de Cassation will apply the European Convention on Human Rights.

Stephen BREYER: Every court in France can apply the Human Rights Convention *except* the Conseil Constitutionnel?

Robert BADINTER: Remember that they are not courts of the same jurisdictional order and that the jurisprudential bases for decision differ. The Conseil Constitutionnel bases its decisions upon the Constitution. But we in the Constitutional Court have referred to the Strasbourg Court's jurisprudence when explaining the grounds for our decisions. This is reciprocal influence. It does not belong to the same unified order of jurisdiction. That is why it is so confusing and difficult to handle. But all that is another matter. At this stage—to continue our discussion—what impression or conclusions do you have about judicial activism and imperialism? Do you think, in terms of the general trend toward activism, that the overall tendency is limited only by the fact that judges can handle only a certain number of decisions each year—which means that they do not want too many? Or do you think that the general tendency is toward not a greater number of decisions, but individual decisions of ever-greater consequence and of ever-greater scope? The growth in a judge's exercises of power need not be measured quantitatively, for it often consists simply of a broader field of action. Is that it? I think so. But are you aware of other examples or instances in which the judge does not want to consider certain matters? For instance, the judge does not want to decide questions about atomic energy or does not want to work on environment law.

Stephen BREYER: I would say that the jurisprudence of American courts would seem a little activist compared to the rest of the world.

Robert BADINTER: You have a long tradition of activism.

Stephen BREYER: We have some counterexamples. In the *Vermont Yankee* case,[15] the Supreme Court tried to stop lower courts from insisting that administrative agencies follow certain procedures. The Supreme Court, in effect, told the courts to grant agencies a greater margin of deference, to refrain from a kind of procedural "activism."

Ronald DWORKIN: Is that true?

Stephen BREYER: I doubt that our courts have been continuously expanding their jurisdiction, at least not recently. But other courts elsewhere in the world may be catching up with some of our earlier, more "activist," decisions. Those decisions include decisions expanding substantive rights. Some argue that today our Court is "activist" in trying to limit the power of Congress, thereby granting states additional power.

Ronald DWORKIN: That is a very important point about the use of these ideas of activism and imperialism and all of these "territorial" metaphors to describe what we are talking about. There is a limitation on the usefulness of these territorial or even military images that are used because it may be the wrong dimension in which to try and measure it. We see that the German Court is, by conventional terms, more active than the U.S. Supreme Court. What we were speaking about earlier would not take place in the United States, I think. We have justices on the United States Supreme Court, who for years denied and condemned activism. In my view, they together form a core that is the most activist in my memory, because they wish to return the United States to what they take to be a period of its history that I think never existed and certainly did not exist in their lifetimes.

So do we call them activists or pacifists? They say, "We are simply returning to the original vision. We are correcting activism." But from my perspective and those of other critics, they are being inconsistently and outrageously activist. I just want to add a caveat against the usefulness of this way of measuring what we are talking about. In Europe, for example, I believe that the Strasbourg Court has in many respects been less active than it could have been. That is certainly true of the international court. Antonio CASSESE gave us a very good example of this.

Robert BADINTER: Ronald, I am sorry to interrupt, but I do not think that you can say that Strasbourg has not been activist. It has been very activist. Always keep in mind that, in the beginning, the Convention was drafted by people who were mostly Christian Democrats (i.e., moderate socialists with traditional religious views). Those people never thought of gay rights or transsexuals' rights fifty years ago.

Ronald DWORKIN: Is this not another example of the sponginess of the concept of how to measure what is active and what is not? If you measure it against the expectations of the generation that created the law, then it looks very active. If you measure it against the expectations of the litigants or against the possibilities presented by the doctrine, you and I might think that the freedom of expression sections have been underutilized in the Strasbourg Court. The Strasbourg Court has deferred to—I forgot what the phrase is—the interest of the various nations and the special problems and circumstances of the various nations, in my view, more often than it otherwise might have done. If you measure it against what a genuinely active judiciary, following Dieter's logic of taking rights and expanding them to their limit, would do, then I will say that it has not been so active. If you contrast it to what would have been expected by the people who laid down the Convention, it has been extremely active.

Robert BADINTER: We should take up this matter again because, Ronald, I would not agree with your statement. Remember one essential thing: You cannot compare the situation of the all-powerful German institution at Karlsruhe (the German Constitutional Court) with that of Strasbourg, which has only jurisdictional authority delegated by Convention. The member nations agreed to the creation of that jurisdictional authority only within limits set by the Treaty. The agreement by those nations to create what was for them a foreign legal jurisdiction and to submit to the authority of that foreign jurisdiction, particularly with respect to an issue as critical and fundamental as liberty, was a highly sensitive matter. You cannot, as a member of a court created by convention, forget the fact that you can exercise only this kind of power. Your court is not integrated structurally within a country; it is not part of a country, it has been placed above other countries simply by a convention.

Ronald DWORKIN: Perhaps we are not disagreeing. I am saying that they have been cautious. And you say that, of course, they have been cautious.

Robert BADINTER: No. What I mean is that they have been bold up to the limit of what is possible.

Ronald DWORKIN: It is really a question of *a priori* or afterwards. Because whether judges can or cannot get away with it is always an argument before and after. For example, in the United States, Alexander Bickel, who was the protégé of Justice Felix Frankfurter, wrote a book saying that there are limits to what the people will accept from the Court, and that the Court must be very careful. It was Frankfurter's message that the Court must be extremely careful.

And yet we have not come to any case in which, in retrospect, when the Court did take a step of the kind that Frankfurter thought was wrong, these predictions turned out to be real. I am thinking of the cases that raised the question of the constitutionality of miscegenation laws, when Frankfurter wrote Learned Hand and said, in essence, that a court better not take the step of hearing the matter.

Stephen BREYER: I still suspect that a civil law judge, compared to a common law judge, believes that he must decide whatever case is put in front of him. If a written law says x, and a case arises in which the meaning of x is at stake, the civil law judge will decide the case, no matter how political the ramifications. There are no principles that allow him to avoid deciding, for example, the legality of the Vietnam war. Is that so?

Antonio CASSESE: Not necessarily. Listen, you do not decide necessarily. What Dieter said is true because a judge can find that it is not a duly presented question.

Stephen BREYER: I refer to a properly presented case with proper parties with a code provision that seems to cover the matter.

Robert BADINTER: No. It is not possible.

Stephen BREYER: My question is whether the civil law judge is more likely to decide a legal question simply because, conceptually speaking, the case before him presents an issue that falls within the scope of words in a legal document. If so, then, if you present that judge with a document, say, a constitution that has a very broad text, perhaps that judge will decide more matters than his common law counterpart, who is bound by principles telling him not to decide, say, political matters, foreign affairs, or matters committed to agency discretion by law, even if the case and parties are otherwise proper. To what extent do the conceptual task, democratic theory, and other factors account for comparative "activist" differences?

Robert BADINTER: Could we come to a conclusion on this discussion? Let us leave aside the word "imperialism" and use "activism." Do we believe that there is a tendency not only toward accruing ever-greater jurisdictional authority, but also toward accruing greater power for the judge within the bounds of existing jurisdictional authority? The more activism there is, the more that the court will decide. Is that a general tendency? I am convinced that it is. I am convinced that it is throughout Europe.

Gil Carlos RODRIGUEZ IGLESIAS: It is a general tendency, but a tendency that has exceptions. I believe that there are times when judges believe that courts are not the legitimate institutions to decide certain matters. They express, through the use of technical legal arguments, their conviction that they should, or should not, decide certain matters. For example, for a number of years we have avoided considering abortion in Ireland.

Robert BADINTER: That is a very important example. When I look at it from the outside, the U.S. Supreme Court decided a case about the freedom of abortion in *Roe* v. *Wade*.[16] Then there were many attempts to change that decision, including some within the Court itself. But Congress did not settle the question. I have the impression that Congress was perfectly happy to leave the issue to the Court. It is more convenient for the politicians to leave the matter to the Court than to take it into the political or legislative field. It is a form of political retreat. The politicians consider the matter a hot potato, and they realize that they have nothing to gain by deciding it, but much to lose. They think, by contrast, that judges are fit to decide such a matter. It is a salient example.

Ronald DWORKIN: I think that is not exactly right because lurking in the backdrop is a very vigorous group of politicians who would love to reintroduce this issue. We saw it once again in the platform committee of the Republican National Convention for the 2000 presidential election, against the absolute strenuous urging of the candidate's team. The latter insisted that in the Republican plan would be a promise to appoint judges irrespective of their views on abortion. I would be quite happy to see this happen. As in most cases, we have to qualify everything that we say. But if there is any sort of conclusion as to what we think about this, I know that it is unfortunate. I do not think the word "activist" is the right word to use at this point partly because, at least in some places, it is a derogatory term. That is, judges should not be activists partly because, as the recent history of conservative judges shows, it is very unclear what counts as being activist. I think that we should aim at some formulation that says that a growing number of issues are regarded as issues that are promptly subject to adjudication or properly subjects for judges to decide.

Robert BADINTER: Yes, but consider this. Judicial "activism" is a fact, and we agree about that. But what are the factors that are driving the current reality? Is it that public opinion at this moment favors such a transfer of power? Does it reflect a certain lassitude or a willingness to transfer responsibilities on the part of the political world? Or is it the judges themselves who simply seek to extend the scope of their authority? It is a very important issue, practically speaking, because it helps the judges to remove barriers.

Ronald DWORKIN: It is almost a conceptual truth that you have to decide. If you were to take a public opinion poll, say, in the United States or Britain, and you asked: "Is it right that judges have assumed responsibility for this or that?" I think that you will get a lot of people saying yes. If you once asked, "Do we want our judges to be more activist?" then they would also say no. That is why I am saying that it is a word we need not use.

Robert BADINTER: I find interesting the realities that underlie the words, and not the other way around.

Stephen BREYER: Ronnie wants to ask the following: To what extent does a certain consequence (judges deciding more matters) flow from a certain kind of cause, namely, judges themselves "pushing the envelope" of their jurisdiction? I suspect that we would say that this factor has played some role in Germany, in international courts, and in the United States if we go back to the 1960s. We still do not know the extent to which this factor reflects personal considerations (*e.g.*, "I can decide this as well as anyone"), changes in the written law (*e.g.*, giving courts more matters to decide), and institutional considerations (*e.g.*, treaties or constitutions that ask judges to decide). We ask whether judges have "pushed the envelope."

Ronald DWORKIN: Exactly. It is very hard to avoid these spatial metaphors, but we have to be very careful when we use them. The important thing is that the range of issues that now are regarded, both by the institution and by the public, as appropriate issues for judges to decide seems to me to be increasing.

Stephen BREYER: We simply agree that the answer is yes. But we do not necessarily agree about why.

NOTES

1. 7 BVerfGE 198 (1958).
2. Judgment of February 25, 1975, 39 BVerfGE 1 (1975).
3. *Olmstead* v. *United States*, 277 U.S. 438 (1928).

4. *Katz* v. *United States,* 389 U.S. 347 (1967).

5. *Barcelona Traction Case* (Belgium v. Spain), 1970 I.C.J. 3.

6. *South-West Africa Cases* (Ethiopia v. South Africa, Liberia v. South Africa), 1966 I.C.J. 6.

7. *Brown* v. *Board of Education,* 347 U.S. 483 (1954).

8. *Dickerson* v. *United States,* 530 U.S. 428 (2000).

9. *Miranda* v. *Arizona,* 384 U.S. 436 (1966).

10. Case 8/74, *Procureur du Roi* v. *Benoit & Gustave Dassonville,* 1974 E.C.R. 837, 2 C.M.L.R. 436 (1974).

11. Case 120/78, *Rewe-Zentral AG* v. *Bundesmonopolverwaltung für Branntwein,* 1979 E.C.R. 649, 3 C.M.L.R. 494 (1979).

12. Case 169/91, *Stoke-on-Trent Borough Council* v. *B&Q,* 1992 E.C.R. I-6635.

13. Joined Cases C-267 & 268/91, *Keck and Mithouard,* 1993 E.C.R. I-6097, [1995] 1 C.M.L.R. 101 (1993).

14. *Bowman* v. *United Kingdom,* 26 Eur. H.R. Rep. 1 (1998).

15. *Vermont Yankee Nuclear Power Corp.* v. *Natural Resources Defense Council, Inc.,* 435 U.S. 519 (1978).

16. *Roe* v. *Wade,* 410 U.S. 113 (1973).

2

The Secular Papacy

2.1. Presentation

Professor Ronald Dworkin

I pose three questions about the contemporary role of judges in announcing, interpreting, and enforcing the basic principles of justice and democracy for their communities: (1) Is there any way that judges playing that role can avoid relying on their own personal moral convictions, which may be different from those of most of their fellow citizens and, in any case, will vary from judge to judge? (2) If not, is this judicial role anathema to democracy or otherwise objectionable? (3) Such authority is indeed thought unjustified by many critics and much of the general population, and judges characteristically deny that they rely on their own personal moral convictions in exercising it. Why, then, have so many democracies—emerging as well as mature—adopted constitutions that inevitably give judges the power that the critics deplore and the judges strain to deny that they have?

I

I know that many non-lawyers (and even some law professors, lawyers, and judges) think that law is wholly independent of morality, and that judges who appeal to moral principles or ideals to support their decisions are trespassing on the roles of priests, statesmen, and moralizers, and violating their responsibilities to decide cases according to what the law is, not what it should be. That positivist canon was never defensible. Nor, perhaps, would any of us here defend it. It was not true even when the highest courts of modern democracies were preoccupied almost entirely with enforcing codes or statutes or applying the precedential decisions of the common law to new situations. The strict positivistic sources of law had fuzzy boundaries and left gaps; these had to be sharpened or filled in with interpretation, and interpretation requires judges to decide which way of continuing the story that the legislature or other judges have begun is the most satisfactory, all things considered. That is a judgment that is moral at its core.

In the decades after World War II, more and more of these democracies—except in the United States—gave judges new and unprecedented powers to review the acts of administrative agencies and officials under broad doctrines of reasonableness, natural justice, and proportionality, and then even more surprising powers to review legislative enactments to determine whether the legislatures had violated the rights of individual citizens set forth in international treaties and domestic constitutions. The impact of moral pronouncement on judicial argument thus became much more evident and pronounced.

The new role was different from the traditional one in three interconnected ways. First, the need for judges to confront moral issues is more pervasive in general administrative regulation, and much more pervasive in constitutional adjudication, than it is in either ordinary statutory interpretation or common law development. The law of crime, property, contract, commerce, and personal injury can—and indeed must—be structured by technical rules whose operation can be predicted with reasonable confidence by homeowners, testators, businessmen, and insurance companies. These technical rules raise deep issues of fairness and personal responsibility, and such issues are at the heart of the matter when judges decide novel cases at the boundaries of the rules, and when they undertake some much needed reorganization or reform. But the visible impact of judicial moralizing is often small in such cases. The role of moral judgment is pervasive and undeniable in administrative regulation, on the other hand, because the standards of that task are themselves set out in moral language—the language of convenience and necessity, or reasonableness, or proportionality, for example—and because it requires judges to choose among contested conceptions of economic and administrative efficiency, and to fix an interaction and balance between efficiency and other moral values.

The role of moral judgment is yet more pervasive and less deniable in constitutional adjudication, because the pertinent constitutional standards are even more explicitly moral: They declare rights of free expression, treatment as equals, and respect for life and dignity, and sometimes make exceptions for constraints "necessary in a democratic society," for example. In ordinary code or statutory interpretation, and in common law adjudication, novel or otherwise test cases are hard most often because they lie at the boundaries of what is settled. In constitutional adjudication, on the other hand, cases are often hard not because they lie at the borders of doctrine, but because they call for a fresh understanding of the most basic underlying underpinnings of the doctrine. The question whether the right of free expression, properly understood, protects hate speech or speech insulting or offensive to persecuted minorities, for instance, or whether some prohibition of such speech is necessary in a genuinely democratic society requires reflection on some of the deepest issues of political morality—on the reason why free speech should be protected and on the best conception of democracy. Of course, practice and precedent will shape (in different ways in different jurisdictions) how any particular judge must reflect on those issues. But, particularly in the formative period of a nation's (or a continent's) constitutional law, precedent and practice will be thin. In any case, the question how and to what degree a judge's moral reflection on constitutional issues should be shaped by practice or precedent is *itself* a deep and contested question of political morality, as I shall shortly emphasize.

Second, the moral issues that constitutional judges face are often the most controversial and divisive in the community. Ordinary adjudication raises moral issues, but these are rarely issues that are the subject of wider public notice or disagreement. Whether it is right that a murderer inherit property from his victim or fair that someone whose negligence has caused gigantic damage should bear the entire financial responsibility is not a matter of great public concern or attention. And if these were to become so, they would probably not generate violent controversy. But the moral issues that figure in constitutional adjudication are the most divisive possible: In the United States, they include questions about abortion and euthanasia, about racial and other forms of discrimination, about whether government may favor disadvantaged minorities, and about whether prayers may be said in public schools or at college football games. The notoriety of these moral issues guarantees that the judicial role in deciding them will itself become a matter of public attention and at least occasional hostility.

Third, the moral issues at the heart of both administrative and constitutional adjudication are largely matters of political morality rather than individual ethics. The issues of fairness that occupy ordinary adjudication are matters of how individuals should treat one another in business, or in creating risk and compensating for damage, for example. But the issues for judges in constitutional cases are about how government should or may treat its citizens. When a constitutional court considers how far government may make abortion or euthanasia a crime, it is not considering—at least not directly—whether these practices are wicked or immoral. It is considering whether government may properly decide those questions for everyone subject to its power, or whether it must rather allow individuals to judge the ethics of abortion or suicide for themselves. (The public is often careless about that distinction: Many people believe that the U.S. Supreme Court has decided that abortion is morally permissible and that assisted suicide is morally wrong.) Of course, there are complex interconnections between issues of individual ethics and of political morality—whether the government may properly prohibit abortion depends crucially, for example, on whether abortion is the murder of a human creature with interests of its own. But the central moral issues of constitutional adjudication are nevertheless political, not individual.

The prominence of moral issues in constitutional adjudication has made judges into public figures, particularly in the United States, but also, to a growing degree, in other countries. Even in Britain, which has only just decided (in effect) to incorporate the European Convention on Human Rights into its domestic law, and thus to give the powers and responsibilities that I have been discussing to judges, the background and political stance of individual members of the Judicial House of Lords is already beginning to attract attention. (New Law Lords will be appointed soon, and the question of who will be appointed is receiving much more attention than such promotions used to attract.) The new attention (in the United States, the longstanding attention) is very often, and sometimes fiercely, critical. It is widely thought that there is something wrong with judges pontificating about controversial matters of ethics and political morality. Even sophisticated lawyers and judges who accept that judges must necessarily weave moral judgments into their arguments seem embarrassed by that fact, and they are dogged in their insistence that judges need not and should not invoke what is often called their own *personal* morality. Much ingenious argument has been devoted to attempting to show why and how judges can avoid—or at least substantially reduce—any reliance on their own personal convictions about the moral issues in play. Steve, for example, in an excellent lecture at Oxford a few years ago, described and analyzed a number of features of constitutional adjudication in the Supreme Court that seem to him to have that effect.

It is understandable that the lay and professional public—and the judges themselves—are anxious to insist that, when judges decide whether their countries may ban abortion, or authorize their police to terrorize terrorists, or prevent the publication of racially inflammatory or insensitive literature, these judges are not simply imposing their own personal moral convictions, which may be idiosyncratic, on the multitude of their fellow citizens. It seems undemocratic that such fundamental issues should be decided by a small group of appointed officials who cannot be turned out of office by popular will. Judges disagree about political morality among themselves, moreover. And it also seems unfair that important decisions should turn on which panel of judges was sitting at the time, particularly since judicial appointments are often matters of politics and even luck, rather than a solemn assessment of merit. So the most responsible lawyers and judges emphasize, whenever they can, that when judges pontificate about matters of moral dimension they are not (or at least not usually or often) relaying their own personal moral convictions. They say that the judges are relying on something else: the morality of the community as a whole, for example, or the principles embedded in the nation's history. Or that they need not rely on fresh moral judgments at all because, except in particularly outrageous cases, they can and should defer to the judgment of other officials—the domestic legislature or some international body, for example. It seems unlikely that any lawyer who stated that when moral judgment is necessary he would rely on his own personal convictions would find himself or herself appointed to a constitutional court.

Nevertheless our judges' assurances that they do not rely on their own personal morality, however honest, are delusional: They gain whatever plausibility they have because the convictions on which constitutional judges rely are almost always distinctly political convictions rather than the kind of ethical judgment that most people think of as moral. Consider the popular opinion I mentioned: that when judges define some constitutional right—by deciding, for example, whether freedom of expression includes the right to defame a minority religion or race—they should defer, except in truly shocking cases, to the judgment of a legislature or other elected body. If a national legislature has decided that the constitutional right of free expression does not extend that far, or that an exception condemning hate speech is necessary or permissible in a democratic society, then judges should not substitute their own contrary personal convictions. In that way (it is said), judges can avoid simply enforcing their own personal morality. But that is an evident mistake, for these judges are certainly enforcing their own convictions of political morality—*i.e.*, their own conceptions of how decisions should be made in a genuine democracy. And these convictions are as much moral and as much controversial among judges as the more directly substantive opinions that they claim to have set aside.

Judges who appeal to history or to the supposed morality of the community as a whole are also in two ways plainly relying on their own controversial political convictions. First, these judges have embraced the surely controversial conviction that history or popular opinion should govern what rights individuals have. Second, since there will inevitably be a wide variety of different competing interpretations of the community's history respecting free speech, or of what opinion about free speech is the view of the contemporary community as a whole when individual citizens disagree, an interpreter must rely on his own sense of the point of free speech and the correct understanding of the democratic ideal in order to decide which of these competing interpretations is best. The role of a judge's own convictions regarding justice and fairness may be more obscure in such decisions than it is when the judge pontificates directly about the morality or immorality of abortion, for example. But it is no less decisive. True, opinions about the character of democracy are not often debated, or even recognized, by the general public, so that judges who endorse one or another conception of democracy are not taking sides on hotly contested public issues. But if the public came to understand the importance of such abstract issues of political morality for the more substantive issues they do care about—if the public came to understand the consequences of one or another view for a court's decisions about race relations, for example, as Americans did in the course of a recent bitterly contested Supreme Court nomination—then the abstract issues would become instantly more controversial for that reason.

The educational and professional background of most constitutional judges in our countries and the methods by which they are selected tend to ensure that, at least for the most part, their personal convictions are not eccentric—that they fall (in an expression popular in America) within the "mainstream" of popular opinion. There have been times (I believe that one such time is now in the United States) when history produces a group of constitutional judges whose political morality is in important respects radical by conventional standards. Even then, the opinions of the "non-mainstream" judges reflect an important, if not a dominant, segment of opinion. These political realities no doubt contribute to the legitimacy of judicial review. But the constraints that they impose are *de facto*, not normative: A judge's convictions are none the less personal because they are likely to be popular, or at least not too unpopular.

2

So there is no bedrock of interpersonal consensus or institutional allocation of power or historical fact on which a constitutional judge can rely in place of expressing his or her own personal convictions of political morality. Every decision that a judge makes to enforce the broad moral provisions of a constitution to new issues demands the exercise of the judge's own judgment of substantive justice or the judge's own understanding of what a fair distribution of political power requires. (For those who know the work of the children's philosopher, Dr. Seuss, "It's turtles, all the way down.") This fact raises issues of legitimacy that are much chewed over in American constitutional theory, but fresher in Europe. Is it undemocratic for judges to have what is in effect the final word over large moral issues?

We might consider three responses to that question. The first points out that most people in the nations in which judges have been given that responsibility do not object to it and, from time to time, in different ways, endorse it. But though this states another important political fact, it is not satisfactory as a full answer, because the final question must be not what the people do accept but what they do right to accept. If judicial review means an abdication of the people's democratic right to govern themselves, then that abdication might be wrong even though voluntary. And, of course, not everyone believes that government by judiciary is acceptable: Many people think that it is deeply wrong.

The second response concedes that, at least according to the standard definition of democracy as majority rule, it is undemocratic for judges to have the powers that I have been describing. But it insists that democracy compromised in that way is a better form of government than a purer form of democracy because the former produces a more just community by protecting the rights of minorities. That is a popular view, but once again I find it unsatisfactory. "Democracy" is the name not just of one type of political arrangement, but of an important political value. It stands for equality in the distribution of political power—for self-government in that distinct and special sense—and, if we concede a compromise of political equality, we concede something important and regrettable. How can we be confident that the result of that compromise is greater justice if the compromise is itself a deep injustice? We do better to take the challenge more seriously: Instead of asking simply whether some judicial power is undemocratic according to one traditional understanding of what democracy is, we must ask whether it is undemocratic according to the best understanding of that ideal.

The third response, which is more ambitious than the other two, undertakes that task. Once we notice that the traditional majoritarian conception of democracy is only one among several such conceptions that philosophers have identified and discussed, then we are likely to reject that majoritarian conception, because there is nothing inherently fair, and nothing that provides genuine self-government for all, simply in the fact that more people favor one decision than favor another. Majority rule is fair only when certain conditions are met—only, for example, when people have a genuine and equal right to participate in the public debate that produces the majority decision, and only when issues of distinct importance to individuals, like the choice of religious commitment, are exempt from majoritarian dictate altogether. If we understand democracy to mean not majority rule in itself, but majority rule under appropriate conditions, then it does not compromise but rather protects democracy when effective means are deployed to secure those conditions. It therefore begs the crucial question to say that judicial power undermines democracy: We must look to see whether the consequence of that power is in fact greater democracy because it has helped to achieve a more genuine realization of the conditions that genuine democracy requires. Of course, judicial review of legislation is not the only means that a society may choose to attempt to secure those conditions. I shall shortly discuss another means that was formerly thought superior in most mature democracies: parliamentary conscience and restraint. My claim now is only that whether judicial review is undemocratic is a substantive, not an institutional, question: We must look, at retail, to the particular constitutional provisions that judges enforce in particular jurisdictions, and to how they enforce them, to see whether, all things considered, democracy is improved or worsened by that feature of the society's political arrangements.

3

If it is so widely thought embarrassing that judges have what is, in effect, the final say on fundamental moral issues—if constitutional judges strain to deny or qualify their own power—then why is that power now so pervasive? The dramatic increase in judicial responsibility that followed World War II—a convergence that now embraces Canada, South Africa, Israel, and Eastern Europe, as well as Western Europe and (from the beginning) the United States—signals a widespread desire for constitutional legal protections drafted in abstract moral language. If the people are deeply suspicious of papal judges, then why have they made judges popes?

That question is in the front line of the large issues that Robert has asked us all to keep in mind in our sessions. Of course, the idea that people have rights against government—the *droits de l'homme*—is much older than modern forms of judicial review. We can accept that citizens have rights without also accepting that judges must have the power to impose their will on the elected representatives of the people. The most obvious alternative is the form of parliamentary supremacy championed in the longstanding rhetoric of British political theory. Parliament is at once the voice and the conscience of the people: It pursues the general interest, but subject to ancient constraints of fairness and decency to individual citizens. The balance between these two great political goals—the general interest and fairness to individuals—is a matter of judgment, and that judgment is exercised by the people themselves, through parliamentary representatives chosen for their moral sensibility as well as their legislative skill.

That is the long-cherished model of good government—we might call it the parliamentary model—that is now being swept away, all over the world, by the radically different idea that the two great goals of collective good and individual right should be institutionally divorced, so that the latter is finally the responsibility of different officials from the former. Why does the parliamentary model now seem less attractive? We must distinguish two different strands that contributed to its popularity: It combined the democratic romanticism of Rousseau and the political elitism of Alexander Hamilton. The elitist tradition assumed, with Hamilton, Burke, and the great British parliamentarians, that democracies can and should generate a governing class—either through the aristocracy of birth, wealth, and intelligence, as Hamilton and the British assumed, or a purer aristocracy of intelligence, as became the French tradition—which transcends its own personal interests and seeks the general good while respecting deep-seated traditions of fairness. Such leaders can be trusted to do what is right. The romantic tradition connected these leaders to the larger society: The convictions of a governing class are naturally formed, according to this view, through the organic and informal processes of civil society—processes of collective experience and exchange in which the fundamentally good instincts of the people at large are honed. Civic experience and a progressively more informed and deliberative citizenry produce and refine a political culture that expresses a decent and honorable general will: The people produce their elite leaders through that culture which the people have themselves created. (In our time, that part of the ideal seems to me best expressed through the work of Jürgen Habermas, who distrusts the papal judiciary because he believes that constitutional provisions should be generated, refined, and interpreted by the continuing informal conversations and collective deliberations of the civil society as a whole.)

These two ideas—political elitism and democratic romanticism—may seem contrary, but they were woven together in the old parliamentary model. It was a feature of that intellectual symbiosis that moral and political instinct—judgment deeper and more intuitive than could be explained in reasoned argument—was trusted and valued. The sense of the good and the right that the people develop, and which their leaders can be trusted to protect even in those moments of excitement or temptation when the people have temporarily forgotten it, cannot be captured in any philosopher's system or any code of legal principle. It is a matter of the natural, intuitive judgment of fundamentally good people expressed through conscientious leaders with decent and deep instincts.

That is my understanding of the ideological base of the old parliamentary model. It is not difficult to see how the events and developments of recent decades undermined it. First, the horrifying tyrannies of the short but terrible twentieth century (according to Eric Hobsbawm, that century lasted only from 1914 to 1989) shattered the complacent Whig assumption that the developing political traditions and sensibilities of industrial nations would naturally produce decent government. Second, the citizens of the large democracies became more sophisticated about politics: They understood that it was no longer true (if it ever was) that their elected leaders were statesmen with a noble calling. They were politicians bent on re-election above all else. Third, the increasing ethnic and cultural pluralism of nation states, together with the increasing association of those nation states in larger and inevitably culturally diverse political communities like the European Union, made the old assumptions about social convergence on a moral sense newly implausible. Sharp ethnic and cultural division even within the mature democracies, and certainly among them, called into question, if not the idea of civil society itself, at least the idea that civil society would generate moral ideals neutral and fair to all.

These developments help to explain why people began to distrust the parliamentary model and were tempted by the different (and in some respects older) idea of Montesquieu and of the eighteenth-century American formation—that it is a mistake to use one lever for both ideals of good government and that the moral brake should be separated from the social accelerator. They do not yet explain why so many nations have now turned to judges, among all the institutional possibilities, to hold the brake and to express and guard a political conscience. Part of the answer, I suppose, is the example of the United States, where that assignment has seemed, not just to Americans but to people generally, to have worked on the whole. But we might explore a more basic reason—a reason that might also help to explain the underlying popularity of the Supreme Court itself, even in periods of great public discontent with what it has done. I said that it was part of the parliamentary model to distrust systematic formulations of large principles and to favor inarticulate instinct and discrete Aristotelian judgment instead. Perhaps the new popularity of legal constitutionalism reflects a further shift away from that romantic conception of moral instinct back toward the classical Enlightenment faith in reason, the faith of the older, eighteenth-century American Constitution.

Robert asks us to notice that the role now played by judges—wielding power in service of conscience—was once played by priests and then later by politicians. These were shifts not just in personnel but in moral epistemology as well. Priests ruled by divination from the occult, as they still do, for example, in Iran. Democratic politicians now rule, not by the instinctive wisdom and fairness celebrated in the old parliamentary model, but by representation, which means by compromises, trade-offs, and political deals that do not even aim at coherence. Neither priests nor politicians have a responsibility of justification in principle or of capturing all that they do in more general formulations of right and wrong. Any such responsibility would undermine the emotional base of priesthood, which is mystery, or cripple the accommodating and pragmatic strategies of politicians.

But that responsibility for articulation is the nerve of adjudication. Judges are supposed to do nothing that they cannot justify in principle, and to appeal only to principles that they thereby undertake to respect in other contexts as well. People yearning for reasoning rather than faith or compromise would naturally turn to the institution that, at least compared to others, professes the former ideal. I do not mean, of course, that judges are more rational or more skilled at analytic reasoning than theologians or parliamentarians. We have no guarantee that the political principles that our judges deploy will be the right or best ones, or that they will articulate those principles consistently or coherently; indeed, since our judges disagree among themselves, we know that they cannot all be right and that they will not always be consistent. But the code of their craft promises that at least they will try.

Government by adjudication is newly appealing for a different reason as well: It seems better suited than the alternatives to the cultural and ethical pluralism that is so marked in modern political communities and associations. Adjudication is constructivist rather than oracular: Though judges rely, as I have been insisting, on their own personal moral convictions, they accept an institutional responsibility for integrity with what other judges have done and will do, which means that the body of principle that they together construct by way of constitutional interpretation is more likely to be abstract and less tied to any particular cultural tradition. And the political rather than ethical character of these principles contributes markedly to that result.

You may find these explanations for the choice of judges as popes much too intellectual. Popular culture, after all, hardly suggests a raging appetite for reasoned explanation of anything. But we are trying to explain not an explicit political calculation, but a broad sense of the fittingness of that choice. And we must remember that most people, who are wiser about politics than people were before the terrible century began, have plain reason to reject at least the most natural alternatives to a judicial papacy. The church as Caesar is no longer an option: We are too divided about religion, and too united in our conviction that religion and state should be separate, to permit that. We know that politicians aim mainly at their next electoral success, and while it is sensible to give officials who have that prime ambition the task of benefiting the majority, it seems less sensible to ask them to be the majority's conscience as well. These strictures and doubts are now also part of popular culture, and they make it not so surprising that people are attracted to the idea of one forum, at least where argument matters.

2.2. The Secular Papacy

Discussion

Ronald DWORKIN: Robert would like me to summarize my paper briefly. I found the suggestion of a pontificating judge, which is how I choose to read the topic that I was assigned, intriguing. I took it to mean that, in our day, judges are among the principal, if not the principal, spokesmen for morality or conscience to the nation. That proposition would seem surprising to many people because they think that law is entirely distinct from morality. That was the claim of the legal positivists, who were for a long time the dominant Anglo-American legal philosophers. But I suppose it is uncontroversial among us here that the positivist distinction between law and morality is finally untenable. Judges in all our countries constantly appeal to moral considerations in the course of their legal arguments—they appeal to what is fair, what is just, what is reasonable, what is unconscionable, and so forth. That is part of their ordinary job as interpreters of a code, or as architects and elaborators of a common law system. In some parts of the law, however—administrative and constitutional law, for example—the role of moral argument and reasoning is particularly prominent. I begin my argument with the claim that there are three reasons why the role of moral argument, or at least moral appeal, is more prominent in constitutional law than in the more ordinary business of lawyers and judges.

It is more prominent, first, because constitutional standards are so often themselves drafted in highly abstract moral language—the American Constitution mentions "due" process, "equal" protection, and "cruel" punishment. Second, because the moral issues that constitutional law treats (which include not only the hugely contentious issue of abortion, but several of the other questions that we talked about earlier: whether prayers in public schools are consistent with freedom of religion, whether terrorism properly can be fought with terrorism, and whether the state can properly prohibit racist or hate speech) are among the most divisive and heated that the community faces, so that the public's attention is inevitably drawn to the role of judges in deciding these issues. Third, because these issues are typically of political rather than individual morality—they are not about what one individual owes to another, or what is fair for one person to do to another, or whether certain sexual practices are repulsive or indecent, but rather about what government may properly do its citizens—the idea that judges rather than elected officials should decide these political issues seems particularly arresting.

Judges, then, are assigned the responsibility of interpreting abstract constitutional provisions drafted in moral language to decide the most controversial and divisive issues of political morality. Does it follow that a judge charged with that responsibility must ultimately appeal to his or her own moral convictions? Or is there some way that judges can escape that personal judgment? I find that judges, at least in America and Britain, struggle to avoid admitting (as they might put it) that they ever rely on their own personal moral beliefs. They say, for example, that, in deciding these great constitutional issues, a judge should defer to the moral judgments of the legislature or perhaps the community as a whole, or defer to history, or use some other mode of escape from having to rely in the end on his or her own moral conviction about right and wrong. It is understandable that judges should seek some escape of that kind: It seems wrong in democratic theory that the moral convictions that finally count are those not of the public at large, but of a few unelected judges, appointed in many countries for life, who are not subject to the verdict of the public. Moral issues, including issues of political morality, are not technical judgments that are susceptible to proof. Moral judgment ends in undefended convictions about which people finally disagree, and judges will often disagree not just with the majority of the public, but with one another. It therefore seems particularly unfair that the fate of a litigant or, in the case of great constitutional issues, the fate of the nation, should depend on which lawyers have been appointed to the Supreme or Constitutional Court, and which of these happen to be sitting on a particular case. These are powerful reasons why judges might want to insist that they do not rely on their own personal convictions, but rather on something more public and shared when they decide legal issues that are also moral ones. In my presentation, I argue that this claim is nevertheless delusional: When judges appeal to moral conviction, as they must, that appeal is fundamentally an appeal to their own personal moral convictions. All the energy that constitutional scholars and legal philosophers have devoted to explaining that obvious fact away seems displaced.

If I am right, then we must confront an important challenge. Is it wrong for a legal system to give unelected judges the power—and the duty—to impose their own moral convictions on the nation? To give them the power and the duty to moralize? What reply might we make to the charge that assigning judges that power is undemocratic? In my presentation, I consider three replies. First, we might say that this judicial power and responsibility is not undemocratic because almost all the people seem to accept it. That is, I believe, a very poor response. It is not true that almost all the people accept it: Judicial moralizing is very controversial, even among people who understand that that is what constitutional adjudication necessarily involves. In any case, the question or the challenge that I imagined asks not whether the people accept the practice, but whether they ought to accept it. If judicial moralizing involves some sort of abdication of democratic rights by the people, then the fact that they have somehow been persuaded to abdicate those rights would provide no justification for that act. So we should set aside the familiar response that judicial moralizing does not matter because the people accept it.

The next response that I consider concedes that judicial moralizing is undemocratic but adds that pure democracy is not necessarily the best form of government. Democracy adjusted to include judicial moralizing in order to protect individual rights, in this view, is an improvement on pure democracy. That reply may be persuasive to many people, but it rests on an unnecessary and dangerous compromise with the truth. "Democracy" is not just the name of a form of government that Plato did not like. The word names a very important political value: It stands for political equality. And we should not admit, unless we have to, that the making of moral judgments by judges corrupts political equality. That would be to concede that there is something very bad about that practice, even if we think that, in the end, what is good about it overcomes what is bad.

I prefer the third reply, which I will only briefly summarize now. It begins by noticing that the majoritarian conception of democracy is only one of the conceptions that philosophers have identified and studied over the past millennium. It is not even an attractive conception of democracy, because there is nothing good, even *pro tanto*, about majority rule in itself. The fact that more people favor one solution over another in itself counts as no justification for the community forcing that decision through coercive means on those who dissent from it. Democracy means fair majority rule, and majority rule becomes fair only when certain conditions are met.

These conditions include, for example, freedom of expression, rights of access to the media, rights of privacy, and so on. So whether a community is truly democratic depends not just on whether the majority rules, but on whether these conditions are in place. Judicial review is one means—not the only means and not a necessarily effective means—of trying to ensure that these conditions are met. So we cannot decide whether judicial moralizing is democratic or undemocratic *a priori*, in advance of looking to see what its consequences have been. We must consider, for each jurisdiction, what issues are assigned to the judges, under what standards, and what decisions they, on the whole, tend to make. These are judgments to be made at retail, not wholesale. In my view, on the whole, in the nations with which we are all familiar, judges having the power and responsibility that I described has made the nation more, rather than less, democratic. There is nothing inevitable about that, and, as I emphasized, judicial review is not the only means available for securing the conditions of democracy. But if we are to respond effectively to the anti-democratic objection, we have to do it in the way that I have just described: at retail, by look-ing to see.

My final topic is historical. Given the popularity of the objec-tion that judicial moralizing is undemocratic, then why is it that in our day, following the Second World War, so many states have turned to judges to protect the individual rights of citizens? If peo-ple object to papal judges, why have they made judges popes, as they have in recent decades, if not all over the world, then at least over very large parts of it? My answer is much more speculative (though I hope not less provocative) than my earlier arguments. In the eighteenth century, the idea took root in Europe that individual citizens have moral rights against their government. One of the pre-eminent problems of modern political theory then surfaced. It is necessarily controversial what rights these are, even in the abstract, but particularly when such rights seem to conflict with the public interest as a whole. What constitutional arrangement is best suited, then, to identify these rights and to protect them from the pressure of the public interest? The nineteenth-century answer, across Eu-rope (and even, for much of the century, in the United States), was that parliamentary sovereignty—unlimited power in the hands of the elected representatives of the people—would provide an ade-quate guarantee of individual rights against the people.

That decision was supported, at the outset of that century, by a confluence of assumptions that were doubtful even then and are much more so now. The first is that the parliament will be made up from a natural, well-educated governing class who will not be sus-ceptible to the momentary and ill-judged passions that might in-flame the population as a whole. That was Alexander Hamilton's idea, it was Burke's idea, and it was the inspiration behind France's Grandes Écoles that provided that nation with superbly educated administrators and civil servants. The second assumption had very different roots: in the democratic romanticism that inspired Jean-Jacques Rousseau and flourished in the philosophical idealism of the nineteenth century. That is the idea of naturally good people reasoning together and collectively developing, out of their innate sense of justice, a governing ethos that disciplines the successful de-velopment of civil society. I suggest that we might understand the political theory of Jürgen Habermas as an attempt to recapitulate this idea through what he calls an undominated conversation in civil society, a process through which the nation itself develops—not imposed from on high, but generated from the bottom—its own collective political and social morality. I believe that the fusion of these two ideas—that there will be a governing class, but that the governing class will develop from a civil society that has itself generated an ethos from which it only rarely lapses—provided the ideological base of parliamentary supremacy. Educated and enlightened legislators, it was assumed, would understand the true dimensions of individual rights and hold to them in all seasons; these legislators would be instructed and supported by the community as a whole, exercising its democratic powers in service of a morality constructed together in civil society.

If something like this set of ideas first nourished the idea that a parliament was an adequate custodian of individual rights, then that fact explains why that institution no longer seemed adequate after the Second World War. The tyrannies of the short and terrible twentieth century led to the idea of a civil society in industrial nations whose collective conscience informed an enlightened aristocracy of leadership. Quite apart from the examples of tyranny, the increasing pluralism of states, augmented in recent decades by the growth of international associations of states, made increasingly implausible the idea that a national or international civil society could generate a common and shared moral base. We may hope that national and international communities can settle on a general constitutional structure that all regard as fair. But we cannot hope that such communities will generate moral convictions about particular substantive issues that will be shared by almost everyone.

I now want to add a further claim, though even more tentatively, because I risk being teased. It was a further feature of the political settlement that I have been describing in favor of parliamentary sovereignty—that sound instinct outruns reason, and in particular, that sound instinct outruns articulation. It is still a very common piece of rhetoric to insist that people of good sense know what is right even when they cannot capture what they know in articulate general principles. The terrible twentieth century taught people the danger of that idea, too, and many have returned to an earlier faith in reason and articulation as itself protection against injustice. That new enthusiasm for articulation adds to the case for replacing the older idea of parliamentary sovereignty with a new concern for law and judicial review. For though judges cannot avoid relying, in the end, on their own convictions of political morality, they are nevertheless expected, as a matter of institutional responsibility, to set out, or at least to presuppose, a body of principle that justifies what they do in each case and contains an articulate promise or warning of what they will do in the future. I am not claiming that judges are the only kind of official who can undertake reasoned articulation of the grounds of judgment. That might be a flattering assumption at this table, but even at this table I would not get away with it. Nor do I mean that judges always and everywhere live up to the highest standards of articulation. The opinions that judges write are dictated by conventions of institutional competence and style that vary from nation to nation and from jurisdiction to jurisdiction. My claim is one not so much about actual performance as about expectation. If you want the people's voice expressed in a more or less natural and instinctive way, you do not turn to the judiciary. If you want it expressed in a reasoned and articulate way, then that is where you do turn, even if you do not always get what you wanted. That is my best effort at explaining why it seems so natural now, at the end of that terrible century, to assign to judges the task of protecting the rights that everyone agrees individuals have against the majority of their fellow citizens, and not to flinch when judges have to turn papal to fulfill the assignment.

Stephen BREYER: My comments draw upon my own experience as an American judge. Ronnie says that judges enforce their convictions of "political morality." In a sense, that is so. Continental administrative law judges have long applied broad doctrines of reasonableness, natural justice, and proportionality to review the lawfulness of an administrator's decision. And one could consider them to enforce "moral" convictions when they do so.

But to use the word "morality" in respect to constitutional law decisionmaking suggests that the basic question a judge asks is "What is fair?" And I do not think that is always, or even often, the question. Were I forced to pick one, highly abstract, general question that I ask about the proper result in a case, I would select "Does this interpretation make sense?" where "sense" has a special legal connotation related to the basic purpose of the provision in question.

If your notion of "morality" is broad enough to encompass what I have in mind by "making sense in terms of purpose," then we may be talking about the same thing. Where statutes are at issue, and where the language is not determinative, I think that judges often ask what makes sense in terms of the statute's basic purpose. The judge then returns to the language to make certain that the language is consistent with the "sensible" result or interpretation.

Of course, sometimes a statute cannot be interpreted to reach a "fair" result. A statute of limitations may prevent recovery of damages that "morality" would conclude ought to be paid. And sometimes a statute's language precludes what we might think of as a more "sensible" interpretation. In such a case, judges, after investigating the matter, will apply the statute as written.

In applying the federal Constitution, the "sensible" result is often the result that refers back to the purpose of the entire document—the creation of workable democratic government for a free society. And I believe that applying the Constitution in this way requires a judge to have an understanding of what American society is like, and that understanding is as important, if not more important, than an understanding of, say, moral theory.

Indeed, I suspect that the greater similarity between legal interpretation and political morality lies in method. When two individuals engage in moral argument, they often refer to principles, to facts, to subsidiary principles, and to predicted consequences—all without determined order, as the argument bounces between one level and another. Legal rules, including legal decisions, have ramifications upon other rules, principles, and institutions that create the system, all of which, in turn, have consequences in the world. And legal arguments, like moral arguments, jump back and forth among principle, sub-principle, and consequence—particularly where constitutional interpretation is at issue.

I agree that much of what the American Constitution contains can be explained by appealing to a coherent theory about the nature of democracy. But coherent democratic theory cannot explain all the protections that the Constitution provides. How does one explain, for example, the "right to die" case,[1] the case that asked us to decide whether the Constitution's word "liberty" includes protection for a terminally ill patient seeking to commit suicide with the assistance of a doctor? I suspect that cases such as these arise because the words written into the Constitution to protect the liberties that are necessary for the functioning of a democracy will inevitably cover, and thereby protect, various other important liberties as well. Once words appear on paper, judges must decide how they apply—and it is not surprising that those judges have sometimes interpreted the words as going beyond what the demands of democracy alone may dictate. When the public, through its Constitution, asks judges to decide such matters, it can expect no more than a reasonably thoughtful, lay decision, likely to lie within a mainstream.

I would also ask if reason and reasoning alone, though important, are the most important parts of judging. Judgment too, after all, is a fairly important quality in a judge. When one wishes to compliment a judge's decisions, one might use the word "intelligent." But sometimes a better compliment is to say that the decisions are "sound." I can think of instances in which I suspect that the opinion with the less good argument reaches the more sound conclusion.

Ronald DWORKIN: When this moment arrives, and you think that the better argument is for X, but "she" thinks Y—I think I know the "she" that you have in mind—you may wonder whether she has got the better judgment, but you do not switch your vote, do you, until you find an argument that shows you that, as you just put it, the law permits her conclusion?

Stephen BREYER: The problem is that there are many arguments that are relevant as one searches for the factor that is key to the judgment. In a statutory case involving whether statistical analysis could be used to supplement pure counting to determine the total census—a matter that dramatically affects representation in Congress—I was most interested in whether the statistical analysis in fact worked fairly, a matter that was only tangentially relevant to the many, more legalistic arguments being made. Was the question of "fairness" key to the interpretation? I explained why I thought that it was relevant to a "sound" interpretation of the statute.

Consider a decision by France's Conseil d'Etat: Octobre 1995, Requête de la Commune de Morsang sur Orgues. In that case, the Conseil had to decide whether a nightclub act called the *lancer des nains* (dwarf throwing) violated principles of human dignity. It had to weigh the desire of the dwarfs to work in the act against the undignified nature of the resulting spectacle. It had to consider the effect of the principle that it adopted in other areas, for example, that of laws permitting (or forbidding) prostitution. The decision is only a page or two long, with highly compressed reasoning. And it is a perfectly good example of a continental court decision.

To pose several questions for discussion, I would ask: (1) What is meant by "political morality"? (2) Are there important constitutional protections that have little to do with democracy or its preconditions? (3) Is it reasoning or judgment that we want from the judge? In what proportions? How public should the reasoning be?

Ronald DWORKIN: Steve says that he agrees with me that judges must rely on their own personal moral convictions only if I mean morality in a very, very broad sense. But the way he describes what he does himself seems to me to confirm what I said earlier: that judges try to find locutions to hide their own reliance on morality in its perfectly familiar and ordinary sense. He says that he is interested not in what is fair or just, but in what is "sensible" or what "works" for the nation. But we need ordinary moral judgments about what is fair or just to decide what is "sensible" or "works." Take the great debate about whether the American Constitution, properly interpreted, permits the states to make early abortion a crime. Many American lawyers say (in the spirit of what Steve has said) that we should set aside all the divisive questions about whether abortion is murder or whether justice requires that a woman be able to make up her own mind about abortion, and just ask whether it will work better to permit or forbid states to outlaw abortion. But how can we decide what works or what is sensible without taking sides on the divisive questions? People who think abortion is murder will not think that permitting abortion has "worked"; people who think that government has no business dictating morality to women will not think that forbidding it is "sensible." The same holds for homosexuality, or assisted suicide, or hate speech, or any of the other heated issues that constitutional courts must rule about. Saying that judges should aim at what "works" may sound more judicious or practical, but it is only a smoke screen.

Stephen BREYER: I think that there is less disagreement than you suggest. The more central the principle, the less likely that they are to disagree. And what seem to be arguments about secondary principles are often disagreements about consequences. We often make progress in such arguments.

Ronald DWORKIN: Yes, it is desirable for judges who disagree to come to agree, and that is often the result when the two sides come better to understand the facts and the consequences of a decision one way or the other. There may be convergence then, but we must not try to hide the fact that it is convergence on an essentially moral position, and that it will almost always be one that a great many people in the community would nevertheless reject.

I agree that some constitutional issues are not helpfully understood as questions about the structure of democracy, but a great many are. We need to understand the dimensions of religious freedom, for example, in order to understand democracy because majority rule is unfair unless it leaves to individuals those decisions that we must make for ourselves or forfeit self-respect. Steve and I disagree about the constitutional status of the right to die, but I do not mean to take sides about that issue or any other now. I only mean to say that any comprehensive democratic theory must, in the end, take sides about the extent to which people should be left free from the collective morality of the community.

Steve's remarks about the need for judgment remind me of Learned Hand, a famous American judge whom I worked for. He used what I am going to call (in this company) the "Oh, hell!" test. He would often say: "I have studied all the arguments, I keep changing my mind, I go back and forth, but oh, hell, this is what I think now!" Bang! There came the decision, and I had to hand it to the clerk. The question of the connection between reasoning and conviction (or judgment, as Steve calls it) seems to me one of the deepest issues of epistemology generally. The only thing that he and I might disagree about, and I bet we really do not, is his suggestion that "arguments are cheap." I do not believe, and I do not believe that he believes, that even when it is close, one argument is not, all things all considered, better than another. What Hand meant by his "Oh, hell!" was not that no argument was really better, but that he was not sure which one was, and he knew that he would keep changing his mind until he finally acted on his conviction of the moment. That is the opposite of thinking that no one argument is the best one.

Stephen BREYER: That last point is important. More often now than in the past, I find a decision extremely close and difficult. Yet once I tentatively make up my mind, the more time passes, the more convinced I become that I was right. Perhaps that is just human nature.

Ronald DWORKIN: Absolutely correct. You end up saying to yourself the famous phrase, "There is nothing else to think!"

Stephen BREYER: Still, I can wonder what I would now think had I devoted the same intellectual energy to the path not taken.

Ronald DWORKIN: Yes. But you should not divorce conviction about reasoning and about result. These lock together, and when you have (let us say) fooled yourself into thinking that there is only one thing to think, you will also think that the argument that got you there is the only one to hold. There is not much space between argument and result.

Dieter GRIMM: May I tell a story? It is a very short story from my experience on the bench. I was the judge *rapporteur* in what the Americans would call First Amendment cases and, among these cases, freedom of assembly used to be a difficult issue before the Court. Once we had a case in which someone had been convicted for his behavior at a demonstration. I suggested that we reverse the judgment of the criminal courts. And my seven colleagues said, "We agree with the result, but the way that you reach it is not viable." I defended my way, but I could not convince them. So I asked which way they had in mind. It was not very clear what they had in mind, but they roughly sketched their approach, and I said that I would try to write the opinion on that basis. I tried but I was unable to do it because it would have meant sacrificing three or four principles that had not been contested up to that time. So I returned to the Court and said, "If anyone can write it on the basis that you have described, I am ready to leave it to him or her. I cannot write it because of reasons A, B, etc." They admitted that there were some obstacles to their approach, but still did not support my way. So finally, we upheld the judgment of the criminal court.

Each time I have told this story—and I have told it three or four times, trying to hide which case it was—the reactions have been different. One reaction has been: "Well, this is not a sound understanding of the judge's job. They all agreed that they had found the just result, but since they did not have the right arguments, they turned it around." The other reaction has been: "These people really take their job seriously! Methodology, text, and legal reasoning matter." Now, why do I tell this story? I tell it because I agree with you, Ronald, that ultimately, as a judge, one cannot avoid relying on one's own moral judgment. But before it comes to this point, other factors intervene. The text of the constitution matters. It may not exclude very much, especially in the American case of a very short and broadly framed Constitution, but it does not allow just anything. Second, methodology matters. Methodology may also leave many ways open. And methodology can change, but you cannot totally change an accepted methodology at once. Thirdly, there is the legal context and the legal culture in which you handle legal matters. So what you neglected a little bit is the professionalization of the legal field. In my experience, the point at which you really have to rely on your own moral judgment in many cases does not arise at all and, in other cases, it comes in very late. Hence, although I basically agree, I think that you did not sufficiently take into account the period before it comes to that point.

Ronald DWORKIN: Certainly, there are many cases in which the moral assumptions in play do not show; they are in the iceberg beneath the water. But over time, when other judges whose professional formation and background assumptions are a little different are appointed, then what was beneath the iceberg, what went without saying, what was part of the legal culture, and what never rose to the surface suddenly does. Nothing is immune from this process, and I should have made that more explicit. At any given moment, there will be a great deal that seems beyond question, but any of that could suddenly be put into question. And if we wait long enough, it probably will, even while the assumptions go without saying. Moreover, it is a set of *moral* assumptions that go without saying.

Stephen BREYER: There are constitutional principles decided in past cases that lie like icebergs under the water, invisible but waiting to re-emerge at an appropriate time. The "rate-setting" cases of the early twentieth century may be like that. They guaranteed a "fair return" to investors in regulated electricity companies. They simply disappeared, rarely cited, for many years. They have never been explicitly overruled. Our Court's recent holdings on federalism appeal to cases and principles that, for many years, have lain dormant.

Ronald DWORKIN: That is a good example. Most constitutional lawyers thought that certain basic issues of federalism were settled, but a majority of your Court is bringing them back into controversy.

Antonio CASSESE: May I also cite a case from my experience as a judge in a criminal court? I think that criminal cases may be extremely interesting as a matter for judicial decision, and I agree with you, Ron, that in fact judges rely on their moral convictions. However, they unwittingly find legal arguments to support their moral convictions. Let me give you an example.

It was the case of a young man, Drazen Erdemovic, who in 1995 was a member of an execution squad in Srebrenica when the Serbs rounded up a lot of Muslims in a United Nations–designated "safe haven."[2] He was a Croat, a young man of 23, and a member of a Serbian execution squad. They went to a village and buses full of old Muslim civilians and women were taken to a particular place. In one afternoon, in a matter of four hours, about 1,000 people were executed. Erdemovic was a member of a seven-man execution squad, shooting at the backs of these Muslims. He was arrested, and when he pled guilty, he said: "Yes, I probably killed between 70 and 120 people myself. However, when I was given orders to shoot, I said, 'No, I refuse because these are elderly people, and the Muslims have done nothing.' The commander of the execution squad said, 'If you do not shoot, I will shoot you, also because you are not a Serb, you are a Croat.'" Erdemovic was a sort of mercenary, he was very young, and he had to earn some money because he had a child. He came to our Court and said, "I plead guilty. Of course, I committed horrible crimes." And he then started crying. But he pleaded duress.

We, the judges, had a huge problem. What should we do with duress? Is it an excuse? And then, within the tribunal, there was again the divide between judges coming from common law countries and those from civil law countries. All my colleagues, particularly my American colleague, said, "Well, it's very easy," because, in common law countries, you have a famous case involving *The Mignonette* (a ship) called *The Queen* v. *Dudley and Stephens*.[3] There was a shipwreck in which four people survived. There were two people, Dudley and Stephens, who I think spent 17 days on a raft or on a lifeboat. One day, they decided to kill and eat the cabin boy. They were subsequently arrested and sentenced to death by a

British court, but later on the sentence was commuted to six months' imprisonment. That was a moral decision—that life is sacrosanct. You cannot kill anybody, even if you are under duress or by necessity. Therefore, my fellow judges from common law countries found an easy solution based on the common law approach. However, it was actually a moral conviction. They found Erdemovic guilty. According to them, he should have refused to kill the 70 or 120 people over the four-hour period. In my view, however, this means asking people to behave like heroes. A young man of 23 cannot be asked to be a hero. He cannot be asked to say, "Look, kill me because I refuse to kill other innocent people." My colleagues from common law countries said, "The common law approach is quite clear. The *Mignonette* is clear." And all the British courts take the same, I would say, moralistic stand, namely, that you must be punished because you have taken the life of an innocent person. I did some research and I found a French case, *Le Radeau de la Méduse*. Do you remember the painting by Géricault? I went through all the documents in that particular case: There also was a shipwreck, and some of the survivors on a raft killed and ate others. This incident took place off the coast of Senegal in the nineteenth century. When the survivors came back to France, criminal proceedings were instituted against the captain of the ship only, alleging negligence because he had not been careful enough to avoid the ship running aground. I think that was a much better and more humane approach.

I wrote a dissenting opinion in the Erdemovic case. There was, in a sense, a rift or a clash between seemingly legal arguments, but, in fact, the rift was between moral convictions. I thought that it was simply preposterous to ask a young man of 23 to behave as a hero. My solution, based on some cases in Germany and Italy, was as follows: If you are a member of an execution squad and you know that innocent people are going to be shot, there is no point being a hero because, in any case, you are among 7 or 10 people all shooting at the poor innocent people. I said this, and my colleagues said, "You are totally wrong because it is much better to give him the stigma of guilt, and then we will give him a very lenient sentence, as was done for Dudley and Stephens in the *Mignonette* case." They said, "It is much better to do so than to simply say that he is not guilty and acquit him."

Stephen BREYER: What did you do when you found a clash between common law and civil law approaches, between, for example, the common law's reliance upon precedent and the civil law's willingness to re-examine the meaning of a code provision?

Antonio CASSESE: Either one applies treaties or rules of international customary law. In this case of duress in the killing of civilians, there were no treaties and no customary international law. In such cases, you have to rely on the common principles that may be derived from the two main legal systems of the world—the common law system and the civil law system. If you can harmonize both of them, then you can apply a principle shared by the two major legal systems. In this case, there was no real harmonizing of the two systems, so each judge decided according to his or her moral convictions. I thought that the attitude taken by my colleagues from other countries was based substantially on a rather moralistic attitude about the value of human life. I thought that it was more realistic to come to my conclusion. But I was probably wrong. It is interesting that you have, in a way, to decide on the basis of your moral convictions, but then you move on to legal arguments.

Ronald DWORKIN: This does not sound to me, however, like a case in which your legal argument was only a rationalization for an independent moral conviction. The argument that you just made, that it is unfair to hold someone responsible when the person was in an impossible situation, strikes me as a good argument in a legal context as well as a moral one.

Gil Carlos RODRIGUEZ IGLESIAS: In my view, personal convictions are indeed important, but only in a minority of cases. Most often, the law does not allow you any significant choice. You just have to decide the case within an objective framework. Whether you like it or not, you are bound by the law.

Now, let me make a few remarks drawing upon my experience in the European Court of Justice. As you know, one of the reasons why the European Court is considered to be an activist court is because it often relies on the goals of the Treaty. In my view, that is not activism. Relying on the goals of the Treaty as an interpretative criterion rather than on personal convictions is just commitment to the law and commitment to our constitution, which is the Treaty. There is more subjectivity when it comes to general principles. We have a lot of experience in this respect because, on the one hand, there is a provision in the Treaty that expressly refers to the principles that are common to the legal systems of the member states as the applicable law in the area of non-contractual liability of the Community and, on the other hand, the Court relies on such principles in many other areas—in particular in the field of fundamental rights—as a means to fill up lacunae.

If you look at the case law of the Court in the area of non-contractual liability, you can easily see that, very often, there are no principles that are effectively common to legal systems of the member states. So the Court is actually called upon to develop the rules. It has to compare the solutions offered by the different legal systems and to choose the one that it considers more appropriate. In such a situation, there is, of course, much room for subjectivity.

The personal convictions of the judges are most important in highly ideological cases, but this happens, I think, less often in the European Court than in national supreme or constitutional courts.

From a different perspective, I would like to note that, in our Court, there is an important element that moderates subjectivity: It is the collegial character of the decisionmaking, which is enhanced by the absence of dissenting opinions. When you cannot express your dissent, even if you are in the minority, you try to cooperate in the reasoning of the decision and you try to persuade the majority not to rely on arguments that you find particularly objectionable.

In difficult or controversial cases, we have a preliminary exchange of views—what we call a *tour de table*—in order to establish a basic orientation for both the decision and its reasoning. After the opinion of the Advocate General has been delivered, the judge *rapporteur* submits a written proposal as a basis for the general discussion among the judges. It is interesting to note that, in some particularly controversial or difficult cases, the majority changes once the *rapporteur* submits a draft judgment, because some judges realize that the solution that they initially favored cannot be justified persuasively.

Antonio CASSESE: How much does legal knowledge and the powerful personality of a judge count in your discussions? You said that people may also change their mind after this sort of tentative discussion, so the majority may move. Now, how much does the legal stature of a judge count in influencing the other ones? Say, if you have somebody really outstanding, a first-class judge, and sometimes you are full of awe for some of your colleagues, and so whatever they say you tend to agree to because they are so good!

Gil Carlos RODRIGUEZ IGLESIAS: Yes, I think that is quite important. In my experience, you can always see that a certain number of judges have a particular influence because of their moral authority and superior knowledge.

Robert BADINTER: To return to the main points, I recall that earlier we discussed judicial activism. That concerns the point up to which the judge can go or wants to go. We have now examined the following questions: Is the judge a carrier of "values"? Does he bear values for society? Does he interpret them? Does he create them? But before going into that (and related to our prior discussion), we must realize that it is *society*—particularly the minority groups and the individuals who are dissatisfied—who calls upon the judge. *They* confront the judge with the question of morality. And, to an ever greater extent, as the voices of the minorities and the dissenting groups become ever louder, they go to the judge because his is a forum where they find it easier to win compared to the forum of public opinion, which tends to side with the majority. The evolution over the past twenty years of homosexual rights in Western societies provides a striking example. You would be right to say that, if we called people up or held a referendum seeking the public's views about whether homosexuals should be permitted to marry, the answer would probably be no. But there will inevitably come a time, as there has in the United States, when a case will confront a judge with that question. The judge will have to decide it one way or the other. And at that moment the judge will have to answer the question *how* he or she should decide. He can only decide in accordance with certain procedural steps—which we have not yet made much of in our discussions. If Habermas were here, he would have brought us back to that issue.

The judge's method, in my opinion, is one of the deepest elements that explain the judge's ascension, compared to others among society's oracles. There is a technical aspect to the matter. Let us return to the concept of procedural democracy or democracy that involves a continuous exchange of opinions. That, according to Habermas, is the fundamental basis of modern democracy. Obviously, there is no place like a judicial forum for organizing differing, fluctuating opinions for and against a particular matter. It is a place where lawyers representing differing interests publicly have to confront contrary opinions. That helps the public debate along. The fact that a conflict finds itself subject to a judicial approach very much helps the public debate. Up to that point, the judge has not been involved in the matter.

Ronald DWORKIN: You suggest that the larger debate, the Habermasian conversation, is already structured in an argumentative way?

Robert BADINTER: Yes. A society characterized by discussion and democratic controversy—the very bases of democracy—finds its basic (but not its only) expression in the judiciary's procedures. That is what I wanted to point out. The judicial forum is the most favorable spot, the best place, for an organized debate. I would go further. I have experience with public debate in elected legislatures. It is a disaster. One major reason underlying the decline of parliaments is the terrible level of their public debate. That is because most legislators, when they speak, think only of what their own clientele will think of the speech. There is no confrontation of views. There is no effort to convince the other side. There is simply a recitation of arguments designed to impress public opinion or to remain faithful to what your own party or your own group wants you to say. There is a complete absence of dialogue. There are only successive monologues. That is why a "deliberative democracy," a "democracy of discussion," finds in the judiciary a privileged forum. That was not so in the nineteenth century insofar as I have read the debates.

Stephen BREYER: The "right to die" case in our Court[4] presents what many would consider a primarily moral question: Does a terminally ill patient have a right to receive a doctor's help in committing suicide? The question was put in constitutional terms, *i.e.,* does the Constitution guarantee that right? And the issue was argued thoroughly in legal, practical, and moral terms, with more than sixty different groups presenting briefs.

Some commentators thought that a group of judges is capable, and is perhaps more capable than legislators, of deciding such a question wisely. But I noticed that a Select Committee of the House of Lords received equally thorough presentations, and, in my view, was better able to investigate the matter systematically than a group of judges. The New York State Legislature in New York also looked into the question thoroughly. If I were to pick the group that seemed best able to reach a sound decision, on the basis of the information that they received and the thoroughness of their investigation, I would pick the House of Lords Committee, and I would rank the courts third.

Ronald DWORKIN: I have made arguments in different ways to both of those bodies. I thought the argument was better in the Supreme Court than in the House of Lords Select Committee, partly because the Committee acted just the way Robert has said such bodies often do. Four members of the Select Committee said to me, in private, "Your arguments are the better arguments, but I cannot vote that way."

Stephen BREYER: I did not think that your arguments were the better arguments.

Ronald DWORKIN: Robert is pointing out that there is a built-in reason for hypocrisy in such bodies, which was certainly exhibited in this case. One member of the Committee had asked me to testify because she said that she agreed with me. She voted the other way.

Robert BADINTER: All this is simply to say that, within the form that contemporary democracy takes, the judge has found a natural place. That place is not one of "government by judges." Rather, it is a place the need for which has been deeply felt. That place has not been constructed artificially or imposed through a kind of judicial coup d'état. It does not represent a particular caste seizing power. Rather it is a place integrated within the mechanism of contemporary democracy considered as a whole. That is the linchpin of the analysis. It fits into our analysis. It does not run counter to our analysis. It does not revolutionize it. It just tries to make the mechanism, as you quite rightly said this morning, work a little better or, let us say, a little less badly.

Remember, the Waterloo of parliamentary democracy already took place once, and in a tragic way. When? In 1933, in Germany, when Hitler was brought to power through free elections—even though serious physical violence characterized the electoral campaign. But even so, it was the will of the majority that brought Hitler to power—in a nation characterized by an extraordinarily high level of culture. On that day, in my view, Rousseau's optimism suffered a terrible blow. A democratic system that rested upon the will of an electoral majority produced a regime that, in turn, meant the death of democracy and the deaths of millions. Such a system raises questions. It does not cast into doubt democracy itself, but it does indicate that the simple law of majority rule cannot be democracy's only law. It is necessary that the principle of majority rule, which is necessary for choosing those who will direct society, must, at the same time, take account the rights of individuals, including those of minorities.

Stephen BREYER: What subjects do you believe do not easily lend themselves to resolution through democratic methods?

Robert BADINTER: I believe that, insofar as the rights of minorities or of individuals are concerned, you cannot apply only the basic principle of democratic majority rule. That is a fact. In France, in a moment of wild political debate, just after the Left took control of the assembly in 1981, a deputy of the Left said to a colleague of the Right, "You are wrong legally because you are a minority politically." There you have an absolute negation of the rights of the minority, or of minorities, or beyond that, of individuals, which are not recognized as such by parliamentary majorities. That is why you have to insert into the system judicial intervention and constitutional adjudication. That is the natural counterweight. Even apart from the various advantages I have mentioned, that is part of fundamental political theory.

I put to the side the position held by a judge of an international court, where the problems are somewhat different. At the moment, we must consider the position of a judge of a national court. How does that judge function? Each of us here has participated in those deliberations, even Ronald, so we all know how they work. The judge is truly a hybrid animal. Like a bat, he has both wings and claws. He is a composite. He is a composite because he cannot escape the legal framework. He cannot decide all by himself.

It is true that, as a prisoner of the legal framework and of precedent, he will seek to articulate the best legal reasoning. But it is equally true that, at any given moment, his deeply held convictions will also reappear. A moral temptation appears when the judge must discuss the questions of the right to assisted suicide, the right to an abortion, or the right of homosexuals not only to be left alone but also to be able to marry or to enter into "civil unions," as the

French recently determined. To a certain degree, moral conceptions will enter into the judge's choice—even if the judge does not confess that it is so. One simply cannot escape it.

Do you think it was any different in a council of the Roman curia? I am certain that it was not. Undoubtedly, the council members had a common culture, a framework of principles, and their own feelings. Whenever a group of men and women share something in common, say, a body of principles, they will take moral positions within the framework set by those principles. And that is so with respect to the judge as well. That is where the difficulty lies. The judge has personal convictions and the judge must respond to a moral question that society poses for the judge to answer. Therein lies the immense difficulty in exercising the judge's function. He cannot impose his own convictions upon society, for they are his. If he did so, the public inevitably would react. Because the judge knows that they are his own personal moral views, he also knows that he cannot impose them as such upon society.

Ronald DWORKIN: Can we make a distinction? Of course, a judge must not think that he is justified in reaching a certain result because it is his opinion that the result is correct. But he may think— if I am right, he must think—that he is justified in reaching that result because, in his opinion, it is correct.

Stephen BREYER: Do you mean "correct" morally speaking, or speaking as a judge?

Ronald DWORKIN: My point is that Steve's distinction misunderstands the following point. The question of how far a judge is entitled to rely on his own judgment about what morality requires is *itself* a moral question. It's turtles all the way down. Any answer a judge gives to that question about his own powers is not just a moral judgment in some special or broad sense, but a moral judgment that has all the properties of the moral judgments that many lawyers say that judges should not make. Any description we give of a judge's proper responsibilities is as much problematic, controversial, and undemonstrable as any opinion that we hold about whether homosexuality is or is not wicked. We fool ourselves if we think that the more institutional question has a different epistemic status from more ordinary moral claims. We like the sound of familiar answers that we can give to the institutional question: We can say that it is an administrative question, or a question about what works, or something of that sort. Answers to questions so described may seem less threatening and more comforting. But the comfort is delusional. I said that I meant to be provocative.

Stephen BREYER: I think that you are saying the following: Take a difficult, open constitutional question—for example, whether the "Qualifications Clause" in the Constitution (which states that a Member of Congress must be twenty-five years old, a citizen of the United States, and a resident of the state) prevents a state from adding a further qualification (limiting terms served to three). In answering even this apparently neutral, technical, and unemotional constitutional question, we will discover that different judges reaching different answers do so because of different views about how the Constitution works, which views are deeply connected with the meaning of democracy, which, in turn, is connected with political morality. In that sense, what appeared to be a neutral legal question is in fact a moral question. Am I right?

Still, to stretch the label "moral" to that point makes it difficult to examine a different question of greater practical importance. How do judges avoid writing their own personal moral views into law? In fact, judicial methodologies and objective principles of law—which I recognize can be called "moral," but only in a broad sense—make it difficult to do so.

Ronald DWORKIN: I still do not see that what you call a different question really is different. You believe that you are constrained in how far you can impose your personal convictions about, say, assisted suicide or homosexuality or anything else on constitutional law. Fine. I think that you should feel constrained in that way. But we should be clear that what constrains you is not some neutral convention or universally accepted credo, but just other, more abstract moral convictions that you have about the proper role of a judge in a democracy. These more abstract convictions are not necessarily less controversial; on the contrary, they are often more controversial. They may appear less controversial when you state them sufficiently abstractly, so it is not clear what result they are going to lead to in a particular case. As soon as you spell them out in sufficient detail—if you should say, for example, that the state has no right to dictate to people in matters of religion or conscience—so that it become clear how you are going to rule on school prayer or abortion or homosexual marriage, for instance, then any hope you had of finding something "objective," in the sense of unquestioned, disappears. You give precedence to the political part of your morality. Good, I think that you are right to do so.

Let me go back to something that Robert said. He pointed out that the ideals of deliberative discourse may be easier to realize in court than in a parliament, and I agree with that. But the question then arises: If it is not undemocratic to give judges the last word on fundamental constitutional issues, then why is it not all right to transfer all legislative power to judges or to let them fix tax rates? We need an answer to that question. I have tried to give one elsewhere, but not here.

Gil Carlos RODRIGUEZ IGLESIAS: I would simply like to suggest my agreement with Stephen. There are ideological issues that are nonetheless decided on the basis of arguments that are purely juridical, objective, and basically independent of the judge's own ideology. Then there are other situations in which that is not so.

I should like to mention two subjects drawn from the case law of the European Court of Justice (a.k.a. the Court of Justice of the European Communities): first, the case law concerning the rights of transsexuals and homosexuals; and second, the case law on "affirmative action" in respect to women. The first set of decisions seems to me to have been taken on a purely juridical basis in that the decisions flow directly from the texts of the applicable provisions. Simplifying somewhat, I can tell you that the Court considered that the rights of transsexuals, but not the rights of homosexuals, were protected in light of the provision that forbids discrimination on the basis of sex. Why the difference? Not because of ideology, but because the principle of gender equality written into the Treaty and the legal texts, as literally interpreted, forbids without qualification discrimination as between men and women. Thus the provisions do not cover discrimination against homosexuals due to their sexual orientation. But, in the Court's view, a transsexual—a person who was a man but became a woman and who, for that reason, was expelled from the school where she taught—was covered by the prohibition forbidding against discrimination on the basis of sex, that is to say, discrimination as between men and women. It seems to me that these results were purely juridical. They were based upon an interpretation of the objectives of the texts.

On the other hand, when the Court has faced cases involving "positive discrimination," it seems to me inevitable that the discussion would be influenced by ideological differences—differences between a concept of equality as a strictly individual right and a concept of equality as an instrument for progressively realizing a "true" (rather than purely formal) equality among collectivities, more precisely between men and women.

Ronald DWORKIN: Was there agreement on all that, as you suggest when you call the issues objective, or were there dissenting opinions?

Gil Carlos RODRIGUEZ IGLESIAS: Well, I think here I can say that there was agreement at the end of the discussion, but not from the outset. But there, you know, that it is secret. You know that I am not allowed to say. I think that, at the outset, the arguments were strongly influenced by the judges' own convictions but, at the end, as far as I remember, though I cannot be sure, I think that there was a consensus about the fact that, legally, we would exceed the limits of our role if we decided to read equal protection for homosexuals into a provision that actually addressed only the equality between the men and women.

Ronald DWORKIN: At the beginning of the discussion, there were people on the court who felt a desire to try to bring equality for homosexuals into the more general language about sexuality, but in the end they yielded on this?

Gil Carlos RODRIGUEZ IGLESIAS: Yes, we had a very interesting procedural discussion before the court.

Antonio CASSESE: There may also be cases where I think the court may be strongly influenced by public opinion, by new trends in jurisprudence, in case law, and so on. Let me give you an example. There was a recent case before the European Court of Human Rights involving torture. It is a famous case—the *Selmouni* case.[5] Ahmed Selmouni, a Moroccan, was beaten up in a police station in France and then wounded. It became a case of torture. The court for the first time said clearly: "We now have to take a much broader view of torture." There is a very terse provision regarding torture in the European Convention. It is just one line and a half saying that no one may be subjected to torture or inhuman or degrading treatment. And so, there is a huge question: "What is the distinction between torture and inhuman or degrading treatment?" To cane children at school, so far, has been regarded as degrading treatment in the United Kingdom. The court stopped short of saying that to beat up somebody in a police station and to subject him to degrading treatment may be so serious as to amount to torture. But a different body within the Council of Europe—the Committee Against Torture (a committee consisting of inspectors visiting police stations, prisons, and so on)—has adopted a different view. The Committee has developed a sort of jurisprudence by issuing a lot of reports about Turkey, Spain, Cyprus, and Greece, among others. Under this scheme, a new and broader notion of torture has been developed. The European Court of Human Rights has now said, in effect, "After twenty years developing our case law, we have to take a much broader view of torture and expand the concept and say that, in this particular French case, the French police officers committed an act of torture."

I think that this was done chiefly because of the pressure from public opinion, from several United Nations bodies, and from the European Committee Against Torture, which has produced so many in-depth reports on cases involving torture. For instance, the court, in another case, this time against Turkey, held that rape may amount to torture. This is really a new development. If a police officer rapes a girl during an investigation, it is an act of torture.

Ronald DWORKIN: We should distinguish between the social causes of a change such as you describe and the reason that the judges involved would regard as appropriate for them to give to justify the change. Public opinion is notoriously a powerful cause of change of judicial opinion, and sometimes it provides an acceptable justification for the change as well. But, in general, a judge would be wrong to suppose that the fact that the public has become inflamed by some conduct by itself justifies judges making that conduct a more serious criminal offense. That would be very dangerous. But a shift in public opinion may well cause a judge to realize something that is pertinent, and that he had not realized before, which is that rape, for example, is actually a form of torture. Several years ago, in a decision that became notorious, a state court judge in America decided that a woman wearing a short skirt could not be raped because short skirts are an invitation to sex. The horrified reaction to that decision brought home to lawyers generally (if they needed the lesson) how silly this was.

Dieter GRIMM: I was a little bit afraid that we are moving away from what you said, because, if I understood you correctly, you said that the judicial discourse fulfills in effect the Habermasian ideal better than the political discourse does. This, I think, is a very important argument when we ask why crucial questions for society are handed over to courts. It may be true that the judicial discourse is closer to that ideal, but it has a considerable price. The price is that the judicial discourse is much narrower than the political discourse. Legal discourse is a selective discourse that only allows arguments that can be based on or linked with legal norms that, in turn, can be qualified as legal arguments. By contrast, there are certainly other arguments that are relevant for the political decision. For instance, is the solution useful or detrimental? How much does it cost? Can society afford this solution or not? So I think that we should be aware of the narrowing effect of the legal discourse. Therefore, it should not be used to replace the political discourse, but only to compensate for some shortcomings of the political discourse.

Ronald DWORKIN: That brings us back to something that I also was trying to press a moment ago. Where do we stop this argument?

Robert BADINTER: I will add one remark. One of the most striking differences between the judicial process and the political process is that, in politics, politicians do whatever they can to avoid answering fundamental moral questions. They think that there is very little profit to be gained and much risk of loss. The judge, however, cannot avoid answering such a question when it is raised. He can try to do so through various clever devices, such as saying that the matter is not within his jurisdiction. But, in fact, he has his back against the wall. There is the famous political saying of Cardinal de Retz, often followed by François Mitterand: "When, in politics, you leave the realm of the ambiguous, you surely will suffer for it." The more ambiguous you are in politics, the better. The judge, however, has to answer. He can do so through a dissenting opinion, or he can join the majority, or he can resign (if dissenting opinions are not allowed). But the court itself must answer. And the answer will be publicly discussed.

The judge cannot escape by saying, "We shall see about that afterwards." And that is one of the reasons why recourse to justice as a means of answering ethical questions is so highly developed in Western democracies. People want an answer to their problems, and when they do not get as clear an answer as they would like from the political milieu, they go to the judicial forum, which is the very forum that we speak about when we talk about the media and judges. It is not only a forum in the technical judicial sense, but also in the traditional sense of the word. It is a place of debate, of public discussion and decision.

Ronald DWORKIN: A forum of principle.

Stephen BREYER: I have been making a list. Our discussion suggests some modern answers to an old question: What gives judge-made law legitimacy? After all, judges are not elected, they are not kings, and they have no divine authority. If we ask a citizen of New Hampshire why he should obey the law, he may be convinced by the answer "You voted for it or for those who voted for it or you had the same chance to do so as everyone else." That answer does not explain why judges have gained more power. Here are a few other possible answers:

First: "Judges are making law by default. The other institutions, harmed by media reporting, enjoy the public's confidence even less." One problem with this answer is that media exposure might diminish confidence in the judicial institution as well.

Second: "Judges will decide better than the other institutions. Just as the public gives the army the authority to make war and the health department the authority to protect public health, so it gives judges the authority to decide social questions—because they will do the job better." One problem here lies in our uncertainty about the truth of this proposition. At most, it could be true only in certain areas, such as the protection of fundamental rights. But we have had difficulty defining those rights. Remember our conversation about court intervention into the development of nuclear reactors.

Third: "Judges do not really make any policy decisions. What they do is dictated by legal language in statutes and in precedent." The problems with this answer are that it distorts the true judicial decisionmaking process, and no one believes it.

Fourth: "Judges are guided by reason; reason and logic, along with hard work, dictate their results." Ronnie may believe this more than I do, and I doubt that this kind of reason will convince the ordinary citizen.

Ronald DWORKIN: It is going to convince them, if you say that there is only one possible . . .

Stephen BREYER: Fifth, international courts may add: "We shall only decide matters about human rights, and only in instances where there is near universal agreement about the content of those rights. We shall limit what we call 'torture' or 'genocide' to extreme cases. Nearly everyone will agree about those cases. Hence, nearly everyone will agree that what we judges are doing is right. Given that agreement, the average person, who is not a philosopher, will not mind that we judges, who are not elected, nonetheless have decided the matter."

Sixth, but international courts have not confined their jurisdictional authority to extreme cases. They have expanded the definitions of, say, "torture." Perhaps there is a growing consensus about what counts as "torture." Given similar economic, social and political conditions among modern democracies, a growing area of agreement about the content of fundamental rights is not surprising. The upshot, for present purposes, is an accretion of judicial power.

Seventh, a cynical answer is that a particular class of people has "captured" the judiciary. That class is made up of professionals. Background and training lead it to favor women's rights, homosexual rights, and affirmative action, and to disfavor the death penalty. It does not represent the people's views any more than did priests or nobles in ancient times. It wears the mask of "reason," but that is a delusion that helps it maintain power.

Ronald DWORKIN: The conversation with the voter from New Hampshire started off wrong. If you say to him that he should obey the law because he made it, he will reply that he did not make it or that he voted against the people who made it. Then you say, "You had as much vote as anybody else." And he will say, sensibly, "That does not mean that I made it." It is deeply established in our rhetoric that, in a democracy, people govern themselves. But unless you give that claim a Hegelian twist, or find some other, more persuasive understanding of it, it is simply fictional. I am on the losing side of most political battles in America. In what sense do I govern myself?

Stephen BREYER: The question is, of course, fictional. But my point is that, if you say to an average person, "You had the same chance to vote as everybody else, and you can vote, and the people who are elected will make the law representing you," that seems a satisfactory reply, which is missing in the case of judges.

Ronald DWORKIN: By itself, just as it stands, it is not a satisfactory answer because the fact that I have the same vote as any other single person does not just by itself mean that I have a reason to obey what the majority has decided when I voted the other way. Certain conditions—the true conditions of democracy—must also be met. I must have free speech, for example. And even that is not enough. The majority must treat me with equal concern and respect if I am to be expected to do what it says. It cannot dictate to me on matters of religion and conscience, which my self-respect demands that I decide on for myself, for example, and it must respect my other basic rights. So, Steve, you have pointed the way to a better answer to the New Hampshire voter, when he asks why the Supreme Court has the power it does, than any of the answers on your list. You can say: "The Court is there to try to make sure that all the conditions of democracy, broadly understood, are met. It is there to try to make sure that, when the majority decides what the taxes will be, or who can build or farm where, the background conditions are met for enforcing the majority's decision against everyone." When these conditions are met, incidentally, then I think it does make sense to say that the people are a political partnership that acts together, that, in that sense, I did make even the laws I object to. But unless the conditions are met, it is impossible to say with a straight face that the people are a partnership.

Of course, people will disagree about what the conditions of democracy are, and when they are met. That is why constitutions must be drafted in abstract language, and why judges disagree when applying that language to concrete problems. Constitutions ought not to try to decide too much. They should not lay down a particular policy about interest rates, or how much of a nation's wealth should be spent on medical care or how much should be spent on space research, and so forth. These, we might say, are majoritarian issues. Once the conditions of democracy are met, then it is right that these be decided, directly or indirectly, by majority will. But what those conditions are, and what they require in particular cases, are not majoritarian issues, and we cannot regard them that way without begging the question. They are moral issues, and that is why modern democracies increasingly turn away from parliaments and toward judges to decide them.

Stephen BREYER: I think that you are right. But I am not completely satisfied because I doubt that we can explain why, for example, torture should include rape on the basis of that theory of democracy. That theory can explain many decisions taken by constitutional courts, decisions concerning free expression, for example, but it cannot explain all of them. I cannot use it to explain, as I have said, why the public is willing to have a court in Strasbourg made up of 40 judges from 40 different countries decide whether torture includes rape. It explains why a certain amount of decisionmaking authority has been given to non-majoritarian courts, but not all.

Ronald DWORKIN: Well, we are in danger of collapsing into agreement, which is the worst thing that could happen in a discussion like this. So I will try and avoid it. Yes, the idea of human rights is more basic than the idea of democracy. But democracy is among those rights, and these rights qualify democracy. A government that exercises power through torture, whatever else it is, is not a democracy, even if it has been elected by majority vote. But I want to come back to the question how far the conditions of democracy depend on majority will. I agree with you—and it is a wholly happy development—that there is much more by way of consensus about certain fundamental rights now than even half a century ago. But people are still deeply divided over whether, for example, discrimination against homosexuals violates human rights. But very few people, I think, suppose that whether laws against sodomy violate basic rights of homosexuals turns on what a majority of the people in any particular country thinks.

Stephen BREYER: The proof of the pudding is in the eating. If you show—as you may have done in your writings—that the "non-majoritarian" principles or protections upon which basic democracy depends closely track the increased powers that European nations have given the judges, then your explanation of what has occurred is a good one. Why am I doubtful? Because I suspect that human rights courts, say, in Strasbourg, are deciding matters that are majoritarian in nature, for example, just when the shooting of an escaping suspect by a policeman constitutes a violation of a basic right rather than ordinary murder. And you have heard Dieter describe cases in which constitutional courts decide matters that you believe should be left to the electoral process.

Ronald DWORKIN: I do not mean to propose a one-note theory. I do not think that there is only one basis for deciding whether international tribunals dealing with human rights should be assigned one question rather than another. It is an important reason that the matter is not one fit for majoritarian decision. But there are surely other reasons. Perhaps it is important that we have a common decision across national or even regional boundaries, for example. And I agree that, in some contexts, we should try to develop arguments that are independent of democracy. An argument that begins with some assumptions about the conditions of democracy might not be so powerful in Iran now, for example. I agree with that.

Robert BADINTER: I should like to return for a moment to the main topic of discussion: "the secular papacy." The title suggests that basic democratic theory is not the immediate problem. Rather, that problem consists of the fact that moral problems are ever more readily being submitted voluntarily to the judicial system for decision, and that system is ever more inclined to consider them, even when it is not strictly necessary to do so.

The example of rape and torture is important in this respect. That is because the question is whether to classify rape as a form of torture or, instead, to prosecute rape as would be done in a classical manner in respect to prosecution, conviction, and stigmatization. For those who pose the question of whether rape is torture, the matter is of a moral nature. We find torture in a democracy at a higher (stigmatizing) level than that at which we find crimes against the person. It is consequently not sufficient to categorize rape as a violent sexual attack. We must go further and stigmatize it at the highest level. This is purely a matter of moral attitude because we already have the technical tools to put the fellow in jail for rape. We already consider rape a crime, the perpetrator is a criminal, and he will serve, say, 20 years in prison. In the end, when we say that rape is torture and that the perpetrator is a torturer, he will still serve, say, 20 years in prison. Either way, in the end, he is in jail. But the issue is truly whether, as a moral matter, rape should be identified as a form of the worst crime. What is interesting is that this kind of question is raised and then answered.

What I want to stress is that, in my opinion, this kind of question would not have arisen, or have been answered by courts, 20 years ago. Going back to the homosexual question, the fact that it is even being dealt with in the Luxembourg Court is interesting. After all, that Court was not created to deal with that kind of question. It was created to assure free trade within the Community and then the European Union. That was its initial function. What happened? The forum was opened, and then people rushed to use it. They find democratic discussion and proceedings insufficient. They have to go to court as well. They are aware of that very important, superior, international court in Luxembourg. They believe that, by calling upon it, they will be able to use it. And they do so. The Court does answer. Everything moves in the same direction.

You remember our first topic: the growth in the judge's power. Earlier, we looked at various areas, and you mentioned that we found an example in which that power was at its peak: when judges came to decide whether nuclear energy was better than other methods for generating heat. What in heaven's name has that to do with jurisdiction? As we were taught when we were in our 20s: nothing at all. Such a question is not even posed. Yet that decision exists. It is a fact. The same people who had to decide whether it was better to use atomic energy or gas will have to decide whether rape is a sexual crime as we have always treated it, or whether it is torture. Now it may be torture, perhaps tomorrow a crime against humanity.

This phenomenon is extraordinary in modern democracies. Why do they feel that they need the stamp of justice? They need the stamp of justice not simply to permit an effective prosecution but because of their desire for added "stigmatizing" force. You can put the rapist in prison without characterizing rape as "torture." But we want the stamp, in this case, of "torture," which the system of justice says carries with it the worst stigma possible. And there you have the secular papacy.

The legislative council did not debate whether rape should be called a form of torture. I presided over the reshaping of the French criminal code. That work, which ended 15 years ago—not so long ago—took 4 years. When we rewrote the code, we rewrote the section concerning rape and increased the penalty. But throughout that period, no one asked us to call rape a form of torture. To obtain that kind of categorization, the social movement will go to the justice system. They go to the courts, not only because they think of the courts as a better forum, with better discussion, and providing better answers, but also because they seek something more. And that "more" is the "papal pronouncement."

Why does society regard it as a papal pronouncement? Of course, the judges wear robes, but that is not a sufficient explanation. The costume does not make the judge. Society approaches the judiciary because, in my view, elsewhere it sees only a desert of moral sources and a drying up of moral springs. People need to find someone to tell them what is of moral value. The tablets of the law are tablets of morality. And what is striking is that the judge does not reply by saying, "Why on earth are you calling on me for that?" Highly qualified international judges do not ask why they should investigate matters of transsexuality. They might find a technical reason for not answering such questions, but they do answer.

Then, the third side of the triangle—which as everyone knows is, geometrically speaking, the most interesting figure—is public satisfaction. I have not heard of any political figure introducing into the legislature a bill that says: "No way. We cannot define rape as a form of torture." No. The public seems perfectly satisfied with the judiciary carrying out this function. Thus, today we have a demand for the secular papal pronouncement, a judicial willingness to take on that kind of task and what appears to be a call for more. All this reflects a major change.

Let me now return to the matter of the democratic majority. I believe that you, Ronald, have written that we cannot answer a German Jew as follows: "In 1934, after all, you voted. Hence, you agreed to what later happened." They voted against the Nazis. They in no sense willed what later occurred. But the German people as a whole pronounced, by a majority, in favor of Nazism. There, you put your finger on the limits of majoritarian democracy.

Ronald DWORKIN: You have taken the argument further than I myself would have. I believe that people understand the institutional reasons why courts are better positioned to decide certain fundamental moral issues, like the conditions of democracy, than parliaments are. You add that people will look to the courts not just as the appropriate institutions to decide those issues, but as having a particular insight into the truth of the matter. (That is, after all, why people looked to the church. It was not just "Somebody has to do it, and priests seem well situated institutionally." People thought that priests had a special pipeline to the truth.) I am not yet persuaded of that. It is perfectly true that ordinary legislators do not go around defining rape as torture, but that is possibly because torture does not play such an important role in domestic criminal codes as it does internationally. It can be treated as an aggravated form of other crimes. But suppose the General Assembly of the United Nations were to adopt by a thundering majority the proposition that rape counts as torture. Do you think that would have less of an impact on popular opinion than if some court someplace says so?

Robert BADINTER: No, definitely not, except that—this is the answer— it will not be the General Assembly of the United Nations.

Ronald DWORKIN: No, I understand.

Robert BADINTER: They will evade answering.

Ronald DWORKIN: Yes, but, Robert, I am trying to distinguish now between your claim that, by default, *faute de mieux,* judges must decide issues like that one, and your stronger claim that people think that judges have "a pipeline to the truth." The second supposes that people are more likely to be persuaded of a moral claim if a court has made it than if a parliament of some kind has. I am less convinced of that. Most Americans accept that church and state will be separated in roughly the way that the Supreme Court has decreed, because they accept that the Court is the right place for that decision to be made. But I do not think that the Court has changed the minds of many people who would prefer organized prayer in public schools. They accept that they cannot have it, but not that it should not be. The same is true, for many people, about abortion. Real popes are different. If, when the white smoke next goes up in Rome, a new pope takes a very different view from this one about contraception, for example, that really will change what a lot of people think.

Stephen BREYER: Perhaps we enjoy the prestige of a *marque,* like a trademark. A court must be careful when it commits its prestige— as did the Pope when he committed the Church's prestige in the Middle Ages. But when it does so, its decision will enjoy the acceptance that flows from respect for the institution. That respect reflects a view that the judges are not out for themselves, but rather that they think seriously about the problems at issue and are not biased. Of course, we must be careful not to "dilute the mark." If an international court in Strasbourg says that torture includes rape, it commits its prestige to that proposition. On the one hand, that may make the proposition more acceptable; on the other, it may, if the public believes that the court has overreached, "dilute the mark."

Ronald DWORKIN: Let us not lose sight of the ambitious claim that Robert is suggesting. He is suggesting not just that the judicial imprimatur is a kind of endorsement, like a good housekeeping seal of approval, but also that judges are widely thought to have a more direct line to the truth about fundamental matters. That is more of a papal aura than I myself meant to suggest. I am in favor of pontificating judges, but not because I think that the population as a whole assigns to judges some measure of infallibility. I would regret it if they did.

Robert BADINTER: Ronald, it is not that I believe that the Pope is infallible because he is the Pope. The Pope is tied to the idea of God, whose interpreter he is. The strength of the Pope's voice is not due to the fact that he is talented or that people believe that he is honest. It is not even due to the fact that people think that he is inspired directly by God. It is due to the fact that, for poor human creatures, he represents God on earth.

I turn to the judge. His comparable influence is not due to his intelligence or any belief in his infallibility. It is due to the fact that at the heart of every human being lies a claim for justice. In a letter that I find admirable, for I believe there is great truth underlying its words, Emile Zola wrote to the wife of Alfred Dreyfus: "Un peu de justice sur cette terre nous aurait fait quand même plaisir." "Un peu," not much, "just a little bit of justice would have pleased us so much." How right that is!

When people turn to judges, they seek justice and what they think will be fair for them. And that is why I used the term "secular papal pronouncement." It is a secular pronouncement because it does not reflect a transcendent divinity, but rather the clamor of humanity for a better justice. That is the point at which the judge's moral mission has increased tremendously within society.

Dieter GRIMM: And then there is this famous statement by Bärbel Bohley, one of the leaders of the civil movement in the former East Germany, who said after unification, "We hoped to get justice and we got the Rule of Law."

NOTES

1. *Washington* v. *Glucksberg,* 521 U.S. 702 (1997).

2. *Prosecutor* v. *Drazen Erdemovic,* 1998 W.L. 2014005 UN ICT (Trial) (Yug.), Mar. 1998.

3. *Queen* v. *Dudley E. Stephens,* 14 Q.B. 273 (1884).

4. *Washington* v. *Glucksberg,* n. 1 *supra.*

5. *Ahmed Selmouni* v. *France,* 29 E.H.R.R. 403 ECHR (2000).

3

Supervision of the Political Process

3.1. Presentation
Judicial Checks upon the Electoral Process

Justice Stephen Breyer

This paper will focus upon three areas in which judges, while maintaining strict neutrality with respect to each party's political program, make decisions that may nonetheless significantly affect the political process. The three areas are: (1) the determination and enforcement of fair voting rules; (2) the regulation of campaign finance; and (3) the interpretation and enforcement of ethics laws. I shall draw examples in each area from American law.

Taken together, the three areas illustrate three different ways in which judges intervene in political processes: (1) Judges sometimes directly supervise elections (*e.g.*, "fair voting rules"); (2) they set aside laws voted by legislatures (*e.g.*, "fair voting rules" and "campaign finance"); and (3) they interpret "ethics" laws that regulate the conduct of public officials, thereby affecting the condition of politics and government service. The examples will provide a substantive basis for discussion, suggesting comparisons with European law and (we hope) leading to more general observations.

I. FAIR VOTING RULES

Consider three questions: What are the electoral rules? Have voters and candidates complied with those rules? Has there been fraud, dishonesty, the buying of votes, the use of force or threats of force, etc., during the election? In the United States, the latter two questions (compliance and fraud) are primarily left to the states, which will answer them in particular cases through reference to state election commissions, subject to some form of judicial review in state courts, or through investigations by local criminal prosecutors.

The first question—What are the electoral rules?—is partly but not entirely a matter of state law. The Constitution specifies that "Times, Places and Manner of holding Elections for Senators and Representatives, shall be prescribed in each State by the legislature thereof; but Congress may at any time by Law make or alter such Regulations." Article 1, Section 4. Yet, Congress has enacted important federal voting laws. And the federal courts, including the Supreme Court, have reviewed local, state, and federal election laws to determine whether they comply with constitutional mandates—a kind of "basic fairness" review. I shall list four examples of this kind of judicial review:

A. Race

The (post–Civil War) Fifteenth Amendment enacted in 1870 says that the "right of citizens . . . to vote shall not be denied or abridged . . . on account of race." For nearly a century, however, black citizens were routinely denied the right to vote, particularly in the South. After World War II, the Supreme Court began to hold unconstitutional voting requirements that systematically excluded blacks from taking a meaningful part in elections. See, *e.g.*, *Smith* v. *Allwright*, 321 U.S. 649 (1944) (major political parties cannot hold "all white" primary elections); *Terry* v. *Adams*, 345 U.S. 461 (1953) (nor can they hold "pre-primary" white primaries). Courts began to consider the constitutionality of such discriminatory devices as literacy tests, civics tests, and poll taxes. In the 1960s, the Constitution was amended to forbid the poll tax. And Congress passed a Voting Rights Act, which basically placed the Southern states' election systems under the supervision of the federal Attorney General. The Act forbade voting requirements that had the purpose or effect of discriminating. It gave the Attorney General broad enforcement powers, and it required states with a history of discrimination (particularly the Southern states) to "clear" any new requirement with the Attorney General or with a federal court.

The Act led to much litigation as Southern states, counties, and municipalities sought to delay desegregation, for example, by gerrymandering districts, substituting larger multi-candidate voting districts for smaller single-candidate districts, or by devising complex voting rules that would help maintain a basically white voting electorate. In the process, judges would often hold voting systems unlawful, sometimes set voting rules themselves, and sometimes supervise elections directly. Over the course of 40 years, the Act has worked reasonably well to eliminate discrimination, but Voting Rights Act election cases still arise with some frequency. A locality, for example, may refuse to submit a particular proposed voting law change (to court or to the Attorney General) for "clearance." Or local residents may claim that a local school board was motivated by prejudice when it chose one electoral plan rather than another. Or a group of voters may argue that a change in a state's judicial system (which is elected) has the "effect" of discriminating against a particular minority.

The upshot is that considerable supervision by federal judges of election processes is necessary to guarantee that those processes are not discriminatory.

B. Reapportionment

But judicial supervision of electoral processes is not limited to ensuring that voters are not treated unfairly because of race. The courts also enforce the constitutional principle that each person's vote should carry equal weight ("one person/one vote"). Each Member of Congress and each member of a state legislature is typically elected from a single-member voting district, the size and shape of which are fixed by the state legislature. Prior to 1963, voting districts within a single state might vary dramatically with respect to population, thereby typically giving greater influence to rural voters whose voting districts often contained fewer people. In the 1960s, the Supreme Court, overturning previous case law, held that courts had the legal power to consider the make-up of a voting district, that different sized districts violated the Fourteenth Amendment's guarantee of "equal protection of the laws," and that voting districts must have approximately equal population. The result was that courts, for 15 years or more, supervised the "reapportionment" of voting districts throughout the nation, striking down legislative districting plans, requiring legislatures to adopt different plans, and sometimes ordering "at large" elections (i.e., without districts) where the legislature failed to adopt a proper districting system.

C. Gerrymandering

Legislatures may produce equally populated voting districts that nonetheless favor one party or another. They can manipulate the district's shape, so that, for example, Party A's adherents are divided among several districts in each of which Party B maintains a majority ("splitting") or so that Party A's adherents are all packed into one district where they can elect one, but only one, legislator ("packing"). Such practices, called "gerrymandering," have long been thought immune from judicial review, in part because of political tradition. Another reason is that many believe that the courts lack the ability to separate legitimate from illegitimate practices, and that review of the drawing of political boundaries seems a factual/political/time-consuming morass, which may force courts to draw political boundaries themselves, thereby threatening the perception of political neutrality that underlies their legitimacy. Until recently, courts would intervene in such matters only when gerrymandering was linked to racial discrimination, *i.e.*, when it amounted to a method of disenfranchising minority voters.

Recently, however, the Supreme Court has considered instances in which legislatures have drawn district lines with the benign object of electing more minority legislators—a kind of electoral affirmative action. And it has determined (typically by a 5-to-4 vote) that the Constitution's Equal Protection Clause forbids using race as a criterion for drawing boundaries, whether the object is to help or to hurt minority voters. *Bush* v. *Vera*, 517 U.S. 952 (1996). Where efforts to achieve greater minority representation are at issue, the Court has held that the Fourteenth Amendment's Equal Protection Clause forbids a districting plan in which race, rather than "traditional" districting considerations, "predominate" (except, perhaps, where the plan represents an effort to avoid districting that discriminates against a minority). *Abrams* v. *Johnson*, 521 U.S. 74 (1997).

These "benign racial districting" holdings will require the courts to determine case by case whether a legislature has, in fact, used predominantly racial, rather than "traditional," criteria. That is not easy to determine, where, for example, black voters vote Democrat, and a Democrat-dominated state legislature redistricts in order to favor Democratic candidates. The ruling has led to significant judicial involvement in the drawing of electoral district lines in several Southern states, and the consistency of these holdings with basic values of fairness has provoked debate. It remains to be seen whether the Court's rulings will lead to even greater judicial involvement in the electoral district line-drawing process. At an extreme, the underlying constitutional rule would forbid the use of gender, national origin, and political party affiliation itself—in which case the rule will become one of "equal" district "compactness," which requirement courts conceivably could enforce, but only with the aid of electoral mathematicians.

D. Political Parties

While the Court has scrutinized districting decisions based on equal protection principles, it has found constitutional protection for political parties in the First Amendment's prohibition against "abridging the freedom of speech." The Constitution itself does not mention political parties. And the states may regulate parties when they exercise their power to regulate the manner in which elections are held. Nonetheless, the Court has used a balancing test to determine when a state election law affecting a political party goes too far and violates the First Amendment.

Courts "must weigh 'the character and magnitude of the asserted injury to the rights protected by the First and Fourteenth Amendments' against 'the precise interest put forward by the State as justifications for the burden,'" taking account of the need to impose that burden. *Burdick* v. *Takushi*, 504 U.S. 428 (1992). A "severe burden" must be "narrowly tailored and advance a compelling state interest"; a lesser burden will "trigger less exacting review." *Timmons* v. *Twin Cities Area New Party*, 520 U.S. 351, 358 (1997).

Applying this test, the Court has found lawful state requirements that, for example, (1) require a party to select its nominee in a state primary election, *American Party* v. *White*, 415 U.S. 767 (1974); (2) deny a place on the ballot to parties that lack a "significant modicum of support," *Jenness* v. *Fortson*, 403 U.S. 431 (1971); (3) ban write-in voting, *Burdick* v. *Takushi*, 504 U.S. 428 (1992); and (4) forbid a candidate from associating with more than one party, *Timmons* v. *Twin-Cities*, 520 U.S. 351 (1997).

Conversely, the Court has struck down state requirements that (1) required candidates not associated with major parties to file for election early, *Anderson* v. *Celebrezze*, 460 U.S. 780 (1983); (2) forbid party officials from endorsing (or opposing) primary election candidates, *Eu* v. *San*

Francisco, 489 U.S. 214 (1989); (3) restricted voting to choose among Party A's candidates for nomination (in a primary) to members of Party A (where Party A wanted to permit any voter, regardless of party affiliation, to choose among its candidates), *Tashjian* v. *Republican Party of Connecticut*, 479 U.S. 208; and (4) required delegates to a Presidential convention (selected at a state primary) to vote for the candidate to whom they had pledged (where the Party wanted to leave them free to change their minds), *Democratic Party of the United States* v. *Wisconsin ex rel. La Follette*, 450 U.S. 107 (1981).

More recently, the Court (by a vote of 7 to 2) struck down a California "blanket primary" system in which a primary voter would obtain a single ballot containing every candidate of every party for every office. *California Democratic Party* v. *Jones*, 530 U.S. 567 (2000). The voter would vote for one person for each office (from whatever party the voter wished). The final election would consist of a run-off among whomever, within each party, received the most votes. The Court held that this system permitted persons totally unaffiliated with Party A to choose Party A's nominee. Consequently, the blanket primary severely impaired the ability of Party A's members to choose a candidate, thereby infringing upon a constitutionally protected right to associate for this important political purpose.

The Court's holding throws into question the lawfulness of "open primary" systems followed in more than 20 states. Those "open primary" systems, while similar to the "blanket" system, permit a primary voter to pick whatever party ballot the voter wishes, but require the voter to declare at least a temporary affiliation with one party at that time.

E. Questions

1. Are the examples mentioned unique to America? Can one find comparable European examples of judicial control of the election process?
2. What explains the increasing judicial involvement described? Greater concern for fair and equal treatment? Special concern about unfair treatment of minorities? Less trust in the fairness of politically created electoral systems? Greater public exposure (via the media) to systemic unfairness?
3. Will growing minority populations in Europe or growing distrust in the fairness of electoral institutions lead national or in-

ternational courts charged with enforcing basic human rights guarantees to intervene similarly in the electoral process?

4. Can courts develop judicially administrable legal principles that permit them to strike down seriously unfair electoral procedures? The "reapportionment" cases ended up with a simple clear principle: "one person/one vote." The principle of "no discrimination against minorities" is also reasonably clear. But the courts have had difficulty administering this principle when the "adverse effect" (rather than the purpose) of a voting rule is at issue. And it may prove particularly difficult to administer a rule that forbids the use of "positive discrimination" in drawing district boundaries. Will the courts eventually try to enforce a mathematical "compactness" rule designed to eliminate gerrymandering?

5. In what other ways might courts intervene in the electoral process in order to avoid serious unfairness?

II. CAMPAIGN FINANCE

Another way in which courts affect the political process is by setting limits on campaign finance regulation. Campaign finance laws seek to limit the influence of money, but they may vary in their more specific aims. They may seek to "level the playing field" by, for example, limiting campaign expenditures, thereby giving less well financed candidates a better opportunity to win. Campaign finance laws may also seek to diminish corruption, or the appearance of corruption, that can occur when those with money wield enormous political influence, by limiting campaign contributions. Judges, particularly those of constitutional courts, typically become involved when asked to determine whether a specific statute violates guarantees of free expression.

A. The American Statute

Congress enacted the basic campaign finance statute in 1974, immediately after Watergate. To achieve the first goal ("level playing field"), Congress imposed limits (measured in cents per voter and usually tied to inflation) on the amounts that candidates, corporations, labor unions, political committees ("political action committees," or PACs), and political parties can *spend* to help a candidate win a federal election. To achieve the second goal ("diminishing the appearance of corruption"), Congress imposed limits on the amounts that individuals, corporations, PACs, and political parties can *contribute* to a candidate for federal office. The Act also makes clear that an "expenditure" (say, by a PAC or by a person not affiliated with a candidate) is a "contribution" if, but only if, the expenditure is "coordinated" with the candidate, *i.e.,* if the candidate or his organization is somehow involved in planning the expenditure. The Act additionally sets up a system for public financing of presidential campaigns, it imposes disclosure requirements, and it creates a six-member, politically appointed commission to supervise what amounts to a highly complex regulatory system.

B. The American Courts

The Supreme Court has had to determine the extent to which the Act is consistent with First Amendment guarantees of free speech. In *Buckley* v. *Valeo,* 424 U.S. 1 (1976), the Court held that, because political speech and association lie at the heart of the First Amendment, it should review finance restrictions closely.

It determined that, in general, expenditure limits are unconstitutional, but contribution limits are constitutional. Specifically, the Court said that restricting the "amount of money a person or group can spend on political communication during a campaign necessarily reduces the quantity of expression by restricting the number of issues discussed, the depth of their exploration, and the size of the audience reached." Moreover, expenditure limits are not needed to prevent "the appearance of corruption." Consequently, in general, they violate the Constitution.

By way of contrast, contribution limits help to eliminate corruption, or the appearance of corruption, for they minimize the appearance of "quid pro quo." They involve "little direct restraint on political communication" for they permit "the symbolic expression of support evidenced by a contribution" and do not interfere with one's freedom "to discuss candidates and issues." Consequently, in general, they do not violate the Constitution.

The Court subsequently has implemented its basic expenditure/contribution distinction. On the one hand, it has struck down other statutory limits upon PAC expenditures, *Federal Election*

Commission v. *National Conservative Political Action Committee,* 470 U.S. 480 (1985); limits upon expenditures by non-profit corporations, *Federal Election Commission* v. *Massachusetts Citizens for Life, Inc.,* 479 U.S. 238 (1986); and limits upon the independent (*i.e.,* "non-coordinated") expenditures by a political party, *Colorado Republican Federal Campaign Committee* v. *Federal Election Commission,* 518 U.S. 604 (1996). On the other hand, it has upheld limits on contributions that individuals and groups may give to PACs, *California Medical Association* v. *Federal Election Commission,* 453 U.S. 182 (1981), and a state law limiting an individual's contribution to $1,000 (despite claims that there was no evidence that a higher limit would create an appearance of corruption), *Nixon* v. *Shrink Missouri Government PAC,* 528 U.S. 377 (2000).

Despite the Act's effort to control campaign spending, an estimated $500,000 was spent on a typical House of Representatives race in 1992, an average Senate race cost over $3 million, and an average closely fought Senate race cost over $5 million. The *New York Times* estimates that a contested House race will cost more than $3 million this year. It estimates that all federal races this year taken together will cost a record $3 billion. To what extent are the Court's decisions responsible for this problem?

On the one hand, the decisions struck expenditure limits from the statute. And, in light of the Court's holdings, a candidate can spend as much of his own money as he wishes (which may help account for multi-millionaire candidates, such as Steve Forbes and Ross Perot). On the other hand, the Court's cases permit contribution limits and, in general, limiting contributions should help to limit expenditures. Of course, the Act's limitations apply only to individual contributions, not to their sum total; and, in theory, one could obtain, for instance, $100 million, with one hundred thousand $1,000 contributions. But that is easier said than done.

Furthermore, the contribution limitation is not effective because the statute itself contains loopholes. It permits contributions of any size to be made to political parties, ostensibly for the purposes of encouraging voter registration or publicizing positions on issues as opposed to asking for candidate support. Vast amounts of money (called "soft money") have been raised for these purposes. Moreover, "issue-oriented" organizations can spend as much as they wish to promote their issue-related positions (which in practice may well favor one party or candidate).

C. Europe and Canada

American courts are not alone in placing boundaries on campaign finance regulation. The European Court of Human Rights (ECHR) has struck down a British statute that limited the amount of expenditure that an individual might make on behalf of a candidate within four to six weeks prior to an election. In that case, an anti-abortion group violated the statute by distributing leaflets urging the election (or defeat) of certain candidates. The ECHR concluded that it was "not satisfied that it was necessary thus to limit . . . expenditure in order to achieve the legitimate aim of securing equality between candidates, particularly in view of the fact that there were no restrictions placed upon the freedom of the press to support or oppose the election of any particular candidate or upon political parties and their supporters to advertise at national or regional level." The restriction on expression was "disproportionate to the aim pursued," and, hence, unlawful under the European Convention. *Bowman v. United Kingdom*, 26 Eur. Ct. H.R. 1 (1998).

The Canadian Supreme Court also considered campaign finance in the context of a highly complex campaign financing scheme associated with a referendum on independence for Quebec. The scheme set up committees, each of which could take a different position on the referendum, and it provided for associated groups, each of which would have views somewhat similar to those of its committee. It provided relatively generous expenditure limits for all such groups. But it virtually forbade expenditure by non-associated individuals. The Court approved the statutory scheme in principle, but it faulted the scheme for failing to find a way to permit individuals who did not agree with any associated group to spend some of their own money to publicize their views. The Court explained how this might be done, and it held the whole scheme unconstitutional (as having violated the constitutional guarantee of free expression) unless and until the legislature made those modifications. *Libman v. Attorney General of Quebec*, 151 D.L.R. 4th 385 (1997).

D. Questions

1. Is the contribution/expenditure distinction convincing? The Court apparently minimized the importance of the "level playing field" objective when it rejected, in *Buckley*, "the concept that

government may restrict the speech of some elements of our society in order to enhance the relative voice of others." Are there good reasons for rejecting that concept?

2. To what extent is the Court, and to what extent is the Congress, responsible for the high cost of American political campaigns?

3. The ECHR decision suggests that the British system places no limits upon contributions or expenditures made to political parties (rather like "soft money"). What campaign finance limits exist in European countries? Do unregulated "soft money" contributions significantly undercut the effectiveness of other forms of regulation? How different is the European problem?

4. The ECHR came to a *Buckley*-type conclusion. Will its decision, permitting single-issue-type expenditures, seriously undercut European efforts to control campaign finance?

5. How easily can courts review highly technical campaign-finance regulatory systems? Should they go so far as to rewrite the details, as the Canadian Court has done? How easy is it to determine just when campaign finance regulation goes too far? How can a court determine whether a particular system offers too much protection to incumbents?

6. What about lowering election costs, or lessening the impact of personal wealth, by publicly financing political campaigns or requiring the media to donate free time? Or do these proposals also raise "free expression" problems?

7. It is sometimes claimed that any regulation, other than disclosure, will simply increase the political power of the media, protect incumbent office holders, or both. Hence, only disclosure requirements are consistent with the principle of free expression. Is that so?

III. ETHICS REGULATIONS

In the context of federal ethics regulation, the Court has also intervened to promote the values of basic fairness and free expression. Federal ethics regulation consists of a highly complex set of statutes and regulations. I shall set forth the major federal statutory approaches, describe their enforcement, list several related problems, and discuss how the courts have responded to some of those problems.

A. Approaches

Most federal ethics laws fall into the following five categories:

1. Financial Conflicts of Interest. Federal criminal law prohibits an official from (a) receiving a bribe; (b) receiving a gratuity (payment for having made an official decision); (c) participating "personally and substantially" in any "particular matter" in which he "has a financial interest"; (d) accepting a gift worth more than, say, $50 (except from family); and (e) receiving a contribution or supplement to salary.
2. Financial Disclosure. Executive and judicial officials must file forms each year reporting (in excruciating detail) all income and all assets owned by the official and all family members.
3. Outside Activities. Officials normally cannot engage in any outside paid activities, nor can they receive honoraria (*i.e.*, payments) for speeches, appearances, or articles. Teaching is sometimes permitted, with compensation limited to no more than about $20,000 per year.
4. Post–Government Employment Activities. With various exceptions, Executive Branch officials who have left the government typically cannot appear (for example, as a lawyer) during the next year before the department in which they worked. They can never act in a "particular matter" in which they were involved as a government official.
5. Workplace Environment. In general, Executive Branch employees cannot participate in political activity. They cannot use government resources for personal activities. They cannot give gifts to fellow employees.

B. Enforcement

These various provisions are typically enforced in three ways. First, ordinary federal criminal prosecutors in the federal Department of Justice may bring criminal prosecutions. Second, a special statute (now expired) requires the Attorney General to ask a three-judge panel to appoint an independent special prosecutor when she has received evidence that any of certain designated high officials (*e.g.*, the President) has committed a crime. A Special Prosecutor (such as Ken Starr) might undertake a prosecution under these laws. Third, an Executive Branch Office of Government Ethics or ethics officials (or "inspectors general") in each government agency may interpret the laws and regulations, issue new regulations, and enforce existing regulations through administrative sanctions.

C. Problems

The ethics statutes and regulations have raised such problems as the following:

First, many of the relevant criminal statutes use language that potentially brings a vast range of ordinary conduct within their reach. The bribery statute, for example, forbids "corruptly" promising "any thing of value to any public official" "with intent to influence any official act." Literally interpreted, that language may encompass at least some campaign contributions. The gratuity statute forbids "directly or indirectly" offering "anything of value to any public official . . . for or because of any official act performed or to be performed." Does this forbid a group of farmers from paying for the Secretary of Agriculture's hotel and lunch when he comes to speak? Common ethics often distinguishes "right" from "wrong" in terms of the amount of money or kind of gift at issue—but these distinctions are not apparent from the statutes themselves. Rather, the statutes leave these matters to prosecutors to decide, when they decide whether to prosecute.

In some cases, because of the breadth and ambiguity of many ethics provisions and the constitutional requirement that the criminal laws provide fair warning of what is prohibited, the courts have interpreted such laws narrowly. For instance, in one case, the Court interpreted a law prohibiting private entities from supplementing the salary of government employees not to apply to a lump-sum payment that the defendant received from his former employer right before commencing federal service. *Crandon v. United States*, 494 U.S. 152 (1990). The courts have also reviewed ethics laws to ensure compliance with the First Amendment. A couple of years ago, the Court invalidated a law that prohibited federal employees from accepting any compensation for making speeches or writing articles on matters of public concern because it did not comport with the constitutional guarantee of free speech. *United States v. National Treasury Employees Union*, 513 U.S. 454 (1995).

Second, the statutes, if broadly interpreted, along with regulations that seek "perfectly" ethical behavior, sometimes produce extreme rules that lack perspective or common sense. The rules frequently fail to distinguish between minor, reasonable, personal use, and abuse of government resources. Executive Branch offices, for example, lock office Xerox machines with codes to prevent personal use; with limited exceptions, federal officials cannot use phones for personal calls or government-purchased stationery for personal letters; use of official autos requires considerable paperwork designed to prevent any personal use (or any use by family members). Disclosure rules require entering hundreds or thousands of items on lengthy forms each year. The result of these exacting rules, of course, is that minor violations frequently occur.

Third, although media scrutiny has the potential to build public confidence by exposing serious instances of misconduct, the media's focus on the many minor violations that occur can leave the public with the erroneous impression that the government is filled with instances of "corruption." The result is a diversion of public attention and of the attention of public officials from the basic job of government, further public disenchantment with government, and greater difficulty in attracting highly qualified personnel (particularly important in America, which relies more than European nations upon private-sector personnel to perform temporary public service). The Court has noted this latter concern as a reason for not interpreting the ethics laws too broadly. *Crandon*, 494 U.S., at 167 & n.22.

Fourth, press publicity also can make it difficult for prosecutors to decide against prosecuting a minor ethical violation. At the very least, public disclosure of even minor violations can seriously embarrass the official involved. In some cases, however, publicity may destroy a public official's career, even when the charges later prove unfounded or too minor to warrant prosecution. And even when an official is acquitted, he may be driven to the brink of bankruptcy by the cost of defending himself in court.

Fifth, the creation of a Special Prosecutor, charged with prosecuting violations by high public officials, magnifies these problems. Considerable publicity for the prosecutor himself, along with lack of any outside control, can produce strong pressures for continued investigation and prosecution—even where prosecutions (in the course of ordinary individuals) would not take place. (The Special Prosecutor's office, for example, when prosecuting an agricultural organization for having paid the expenses of the Secretary of Agriculture at a European Conference, argued that the gratuity statute would forbid farmers from providing even a lunch for the Secretary of Agriculture.)

The Ethics in Government Act presented a novel constitutional question in that it gave a special court the authority to appoint a Special Prosecutor (an Executive Branch official) who could investigate the President. Moreover, the Act permitted only the Attorney General to remove the Special Prosecutor and only for "good cause." The Supreme Court rejected a challenge that claimed that those aspects of the statute violated the constitutional separation of powers. *Morrison* v. *Olson*, 487 U.S. 654 (1988). Although the Court said that the Act was constitutional, Congress, after the Ken Starr investigation, opted not to renew the law.

D. Questions

1. Disclosure, publicity, and rules of ethics all are necessary to avoid corruption, to maintain ethical behavior, and to build public confidence in government. Can we reconcile these objectives with common-sense rules that avoid zealotry, while also preventing the use of "ethics violations" as a political weapon?
2. How can we maintain sufficient independence to assure that powerful governmental law-violators will be prosecuted without giving the prosecutor himself the power to pursue unwarranted prosecutions for improper reasons, *i.e.*, *Quis ipsos custodiat*?

IV. CONCLUDING OBSERVATIONS

Although it generally describes American practices, this paper intends its examples to facilitate a more general discussion. Perhaps each reader should consider how his or her own legal system deals with comparable issues. Are the problems similar? How do problems or solutions differ?

Once we have comparative examples, some generalization may prove possible. For example, in each area how has the role of judges or prosecutors changed over time? (Fifty years ago, for example, American courts would have thought electoral district apportionment was a political question beyond their judicial competence.) Can our legal systems cope with the political problems that underlie the law in each of these three areas? How might they do better?

Consider the following general questions:

1. Why has judicial intervention into the political arena proven acceptable to the public?

(a) Does that acceptability reflect the comparatively greater esteem in which the public holds the courts? On the one hand, the public has lost confidence in the other branches of government. Public opinion polls show a dramatic decline over the past three decades in the degree of public trust in the Executive and Legislative Branches (with about 30 percent of the public having great, or moderate, confidence, compared to more than 75 percent in the late 1960s). Yet confidence in the courts (particularly the Supreme Court) has remained comparatively high (now running at something over 50 percent).

Why? Does the decline in confidence reflect diminished need for government (the end of the Cold War)? The "end of ideology" (increased reliance upon market solutions)? Greater media attention to political figures (focus upon individual instances of misconduct, focus upon the politician's "human" qualities, less reliance upon general reputation, the end of "mythmaking" about leaders)? Less competent or less honest politicians (seems unlikely)? "Impossible" working conditions for political figures and political parties (the media permitting the public to understand, and therefore to judge, innumerable details rather than overall end results)? More fractious societies (immigration)? A thinner culture (Hollywood)?

Does the higher standing of courts reflect the fact that judges are anonymous (leaving the public to judge via reputation rather than personal foibles)? That judges are seen to do their job properly? That judges (because of low pay/conflicts-of-interest rules/tenure) are seen as not being "out for themselves?" That the media, so far, has tended to ignore the judiciary?

(b) Has the public become more interested in protecting basic human rights and more aware of the link between independent judicial decisionmaking and that protection?

(c) Has the public been favorably impressed with judicial success ("desegregation")?

2. Will the courts prove capable of producing reasoned, principled decisions in these politically sensitive areas?

3. What will be the likely long-term effects upon the political (and judicial) processes? Will the judicial system itself become more politicized? Will the political system become more professionalized (or bureaucratized)?

These observations are meant to suggest, but not to restrict, the direction that our discussion might take.

3.2. Supervision of the Political Process

Discussion

Robert BADINTER: We have discussed the rise of judicial activism, and have considered the extent to which issues of morality and values in modern society are reflected in, and steered by, the judiciary, creating what we called the "secular papacy." We will now address the incursion of judges into the political sphere, a realm into which judges have ventured only timidly, and out of which the other political powers want to keep them. The political sphere, particularly the electoral process, is a closely guarded one. It is, after all, the means to gain power. The primary goal of a political figure is to be elected, or re-elected. That is how politics work. We will also discuss an important phenomenon relating to the influence of money, as well as issues relating to judges and politics, and ethical questions. This discussion is also about rediscovering virtue. It is one thing to say, "I am the Church. I know—and I tell you—what is good and right." The other approach is accusatory: "You are the sinner," and, because I am the inquisitor, I send you where you deserve to go, be that jail or to the stake. In these perspectives, I see, if not activism, at least judicial imperialism.

Stephen BREYER: My presentation discusses three areas in which judicial decisions significantly affect the political process: (1) fair voting rules; (2) campaign finance; and (3) ethics laws.

In today's world, democracy legitimates government. But the democratic government must be of a special kind, which we might call a "basic rights democracy." That means that there must be guarantees for the preconditions, or structure, of democracy, such as free speech, a degree of equality, and other basic rights that create democracy's preconditions. A document, such as a constitution, that guarantees those preconditions, will likely also guarantee certain other important human rights that are not necessarily democratic preconditions.

In the United States, judges enforce the rights that this kind of constitution contains. That judges should do so is not inevitable. Judicial enforcement is, in a sense, a means to an end, namely, that the members of the society understand, and accept, that basic constitutional rights are unusually important and that they must be guaranteed in practice. Where that view is generally accepted, we say that those basic rights are embedded in the structure of the society. Broad acceptance of this view itself helps to guarantee those rights.

That ordinary members of society themselves understand that "democracy qualified by the protection of basic rights" constitutes society's basic structure is the key to assuring that those rights will be enforced in practice. Whether the best way to embed this basic democratic ideal is through *judicial* enforcement of constitutional rights is unclear. But in the United States, judges do enforce constitutional rights, and that fact may have helped our society accept the importance of the "basic rights democracy" that our Constitution guarantees.

To understand the importance of embedding those rights in the public's consciousness, consider the following. The United States Constitution in 1832 was very much the same document as the United States Constitution today. Yet, in 1832, the Supreme Court held that the Constitution prohibited Georgia from taking land from the Cherokee Indians. President Jackson then said, approximately, "[Chief Justice] John Marshall has made his decision, now let him enforce it." And President Jackson, in effect, evicted the Cherokee Indians from Georgia contrary to the Court's determination. Today the Cherokees live in Oklahoma. That would not have happened today. Consider too that one of our Court's finest decisions, *Brown* v. *Board of Education*, ending racial segregation, would not have been necessary had it not been for our Court's earlier decision in *Plessy* v. *Ferguson*, holding that the Constitution permitted racial segregation. My point is that judges can make major mistakes about human rights; and, in any event, what matters most is that society in general, not just the legal community, accept the importance of protecting those rights. John Marshall said that the "People made the Constitution, and the People can unmake it."

I am far from certain that granting judges the power to enforce basic constitutional rights is a necessary condition, and it surely is not a sufficient condition, for protecting those rights. But it is one important way to do so; and we have chosen that way in the United States. Perhaps our discussion of the impact of judges upon the political process—like other discussions we are having—will help us evaluate the role of judicial enforcement of basic rights, seen as a means toward the accomplishment of that end.

Now let me turn to the three areas in which judges increasingly have had an impact upon the political process. I begin with judicial enforcement of fair voting rules. In the 1940s, the Court was faced with election district boundaries that had been unevenly drawn. Some rural districts contained only a few voters; other urban districts contained many voters. Yet each selected one state representative. The Court refused to intervene, despite a constitutional provision that guaranteed everyone "equal protection of the laws." Justice Frankfurter said in an important voting rights opinion, *Colegrove* v. *Green*, 329 U.S. 825 (1946), that judges simply should not become involved in drawing election district boundaries—no matter how unfairly legislatures had drawn them—for that was a political job for politicians, not a judicial job for judges. In saying this, he was continuing to state the Court's traditional reluctance to become involved in political matters—reflected in the fact that the Court (including even Justice Holmes) refused to stop Southern states from disenfranchising black citizens, despite a constitutional amendment specifically guaranteeing voters of every race the right to vote. In both instances, the Court feared that, once judges intervened, they would find it impossible to decide how to draw fair voting district boundaries, and, what is worse (and was particularly true of race), political officials might ignore their decisions. Hence, they stayed out of the "political thicket."

In the 1960s, this judicial attitude changed. Courts entered the thicket. The Supreme Court enforced the Fifteenth Amendment, making clear that Southern states must permit their black citizens to vote, while Congress passed the Voting Rights Act, which enforced that basic principle. The Court, in the reapportionment cases, held that all voting districts must be of equal size, *i.e.*, they must contain the same number of people.

Until recently, the Court, while insisting that each voting district be of equal size, permitted legislatures to "gerrymander" districts by distorting their shape, *i.e.,* legislatures draw the boundaries of single-member districts in ways that favor one political party over another, such as by splitting the other party's voters among several districts where they have too few votes to elect a representative. Yet, very recently, the Court held that a legislature cannot "gerrymander," *i.e.,* draw boundaries, in order to favor the election of racial minorities. Accordingly, the legislatures cannot try to place enough black voters in a single district to try to assure the election of a black representative. I have dissented in these latter cases because I do not see how a legislature, which is permitted to discriminate in favor of, for example, Republican voters, can be forbidden to discriminate in favor of black voters. In any event, it is very difficult for courts to determine whether a legislature, which has drawn an oddly shaped district, drew the district's boundaries in order to favor (*a*) a racial minority or (*b*) one of the two major parties. The upshot is that the courts are in the midst of the "political thicket."

For present purposes, one surprising feature of this line of cases is the fact that the public has accepted them with some, but not overwhelmingly, negative comment. Contrary to the predictions made by Justice Frankfurter and others, the courts have entered this highly sensitive area, and both politicians and the general public have accepted and followed the judges' decisions. For present purposes, this is the phenomenon we should investigate.

Why has the public accepted these decisions? I believe that the answer is related to the fact that the general public has confidence in the courts even though the general public lacks confidence in the other branches of government, *i.e.,* the legislature and the executive. The opinion polls bear this out. They show a dramatic drop in the public's confidence in Congress over a 30-year period. (Thirty years ago, perhaps 60 or 70 percent would have ranked Congress "one" or "two" on a five-point "trust" scale; today, only about 20 percent or so of the public would rank Congress in the top two categories.) The public's confidence in the Supreme Court also has declined somewhat, but nowhere near as much (with still more than half the public rating the Supreme Court in the same top two categories). I gather that, in Germany, the public's confidence in courts is even higher. Why?

Dieter GRIMM: For the other branches of government, the same is true: the public's confidence in them is lower, as in the United States.

Stephen BREYER: Yes, it seems to be a universal phenomenon. The only other institution in which the public has so much confidence is the armed forces.

Ronald DWORKIN: After the first Gulf War, that is true.

Stephen BREYER: Various "pop sociology" theories try to explain why confidence in some branches of government have declined. Let me list a few better-known examples of such explanatory factors:

1. Since the Cold War is over, the public may now believe that it no longer needs much government; perhaps business and a free marketplace will satisfy most human needs.

2. Perhaps the media can, and do, cover more intensively than in the past the private and public lives of political figures. The result is that presidents or prime ministers must take care in public to appear to be, or to share the tastes of, "ordinary people," for instance, Mr. Chirac being interviewed in front of a fireplace, or Mr. Clinton seen in the company of baseball players or movie stars. It is an admirable quality in human beings that they wish to judge other human beings on the basis of their personal, human qualities. But will the political system work well when leaders are judged as "people," rather than on the basis of how well they do their job? Regardless, judging political leaders on the apparently "first-hand" basis of knowledge from television, rather than on the second-hand basis of their earned reputations, means that we are somewhat less likely to focus upon how well they do their jobs and somewhat more likely to become aware of their human failings. It may have become harder to maintain myths about political leaders, particularly myths that they are unusually virtuous or without fault.

3. Perhaps political leaders are less competent or less virtuous today than in the past—though I find this explanation particularly difficult to believe. The political cartoons of the late nineteenth century, for example, show Congress surrounded by the Sugar Trust, the Oil Trust, or the Tobacco Trust. Political corruption and bribery were then common. I believe that this kind of corruption is less common, not more common, today—despite difficulties with campaign contributions, which create considerable public distrust.

4. It is more plausible to suspect that television's ability to communicate each political decision—however minor—instantly to an

interested public (say, via C-SPAN) has increased the difficulty of the working conditions for political leaders. That instant communication permits the public to second-guess each aspect of each governmental decision almost instantly. That fact means that political leaders may try to make each aspect popular. Yet it is difficult to make a wise major decision if each minor component aspect of that decision is subject to immediate "second-guessing" by the general public. The public might properly criticize a general for losing the (first) Gulf War; the public would be wrong to criticize each underlying tank corps movement. Since American politicians face the technological fact that each statement they make can be televised and used against them later in political campaigns, it is difficult for a Senator to say, for example, "I am against mandatory prison terms for drug users," even if mandatory terms hurt, rather than help, the overall fight against crime. Perhaps for these, and related, reasons, it is simply harder today for political leaders to do their job well.

5. Perhaps American society is more fractured than it used to be. Our system of government is highly complex. It is difficult to enact laws, and that fact, in part, reflects our society's diverse nature, where different groups do not trust each other. Congress does not simply enact a budget at the request of the President, as happens, for example, in a parliamentary system.

I have listed a few of the "culture-based" explanations for the decline in the public's confidence in the political system. To the extent that they are valid, why would they not also apply to judges? Why has confidence in the judicial system remained comparatively high? I can think of several possibilities:

1. Compared to the members of other branches of government, judges are anonymous. We wear black robes to stress that anonymity, to suggest that we speak not for ourselves, but for the law. Although personality matters, the less it matters and the less the public thinks it matters, the better. In the Supreme Court, where much conspires to identify the judges as individuals in the public mind, it is particularly important to try to diminish what one might call the "cult of personality." From an institutional perspective, I believe that more anonymity is better—for anonymity will help lead the public to focus upon the words that we write on paper, rather than the warmth of a smile or the cleverness of a question at oral argument.

2. The public still believes that judges, despite their failings, do their basic jobs properly. If you believe that the (first) Gulf War—which America's military won—built public confidence in the military, then you must also believe that doing the basic job well—deciding cases fairly and according to law—will similarly help build public confidence in the judiciary.

3. The public may believe that judges are not "out for themselves." Their pay, compared to other members of the legal profession, is low; they rarely advance within the federal judicial hierarchy; and they are subject to strict ethical rules. Indeed, in my presentation, I listed some of those rules, which are written so strictly for fear that even the smallest deviation can hurt the institution because the public will (wrongly) think it is the "tip of an iceberg." The fact that federal judges rarely advance means that, even though presidents or senators are the basic appointing authorities, once a judge is appointed, there is little incentive to distort a decision for personal advantage. The best way, in fact, to secure a higher judicial position is to try to earn a reputation as a good judge, which means trying to do the job properly.

4. Perhaps most importantly, the press does not write very much about judges as individuals and rarely makes an effort to investigate personal scandal unrelated to the judicial job. Will the media continue, in this sense to "let the judges alone"? If not, the result could spell disaster for the institution, since judges find it particularly difficult to respond to charges in the media, placing themselves and the media in an adversary relation.

Why have I made these lists of potential cultural reasons for the decline of confidence in non-judicial institutions? Because I suspect that discussing these factors, which concern the society's current perception of the judge's role, may help us understand how, currently, judges are relevant to the basic constitutional task of helping society, *i.e.*, the public, to embed the protection of basic human, democratic rights.

Let me now turn to a second issue, that of campaign finance. I find judicial action in this area particularly interesting because, in trying to protect one basic freedom, particularly free speech, the courts may have damaged another basic value, that of a fair, democratic election process. In the United States, there are those who trace the rise of the super-rich candidate, Mr. Forbes or Mr. Ross

Perot, to a Supreme Court opinion, *Buckley* v. *Valeo,* that, in part, identifies a constitutional prohibition forbidding Congress to limit the amount of his own money that an individual candidate can spend on his own campaign. The Court held that Congress could limit the amounts that others could contribute to a campaign, but a super-rich candidate, with his own money to spend, does not need outside contributions.

The "campaign finance" problem is nearly universal. The French system, the Chilean system, and perhaps other systems may regulate expenditures or contributions more comprehensively than in America. Even if those systems nonetheless permit large contributions, for example, to political parties, they still diminish the importance of money by lowering campaign costs, for example, by imposing advertising limits or requiring television to provide free, or low-cost, television time, divided among candidates.

But I also see a cloud on the European horizon. The European Court of Human Rights, in the *Bowman* decision, seems to say, as our Court said in *Buckley,* that a government cannot impose financial limitations that would prevent a private individual from distributing leaflets saying, "Vote for Smith because Smith is pro-life [or pro-choice]."

Ronald DWORKIN: Wasn't that a matter of proportionality?

Stephen BREYER: I agree that the *Bowman* court uses the word "proportionality," but it uses that word simply to describe the overall legal test that it will apply to the U.K. statute. The Court then applied that legal test to a U.K. statute that simply had set a low financial limit on the amount that any one person could spend advocating the election on any particular candidate in the few weeks prior to an election. The Court then held that these limits were unlawful—violating basic principles of free expression—when applied to prevent expenditures on leaflets. The Court also noted that the U.K. did not prevent newspapers from advocating the election of particular candidates, nor did it limit contributions to political parties, which could advocate the election of candidates pledged to their programs. To hold the general campaign finance statute unlawful (as applied to leaflets) for this kind of reason resembles what our Court did in *Buckley.* That involves a kind of "free expression"–based, judicial micro-management of campaign finance regulation.

If I am right, *Bowman* raises a more general question, related to international courts. Judges, deciding an individual case, often find it difficult to foresee the consequences of the legal rule applied. Unforeseen consequences produce a demand to change the legal rule. The matter is particularly important in Europe because it is more difficult to change the results of European Court decisions than to change many American Supreme Court decisions. The Strasbourg Court, for example, interprets a Human Rights Treaty. Isn't it almost impossible to change a Court interpretation by amending the Treaty? I doubt that the Court, in *Buckley*, foresaw all the general consequences of its decision.

Ronald DWORKIN: We know that the main author of the opinion . . .

Stephen BREYER: Some believe that *Buckley* may have had several authors. If the job of writing an opinion was divided among several judges, it would be particularly difficult to modify the tentative results determined by the Court at an initial conference almost immediately after oral argument. Here, it would be interesting to know how the French Constitutional Court deals with complex cases, for it often has only 60 or 90 days after a matter is submitted to make a final determination.

Robert BADINTER: But it happens from the start. When an issue is first discussed in the Parliament, we start working. We follow the proceedings closely so that when the issue comes to us, we are already intellectually quite ready.

Stephen BREYER: The problem of changing a decision may be ameliorated by the fact that decisions of the civil courts in Europe are more open to revision, in light of later experience, than are decisions in a common law country. In speaking to one of the judges of a European court, I came away with the thought that a particular judicial decision may be open to judicial revision after four or five years.

Ronald DWORKIN: I am not quite sure that that is right.

Stephen BREYER: Still the question of judicial revision is interesting. Our Court says that a decision interpreting the Constitution is more open to revision than a decision interpreting a statute. Still, the Court cannot revise significant constitutional decisions often, for the public comes to rely upon those decisions. That is why our Court recently refused to modify its well-known *Miranda* case. Some of the Justices who would have disagreed with *Miranda* as an initial matter wrote that they understood the dangers of changing an important constitutional precedent that had become well established in the law. My second subject, campaign finance, leads into these several areas. Shall I introduce a third subject?

Robert BADINTER: Yes, of course. But first, a clarification. You believe it particularly important to maintain the consistency of the Court's case law, insofar as that is possible. I share that sentiment. Without consistency one faces legal insecurity, judicial capriciousness, and law that changes too quickly. We would find ourselves without legal security. But then, the consequence of today's problem, in your view, is that only Congress can change the situation that *Buckley* has created. In other words, to change it requires a new law or statute.

Stephen BREYER: No. It is a decision that interprets the Constitution, not a decision that interprets a statute. And the only way to change an interpretation of the Constitution (unless the Court itself changes it) is to amend the Constitution—a near impossibility.

Robert BADINTER: Yes, that would be impossible. But suppose that Congress enacted a new campaign financing statute. Would it then be possible to limit a candidate's personal expenditures by a particular amount?

Stephen BREYER: In my own separate opinion in our recent case, *Nixon v. Shrink Missouri*, which interpreted *Buckley v. Valeo*, I listed various forms of regulation that seemed open to Congress to adopt, in light of the Supreme Court's cases. These included making television available at low cost, regulating what are called "soft money" contributions, and various others. I added that, if *Buckley* is thought to forbid Congress from adopting these approaches, then our Court should reconsider *Buckley*.

Regardless, I still think an interesting general question—applicable to European courts and American courts alike—arises from the fact that our Court, in trying to protect one basic right, may have hindered the development of legislation that itself would help to protect basic rights.

Robert BADINTER: A question on that particular point, the point of limiting a candidate's expenditures. Is public opinion, as measured by polling, in favor of such a limitation, say $100,000 per candidate? Or is public opinion, after all, of the view that each person has the right to spend his money as he wishes? The richer the better?

Stephen BREYER: Public opinion, as measured by polling, favors limitation. But I am not certain of the strength with which the public
holds that opinion. The media strongly favor limitations. But they
do not often write about limitations on the price of television, *i.e.,*
granting free television time to candidates.

Ronald DWORKIN: They believe, no doubt, that there should be limits
on expenses for television!

Stephen BREYER: They have said that?

Ronald DWORKIN: I am not sure. It would look so self-serving. I think
that it is right that print and television should be treated differently,
but it is very difficult for the *New York Times* to express that opinion
editorially because they might seem to be making exceptions for
themselves.

Stephen BREYER: Then don't you just say that? Why not say, "We think
there should be a limitation on television, not the press, but we recognize that . . ."

Ronald DWORKIN: Maybe they will. There is a great deal of discussion
about what to say.

Stephen BREYER: Let me now turn to the third issue—that of "ethics"
laws. The major difficulty that I see here is that the American laws,
taken together, are not coherent. Sometimes they seem too lenient.
In other instances they seem too strict, to the point where a person
trying to do a public job conscientiously risks inadvertently violating an "ethics law." This latter possibility places great power in the
hands of the prosecutor—say, a Special Prosecutor in the United
States or a *juge d'instruction* in France—who has discretion to decide
whether to prosecute a minor violation, thereby threatening the
public official with the destruction of his career or prison.

Robert BADINTER: They are not special.

Stephen BREYER: In France they are not special. You train the *juges d'instruction* in schools. They work within a system, the institutional
mores of which lead them to take particular care before they begin
a prosecution. Our system of Special Prosecutors for high government officials is separate from the rest of our prosecuting systems
and consequently somewhat different.

We recently heard a case related to the prosecution of a federal
cabinet member, a Secretary of Agriculture. He was prosecuted
criminally for having received from an agricultural organization

payment for his expenses to attend a European meeting of that organization and for having received from a private company transportation expenses and tickets to see a tennis match. The jury acquitted him.

When the related case was being argued orally before us, I asked the Special Prosecutor the following: "Suppose a group of farmers invites the Secretary of Agriculture to speak at a lunch about agricultural policy. Is it a federal crime for them to pay for his lunch?" The Special Prosecutor in effect answered, "Yes." We decided the case against the Prosecutor. But the legal problem arose from the fact that the statutes were not written in terms of amounts. They made conduct criminal whether that conduct involves a lunch or a million dollars. That fact is what gave the Prosecutor power, for the Prosecutor had to decide whether the amounts involved were serious enough to warrant prosecution. And everything turned on the Prosecutor's own sense of responsibility and judgment. Once he claimed that a public official had behaved unethically in accepting a lunch, much of the public likely believed that the official behaved "unethically." Even if the official were acquitted, his public career may have been ruined. I wonder about similar situations in France, which, unlike the United States, has long had experience with what we would call Special Prosecutors.

Indeed, what will happen in France or the United States, if those prosecutors and the media turn their attention and behave similarly with respect to judges? As my presentation makes clear, judges must publicly disclose all income—every penny—received by the judge and his or her family. The accounting fees for doing so are significant, for the forms are extensive, perhaps 30 or 40 pages. Mistakes are inevitable. Yet press articles that focus upon the occasional, inevitable error could easily lead the public to believe that those errors reflect serious ethical problems in the judiciary as a whole. Since there are ethical lapses that should be exposed, one cannot conclude that it would be better not to have a disclosure system. But how to design an ideal system that both catches significant wrongdoing but does not lend itself to destroying public confidence wrongly is, in my view, a major problem. And, like the other problems, it is worth considering here, because that system must be part of a judicial system that itself helps to guarantee basic rights.

Robert BADINTER: With respect to the emergence and development of the judge's role, keep in mind the fact that elections amount to what those involved in politics consider an extraordinarily sensitive matter, a kind of "no trespassing" zone. Because all power flows from elections, we find the relevant movement a general movement. From the perspective of comparative law, we find that all judges have become more and more involved in considering electoral laws. The same is true in Germany and in Spain. We supervise the legality of electoral rules; not surprisingly, we use basic principles in doing so; and the first of those principles is equality. Then we are faced with the problem of equality in shaping electoral districts. We have had a difficult time, for many of the reasons Justice Breyer mentioned.

The Ministry of the Interior initially draws the boundaries of the electoral districts. They are then voted upon by the Parliament. That means that the majority votes for the district boundaries, looking at the matter with a certain prejudice: Everyone is for himself; the law is for all. A President of the Council of the Third Republic, at the beginning of the twentieth century, when Masonry was at its peak, made a marvelous statement to that effect. He said from the Speaker's podium: "La loi pour tous; les faveurs pour nos amis" ("The law, for everyone; favors, for our friends").

The legal principles involved are not original, and I need not dwell upon them at any length. Obviously, the districts must comply with the principles of equality and "one man, one vote." Boundaries must be drawn so that, arithmetically speaking, the districts comply with these principles. There is leeway to take account of some differences that reflect historic or socio-cultural factors. Doing so does not significantly undercut the equality principle so much as it simply reflects very old cultural and historic affinities. I can say that the Conseil Constitutionnel in France has been, what I would call, prudent. It has tried to ensure that there is no visible effort to skew the district for some hidden motive, without going beyond mathematical verification of the boundary drawing. In one area, perhaps there is a pocket of public housing, which means "left" votes; in another, there might be predominantly residential suburbs, which means "right" votes. We check, but we cannot explore the details of each individual house. That is because, in my view, the latter would prove impossible for a constitutional judge. We can stop fraud that reaches a certain level, but we cannot prevent a limited measure of partiality in the drawing of new district boundaries to reflect changes. That is how it is. Perfection is not attainable.

But why are judges involved? I do not believe that there is any problem in understanding the need for a judge's intervention in this kind of matter. If we left the matter to the political majority, we would end up with a purely political drawing of boundaries. That, by definition, would be partial. By permitting it, we would deny a democratic demand of which we all are aware. It is simple. I do not think that we need consider the matter of boundary-drawing further.

A second matter relates to the judicial supervision of the elections themselves. Here too, from the perspective of comparative law, we find that judges throughout the European continent have been exercising ever-stricter supervision of electoral regularity. This a very noticeable feature of the role of the contemporary judge. Consider the fact that, whenever there are elections in Eastern Europe or in the former Soviet Union, the OSCE (Organization for Security and Cooperation in Europe) considers it essential, in order to guarantee the regularity of the electoral process, to send observers; and among those observers are judges. Many judges are sent as part of election supervision missions. The fact that judges are sent abroad to help supervise electoral regularity, for example, to Bosnia at the time of its first elections, tends to prove that there is an international consensus among democracies that judges supervise elections. I do not perceive any difficulty in that fact. It is in the nature of things. It is, moreover, a task that the general public is satisfied that judges assume.

I am not going to go into the details of the French system. That system is complicated by the fact that there are different levels of elections: local, municipal, regional, cantonal. The Conseil d'Etat supervises administrative jurisdictions. The Conseil Constitutionnel supervises national elections, as well as those for Parliament and for the President of the Republic. The supervisory rules are defined in terms of these two levels. And the Conseil Constitutionnel plays the role of a judge with power to set aside or to validate these elections.

Next, the question of finance seems extraordinarily important because it lies at the heart of a problem that is fundamental to democracy, which is "equality." The problem is not, as is commonly believed, that money rots whatever it touches. Rather, it is the following: If candidates are simply means through which opposing financial forces compete, then the winning candidate in our media-driven democracy and our democracy of opinion will be the candidate who enjoys the largest war chest. And, obviously, as methods of spreading campaign propaganda proliferate and the costs of electoral campaigns increase (and since not everyone is Ross Perot, far from it), the result, particularly in France, is greater corruption.

Many politicians have given in to corruption, not for their own pocketbooks, but to obtain the necessary campaign funds. They do not earn much in their official capacities; and, in fact, the great majority of them are honest. A parliamentary deputy is paid exactly the same salary as a state councillor. There is no distinction with respect to income. But when the deputy has to confront the costs of campaigning, he finds that this salary amounts to very little.

Before 1990, each political party obtained the funds needed to defray campaign costs through gifts provided by wealthy contributors, particularly companies; or, what is yet worse, by selling favors—building permits, for example. That was also true in other countries, in Italy, particularly, where the practice was widespread. As we perfectly well understand, every place is susceptible to corruption. That money would arrive, and it would be spent on the election campaign. The practice seriously changed democracy itself in a sense, for it was the financing, *i.e.*, the corruption, of the political parties that assured the functioning of democracy. And it all took place within a kind of consensus, a kind of general silence.

Then, in 1990, the whole system fell apart. The police and the investigating magistrates seized the accounts of the Socialist Party, a party that had directed its own financing practices more honestly than had other parties. In fact, the Socialist Party had kept records of where the money came from and where it went in order to make certain that party members were not enriching themselves personally. It was a great scandal.

Subsequently, necessity made law. The country enacted an initial law on campaign finance, then a second, and then a third. Though I am a pessimist by nature, I am an optimist on this point. We are now in the process of cleansing what remains of those former general campaign practices. There will always remain some small amount of corruption, but I am an optimist on this issue.

The campaign finance measures that we have taken are obviously very strict—a matter of interest to Ronald Dworkin. I shall give you a few examples. A series of laws enacted between 1988 and 1996 contained many of those measures. The Conseil Constitutionnel reviewed most of them. There are two distinct aspects. First, there is the financing of the political parties. If you suppress private financing, you must have public financing. That is the solution that we have chosen. I shall not go into all the details. But generally, a party is entitled to a government subsidy, the amount of which depends upon the results of previous elections and the number of votes obtained. Adding on contributions made by members of the party, particularly the Members of Parliament, which the party can do if it wishes, creates a sufficient amount of financing. Hence, there is no longer any excuse. "Sufficient," of course, does not mean considerable; it means sufficient. That is generally accepted.

Second, and much more interesting than the financing of political parties, is the problem of campaign contributions. There, limitations are very strict. We have a limit that, for the election of deputies, amounts to 250,000 francs per candidate, indexed for inflation. It is augmented by one franc per electoral district inhabitant. It amounts to about 300,000 francs in most elections. Although it is adjusted for inflation, there has been almost no inflation.

Let me make a personal parenthetical comment about senatorial elections. There are no limits. But rest assured that, since the elections are indirect (senators are elected by mayors, etc.), campaign spending is almost nil. The senatorial campaign consists primarily of personal visits to the "key electors." It is out of the question to do more than simply see them and speak to them. I shall make a private confession. I always have my campaign finance account carefully checked. I have spent less than 50,000 francs. Everybody can afford that.

With respect to the financing of presidential campaigns, there are fixed amounts of expenditure. Let us be clear. The path we have chosen to avoid corruption requires, first, limiting expenses, and then, second, working out how to provide the financing for that amount. In the last election, the expenditure limit for the first round was 90 million francs. For the second round involving the two leading candidates, the expenditure ceiling was 120 million francs. Not all candidates spend those amounts. Small parties do not. They may spend about 25 million francs. The candidates have a contractual right to governmental reimbursement. If a candidate obtains 5 percent or more of the vote, he is entitled to a 25 percent reimbursement. The state will pay 25 percent of the expenses. The rest is paid by the parties or by individual contributions, which cannot exceed 50,000 francs per person, which is not very much. There is an absolute prohibition against any contributions by purely legal entities. No money is to come from corporations.

It is also forbidden to pay more than 1,000 francs in cash. That is very important. To guarantee its enforcement, an incentive is provided. You can deduct up to 40 percent of your contribution of up to 50,000 francs from your income tax. That helps encourage people to be generous. At the same time, a maximum deduction has been set.

Each candidate's account is strictly supervised. At the outset the account is in the hands of a representative. Subsequently, it is reviewed by a special commission made up of administrative judges and members of the Court of Accounts. Thus the accounts are held by a representative, reviewed by an account commission, and submitted, if necessary, to the Conseil Constitutionnel. Strict sanctions are available, including annulling the election and disqualification. That means that, if you have cheated or spent more than you should, there may be a new election in which you cannot take part. You will have lost your money and the election too.

Ronald DWORKIN: Is there a statute of limitations on this? How long do you have to discover this?

Robert BADINTER: Immediately after. It is always the same. The losing party brings the matter up for discussion.

Ronald DWORKIN: Yes, but how long after? Ten days?

Robert BADINTER: Yes, but you file it, then you produce your evidence.

Ronald DWORKIN: This is an assumption!

Robert BADINTER: No, no, no. These are very strong measures, and they have been truly effective. Because we have been very firm, they have created a lot of problems for violators. We had a very difficult time with the Minister of Culture, Mr. Jack Lang, whose election was annulled. He did not care how much money he spent. He went far above the limits, so we had to declare his election void.

Ronald DWORKIN: And he was ineligible . . . ?

Robert BADINTER: For a year. He went to the European Parliament, and then he came back to the Assembly. But the matter is not taken lightly, and the public resented it. At the end of the day, everyone is more or less satisfied, except for those who are declared ineligible. Each deputy declared ineligible announces that the decision was obviously political, dictated by hatred and partiality. That is a normal rule of the game.

I must say that we have made considerable progress in 10 years. The key to the matter is a prohibition on radio and television advertising. That was the decisive matter. I do not think that decision could be reversed in France. I doubt that we shall ever have political advertising. It runs contrary to public sentiment. You do not sell a candidate as you might sell soap. The public thinks doing so is disgraceful. The horrible American example shocks us. We consider advertising on behalf of a candidate on television, the political spot, to be a complete disgrace. Obviously, there is very strict supervision. The audiovisual campaign, even before the election, is strictly regulated. Each candidate has his own representative. I myself was Mitterand's representative in the 1981 campaign. The job requires meticulous care.

Stephen BREYER: You do not forbid all publicity. Rather, each candidate can appear on television and television time is carefully divided and monitored to ensure equality?

Robert BADINTER: Yes, and it is done by a commission with numerous magistrates. The rules of the game are very strict.

Ronald DWORKIN: Are there limits on what a politician may do with the time made available?

Robert BADINTER: No, he may do as he pleases, except defamation or insulting other candidates.

Ronald DWORKIN: So he can have, in effect, the same spot ads that we have in America, except he cannot pay for it. It cannot be commercial advertising.

Robert BADINTER: He should pay for it from his own budget.

Ronald DWORKIN: He is taking it on his own budget but there is no restriction. Once the time is allotted, he can have the nastiest, negative . . . ?

Robert BADINTER: Within the limits of defamation law. There is still the same limitation to freedom of expression. You can say "I am a genius." You cannot say, "He is a crook."

Ronald DWORKIN: No, no, you cannot accuse your opponent of a crime. But can you show a picture of him picking his nose?

Robert BADINTER: No, no, that would not be appropriate.

Ronald DWORKIN: What stops that?

Robert BADINTER: That would be the judge.

Ronald DWORKIN: Now, under what regulation?

Robert BADINTER: The general statute on defamation and ridicule.

Ronald DWORKIN: But this is not defamation. There is no lie; there is no falsehood. You are simply using your time to show an ugly picture of your opponent. Then you run a caption under the picture that says, "He voted to raise taxes," when that is not a lie, but may be deeply misleading and, in any case, lowers the character of the political debate. Is there anything in a judge's power that can stop this kind of ad?

Robert BADINTER: I do not see any legal basis for a judge doing that. I can see the Control Commission letting it be known that these are personal attacks. That would not stop them legally. It would simply amount to an observation. But it would create a political boomerang.

Dieter GRIMM: The cultural framework plays an important role. Basically, we have the same system: Political parties get free time on TV during the campaign, and candidates and political parties always cast themselves in a very favorable light, but they do not say anything about their opponents, although the law does not prohibit it.

Ronald DWORKIN: Is it only a cultural revulsion that protects you? Would there be any legal protection if that cultural antipathy broke down?

Robert BADINTER: Yes. Let us discuss the Dukakis case. It was the most horrible thing that I ever saw on TV against a candidate. Remember, Dukakis was an opponent against the death penalty and they produced a film in which you saw his face become the one of the rapist and the murderer.

Ronald DWORKIN: Yes, those were terrible ads. Grotesque, and they probably worked. Should the law forbid them?

Robert BADINTER: Yes, on the grounds that they alter the truth, for the depiction was designed to make the viewer think that he made the decision that led to a death.

Ronald DWORKIN: Dukakis did play some role, as I recall, in securing the release from jail of a murderer who then raped and killed again.

Robert BADINTER: But he was not a rapist and a murderer.

Ronald DWORKIN: But the terrible ad did not say that he was a rapist, and I doubt anyone thought that it was making that claim. The ad showed Dukakis morphing into the murderer, Willie Horton, when the moon fell on his face. The Republicans said that this was only a vivid way of presenting their argument that his executive decisions led to a rape and murder. I want to press the question whether any country's law would actually prevent such poisonous material.

Robert BADINTER: That is just what I said. The depiction was designed to create the impression that it was he who was the murderer.

Ronald DWORKIN: Would any court actually say that the ad was intended to convey that impression?

Robert BADINTER: There would be a legal risk for the fellow who would even try to produce that, apart from the fact that he would be culturally resented very much.

Ronald DWORKIN: Suppose that the ad only showed the menacing face of the murderer looming on the screen. And then a voice-over declares, "Dukakis made this crime possible!" Would you think it right that such an ad could be made illegal?

Gil Carlos RODRIGUEZ IGLESIAS: How is the control accomplished? Is it strictly judicial? In my country, in Spain, there is an ad hoc committee that exercises control over the propaganda of the political parties during the periods leading up to the elections. But it is not a judicial control. It is a sort of administrative control that is subject to judicial review. But, of course, the judicial review comes later. Most important is the decision of the ad hoc committee, which may, for instance, prohibit a particular spot because it is considered to be untruthful or to imply unfair defamation, even if it is not defamation for the purpose of criminal law.

Ronald DWORKIN: Would the standard be a general standard of fairness? Could the Commission just say, "This attack is unfair"?

Robert BADINTER: It would be closely connected with the method of presentation. The depiction of the substitution of the face would, in my opinion, mean withdrawal. If you start with "This is the fellow who killed . . . ," you then see the fellow, and afterwards you say that Mr. Dukakis freed this man, then I think the ad would pass muster. But the technical system that made the ad horrid and unbearable—that art of selling—would not be permissible.

Ronald DWORKIN: This is a very important issue because these attacks are disfiguring politics, and we should face the issue of what the legitimate limits of any effective regulation should be.

Robert BADINTER: That surely would be the basis for the decision. There would have been an attack on the rights of the individual, and there would have been unfair proceedings in the electoral campaign context.

Gil Carlos RODRIGUEZ IGLESIAS: I recall an instance in which, during an election campaign in Spain, the Socialist Party used a spot ad in which a Doberman was depicted as the symbol of the other party. The appropriate electoral commission reviewed the matter. It banned the ad, but only after many people had already watched it.

Dieter GRIMM: One should take into account that, compared with the United States or Germany, the interpretation of defamation and libel law in France is very broad. So, when it comes to a conflict between free speech values on the one hand and privacy or reputation values on the other, the tendency in France is to protect the latter. This may explain something. Isn't that true?

Robert BADINTER: Yes. But what I should like to emphasize is that, in the past 10 years, we have seen magistrates of various kinds get a grip on the election campaign through the supervision of campaign expenses. We strictly supervise campaign finances through the use of sanctions imposed by judges. If you are found ineligible, you are out of the game. Not only have you lost the election, but you are also out of the game. That is a very powerful device. There is also regulation of the amount of television time that you can use. You cannot use more than the television time allotted. All of these regulations turn into some form of judicial regulation. These laws increase the judge's grip. And the public is satisfied with that.

Stephen BREYER: I have one question. Is television time free for candidates or must someone pay?

Robert BADINTER: It is paid for by the government. It is free to candidates. It is absolutely free! It is paid for by the state.

Stephen BREYER: One criticism of regulation that would control advertising for candidates and other expenditures is that the candidates would then depend on the reporting of the television commentators or other journalists. And it is sometimes argued that those commentators and journalists favor one party rather than another. If both parties receive significant amounts of free television time, however, they would be able to respond to reporting that they believed was biased and that might help to answer the criticism.

Robert BADINTER: You have your free time on official television.

Stephen BREYER: The time must be equally divided and also add up to an amount that is reasonable in light of the parties' needs to communicate.

Robert BADINTER: You organize debates on private television, but that is under the authority of a state body that regulates television. And the regulator watches to make certain that the private television channel is not endorsing one candidate rather than another. Nor do you charge your allotted television time only against time on public television. That is where the official campaign takes place, which, by the way, is very boring. There are forums that permit the major candidates to confront each other. Five journalists, for example, will face each candidate and fire questions at him. Or, there may be face-to-face confrontations among representatives of the political parties. But the state regulatory body supervises all of this to make certain there is no inequality.

Stephen BREYER: But what do you do about "issue advertising"? You prevent the candidates from advertising, you give each candidate free television time, and you create a commission that sees that the time is fairly divided. But what about private groups that want to advertise about issues, for example, labor unions that want to say, "Remember to preserve the minimum wage," gun owners who want to say, "Remember, your gun is at stake," and pro-life groups who want to show pictures of the fetus with the caption "Remember this child"? A group will buy space to advertise about an issue, the viewers know that the candidates have different positions on the issue, and the ad thereby tells them, indirectly, to vote for one candidate rather than another. Is that a problem in France?

Robert BADINTER: In France that could not happen, for you cannot buy . . .

Stephen BREYER: The people who buy the TV time are not candidates?

Robert BADINTER: No, but you cannot buy TV time. You ordinarily can buy TV advertisements, but that is prohibited in politics. It would be considered political propaganda, and you would not be permitted to do it. Neither a trade union nor anyone else has the right to engage in political advertising. Neither political parties nor any other organization may do so.

Stephen BREYER: To enforce that rule, you must have someone who will determine when an ad is, and when it is not, political propaganda. That would seem to be a job for a judge.

Robert BADINTER: We would not even do that. It is so obvious that it is political propaganda that the station would not take it because the station would be liable to the state regulatory body.

Gil Carlos RODRIGUEZ IGLESIAS: I think, in light of this point, that we live in such different worlds.

Robert BADINTER: The cultural patterns are radically different. What is the situation in Germany?

Dieter GRIMM: Within the public television system, we give free air time to the political parties, but not to the candidates. As far as the private television sector is concerned, I am not aware of any political advertising.

Robert BADINTER: But does German law forbid political advertising?

Dieter GRIMM: There is no law prohibiting advertisement by private parties in favor of political parties, but I have never seen it happen on the part of interest groups. Sometimes, some rich individuals buy one page of the *Frankfurter Allgemeine.*

Robert BADINTER: That is another matter. I am referring to radio and television.

Ronald DWORKIN: Yes, television is different from newspapers. In Britain, television is strictly regulated. There are commissions, not just for the BBC but for commercial channels as well, which would stop issue ads of this kind. There is also careful attention paid to fairness even in the regulation of ordinary news broadcasts. They count the number of seconds of exposure given to each major candidate. If a politician cuts the ribbon for a new building during a campaign and television covers it, that counts in fixing how much coverage other politicians must have.

Robert BADINTER: We leave a special provision for governmental duties because if the Minister of Foreign Affairs is being shown going to Luxembourg, you cannot say that we shut that out because he is in an electoral campaign.

Ronald DWORKIN: But if the head of the other party also made a trip to Luxembourg, he would have to be shown making that trip, even if it was a pointless one.

Gil Carlos RODRIGUEZ IGLESIAS: It is always a matter of great controversy. In every campaign, people systematically complain about the fact that, in particular, public television is discriminating against them.

Robert BADINTER: Mr. (Jean-Marie) Le Pen is always barking at the sky, saying that he is the object of the most horrid discrimination because he is not being heard enough.

Antonio CASSESE: Italy is interesting because, as you know, the tycoon Berlusconi owns two private TV channel stations. Until last year, when a law was passed—the so-called law on *par condicio,* which put everybody on the same footing—he could use both the public TV (three channels) and his own private TV under the pretext that anyone could pay and he could afford to pay much more since he was the owner. The new law put a stop to this trend because now they count the seconds or minutes during which you appear on TV.

But it is not controlled by a commission or a body consisting only of judges. Actually, as you said, it is a commission that also includes judges, but there are also experts from the TV industry, the media, and so on. I think that it is much better not to leave judges as the sole arbiters. The president of the commission is a senior judge—he is a member of the Court of Cassation—and there are a few judges, but there are also quite a few experts on media communication and so on. I think that it is a fairly sound way of tackling this issue.

Gil Carlos RODRIGUEZ IGLESIAS: I understand that these decisions can be brought before the judges, but, of course, by then, it is too late.

Dieter GRIMM: But we have injunctions. For instance, we had a case before a state election in which a public television station featured a roundtable discussion composed of journalists and party leaders. Four parties were represented in Parliament, but the TV station selected only three of them. The reason that they gave for not taking the fourth one, which was the Greens, was that they had no chance of entering into a coalition, which may have been true at that time. The Greens brought a constitutional complaint and we issued an injunction. We held it unconstitutional to distinguish between parties in Parliament according to their chances of participating in the government. The injunction prohibited the TV station from excluding the Greens. But then the Christian Democrats said that, under these circumstances, they would not appear in the roundtable discussion.

Stephen BREYER: The "campaign finance" problem has been compared to a sponge pillow; you push in at one place and the problem pops out at another. Add to that fact the very serious "freedom of expression" problems that some of these solutions raise in terms of our First Amendment.

Dieter GRIMM: But you can make a point by saying it is protected by the First Amendment.

Ronald DWORKIN: We keep coming back to the question whether judges or commissioners should have the power to regulate the content as distinct from the financing or the timing of political messages and appeals, not for substance, but for what we might call tone or dignity or taste. That is, as I said, a tempting idea: Democratic politics in the age of 30-second political ads, full of jingles, innuendos, and insults, but empty of ideas, is so often coarse and degrading. The public seems to agree, at least when they reflect on the matter. People do watch the ads, and they must be influenced by them because otherwise savvy political managers, who know what they are doing, would stop running them. (I recently saw an interview with a professional campaign manager who said that he could be sued for negligence if he did not run attack ads.) And yet people, when polled, say negative ads are wrong and that they would be in favor of limits. But still I am frightened of trying to do anything in that direction. The people must decide for themselves what to be influenced by. The people, not the law, must improve the content of politics, though I have no idea how that is going to happen. Perhaps we can resist the temptation to intervene more effectively if we concentrate on the downside, the risks. Can you not imagine a commission of judges one day deciding that ridicule is an unfair political tactic, and banning a latter-day Voltaire or Rabelais?

Dieter GRIMM: Let me just offer one very general observation. This is again the argument of the slippery slope in a way: Once you start, you will find no limits and the result will be worse. By curing some vices, you open the field for others. My observation from many discussions with Americans is that the slippery-slope argument very often closes the debate. It prevents the discussions from looking for possibilities to cure vices that everybody admits are vices and that are detrimental to the democratic process. I do not see why it should be impossible to find reasonable limits and to enforce them.

Ronald DWORKIN: I absolutely agree. I bridle whenever I hear "slippery slope." I did not mean to say that the first steps in any regulation of taste in politics would be unobjectionable, but that dreadful steps might follow later. I meant to say that there is something wrong with the first step because no group should assume the power to decide what kinds of arguments or appeals or even nonsense other people, now or in the future, will be permitted to take seriously. I brought Voltaire in as a warning shot, but it was a cheap shot.

Stephen BREYER: Suppose we assume that judges will to some degree involve themselves in political questions, such as supervising the shape of election districts, enforcing or shaping the content of campaign finance rules, supervising the distribution of television time, and perhaps even (at least in Europe) examining the content of political advertising. After all, you have said that the Cour de Cassation, the Conseil d'Etat, and the Cour des Comptes all become involved in France. Were American judges to become even somewhat similarly involved, that might barely prove acceptable, but in part because the American public retains some control over who its judges are—either through presidential appointment and Senate confirmation in the case of federal judges, or through direct elections in the case of many state judges. Indeed, one virtue of our selection process, which sometimes strikes other nations as involving too much politics, is that it helps to assure that the judges themselves will have some rough understanding of the political process.

The French electorate, however, has little say in who the judges of the Luxembourg or Strasbourg courts are. And Americans have no say at all. Does that fact mean that decisions of those courts will lack legitimacy, when they approach politics, or even when they approach politically significant human rights questions such as that involving General Pinochet?

Robert BADINTER: This is a very important matter. It concerns primarily international justice and sovereignty and less the supervision of campaign finance. With respect to that supervision, I want again to point out the need to be careful when trying to understand the meaning of the *Bowman* case. The more I have looked into it, the less clear it seems.

In my view, the Court there tried simply to use the principle of proportionality to find an answer; it did not try to question that principle itself. It asked whether it is legally possible to impose a financing limit on campaigns, and whether one can limit political campaigns from a financial perspective. It asked whether it is legally possible to forbid a third party from spending money on a campaign. It then pointed out that the English statute, Article 75, aimed at assuring equality as among candidates. One can conclude on that basis, as the Court did, that the statute legitimately sought to protect the rights of some, in particular the candidates and voters of Halifax, by restricting those of others, say from other parts of the United Kingdom. In the Court's opinion, Mrs. Bowman's argument focused on the question whether the statutory restriction was "necessary in a democratic society." That restriction, applicable in England during the final weeks of a political campaign, prohibited spending more than five pounds to help provide a candidate with outside support. The amount is miniscule. The Court then develops at length the theme of necessity in a democratic society. In paragraph 43 of its opinion it says, "In certain circumstances, these rights can conflict, which makes it necessary to foresee the possibility of certain restrictions on free expression before or during an election." The Court recognizes that, in attempting to strike a balance between the two rights, the Member States enjoy a measure of discretion, as is generally the case where the organization of an electoral system is at issue. That is why I would classify the decision as one involving proportionality.

Stephen BREYER: But the problem for me is that I do not understand why the Court concluded that Article 75 did not satisfy the principle of proportionality. Why was it disproportional?

Robert BADINTER: Yes, this is not the best decision that the ECHR has ever made. But the Court did not say that free expression must prevail, and that, consequently, every financial limitation runs counter to the European Convention on Human Rights. Rather, it simply required an adjustment among two opposing principles.

Gil Carlos RODRIGUEZ IGLESIAS: This again shows that the principle of proportionality is an instrument of judicial supervision, which can be pushed quite far in the direction of reviewing the substance of decisions made by the political branches.

Robert BADINTER: As to the third point concerning the supervision of government ethics rules, I should simply like to note the connections between the sanction imposed for violating ethical rules, the confidence placed in the judge who will impose it, and the extraordinary consequences that may follow that imposition, going far beyond what the judge decrees as it reverberates through the media. The case of the Secretary of Agriculture was terrible politically because it led to the opening of a corruption investigation. To consider it corrupt for a Secretary of Agriculture to go to a meeting in Brussels to defend the interest of American farmers! That is an example of lobbying for the interests of American farmers. The Secretary of Agriculture is trying to protect American agriculture.

But I believe, in looking at the entire phenomenon, that it is an instance where the power of the judge goes beyond the judge's exercise of his own power. He is an instrument of the media. That is because the further you go in elaborating ethical rules and in imposing criminal sanctions for their violation, the more you open up the possibility of criminal prosecutions and (from the perspective of those subject to those rules) the more powerful is the threat. In France as in Italy, indeed as in all Western nations, the opening of a criminal prosecution against a very important politician is itself sufficient to ruin his career. In the eyes of the public, no presumption of innocence prevails. The fact that a judge has decided to investigate what has happened, the fact that the judge has found that corruption is possible, that is enough to lead the public to conclude that corruption exists. The fellow is politically wounded, if not dead. Indeed, it is now common practice in France that a member of the French government, should this occur, must resign—until he is cleared.

Antonio CASSESE: When is a prosecutor duty-bound to start criminal proceedings? I have asked a lot of Italian prosecutors why they were instituting proceedings against leading politicians. Their answer is: "I have a legal obligation to start criminal proceedings any time I get a *notitia criminis*, that is, any time I become apprised of a possible crime. If I did not initiate prosecution, I might be prosecuted myself." In contrast, in France, you have a lot of leeway, you can decide that it is a minor case.

Robert BADINTER: The legal notion that you must proceed whenever you have cause to believe that a crime has been committed must be an excuse. Considering the complexity of the criminal law, cause to believe must proliferate. If I may say so, you are free to choose your victims. I recall that at one time an investigation was opened into the activities of the members of the Italian Conseil Superior de la Magistrature because they had drunk some coffee paid for by the Mayor of Rome. No one normally paid attention to who paid for coffee. That sort of thing is ridiculous. That is where a legal obligation to open criminal investigations can lead us.

Antonio CASSESE: The problem is that the law is very clear. As I said before, as soon as the prosecutor gets what we call *notitia criminis*, where there is some sort of reference to a possible crime, he or she must institute criminal proceedings. This should ordinarily be confidential, but then the media get involved. There is a special register of those who are being investigated by criminal judges, it is called *registro degli indagati.* Those who are the targets of criminal investigations must be on this register. Why? Because they must know. They are the only ones who must know, so that they can find an attorney and prepare their legal defense. In theory, nobody should know, but very often, everything is disclosed to the media. So if Berlusconi's name is on this register, the news has already hit the headlines. Therefore, in a way, a prosecutor has no leeway, he has very little discretion because he has to justify if he decides to drop a case or charges made against a particular individual.

Ronald DWORKIN: I wonder, has there been any case of prosecuting a prosecutor for not prosecuting someone else?

Antonio CASSESE: I do not think so, but judging from what some prosecutors told me, they may have a lot of problems. However, I do not think that there has ever been a criminal case brought against them for not initiating criminal action.

Dieter GRIMM: We have the same system. We have the principle of legality, which obliges the prosecutor to investigate. Whenever it is set aside, this is done for pragmatic reasons. Since there is so much

information about possible crimes, the prosecutor certainly has a
choice about when to begin and when to wait or to remain inactive.

Antonio CASSESE: We have a special crime, provided for in our Criminal Code, which relates to the omission of official acts by a state official who is duty-bound to perform. This means that if you delib-
erately refrain from initiating criminal proceedings, you may be accused of the offense of failure to perform official acts that, as a
prosecutor, you were legally bound to perform.

Stephen BREYER: Are you speaking of different things? There is the
crime and the opening of an investigation into the crime. If there is
evidence of a crime, must the prosecutor open an investigation?

Robert BADINTER: No. If there is evidence of a crime, there must already have been an investigation, an *enquête*. By *enquête*, I do not
mean a formal magistrate's investigation, an *instruction*, I mean a
police inquiry.

Antonio CASSESE: A newspaper could report about those politicians
who, say, are alleged to be corrupt.

Robert BADINTER: In that case, the prosecutor will have the police
open a preliminary inquiry. Or the prosecutor may find that a letter arrives in his office saying that Mr. X has done this or that,
along with some documents ordinarily originating from within
Mr. X's business. The letter might say, for example, that Mr. X has
taken money to give to his uncle or his mistress. What does the
prosecutor then do? He calls the Police Judiciare to determine
whether any of this is serious or whether, say, the documents
have been forged. From then on, if there is serious evidence, he
will send the matter to the investigating magistrate, the *juge d'instruction*.

Ronald DWORKIN: He has to . . . ?

Robert BADINTER: He has to.

Ronald DWORKIN: It is the same!

Robert BADINTER: By no means, for he also has the authority to send
the matter directly to a tribunal for determination or to close the
case. Imagine that it was true that officials drank coffee paid for by
someone else—a matter not worth consideration by the criminal
justice system. The prosecutor would classify the matter as one not
to be followed up. There are many cases that the prosecutor classi-
fies as not worth the time of the police or of a tribunal. That is true
of many smaller offenses. Were it not so, the police could not do

their job. The justice system would be buried beneath a mass of cases awaiting decision.

Ronald DWORKIN: All this depends on the press not having access to the story, by leak or any other means. If the politician is a prominent one, then the coffee story will get in the press. So everything is in this delicate balance, judgment and discretion.

Stephen BREYER: It is interesting. In our system, if somebody complained to the Justice Department, it would not necessarily be considered a serious matter. It likely would become significant only if the Department started a serious investigation.

Robert BADINTER: Ronald, here is an example, a very significant example. It is the case of M. Juppé, the (former) Prime Minister. Just after he became Prime Minister, it became apparent that he had rented an apartment from the Mayor of Paris, as had his son, with special terms and conditions that benefited him. Was this a criminal matter? The discussion of that issue was important, particularly as the person involved was the Prime Minister. After an investigation, the Chief Prosecutor said that, because no one had complained, "there might be a minor fault," adding that "if the Prime Minister leaves the apartment and repays what would have been a fair rent, we shall not proceed further."

That was the end of the matter. I can tell you that I believe that the approach was very wise and very fair, for it all would have taken place in the same way for anyone.

Ronald DWORKIN: But were there not people who said that this approach only deepened the corruption? Not only did the Prime Minister get an apartment on the cheap, but when it was discovered this magistrate hushed it up. If something like this happened in the United States it might not be a ten-day wonder, but it would be a two-day wonder. There would be newspaper articles and radio talks.

Robert BADINTER: There were many radio talks and articles, and it was a major political event. He suffered deeply in his political reputation. But the prosecutor said, "This is too small a case according to common standards. I should not make it a worse case because he is the Prime Minister."

Ronald DWORKIN: The issue that Steve raised is not just about whether someone goes to jail for what is really only a minor infraction, but whether he suffers permanent damage, which includes serious political damage.

Robert BADINTER: I just mentioned that because of what Antonio CASSESE was saying about the Italians and the differences in respect to the magistrate's power there and here in France. Of course, the prosecutor could have chosen differently. He had the legal right to say, "Mr. Prime Minister, because of your position, we are sending the dossier directly to the Tribunal."

Stephen BREYER: In our system, there are several stages. If one hears that the Justice Department is investigating Secretary Espy's trip to Athens, then one simply considers it as a negative press story. If the matter is referred to a Special Prosecutor, that is very harmful to Secretary Espy. And if the matter goes to trial, it becomes devastating for him.

Ronald DWORKIN: But, of course, the Justice Department can decide not to appoint a Special Prosecutor, and that is often evidently the right decision to take.

Stephen BREYER: That is a serious problem. We wrote a Special Prosecutor statute that somewhat resembles the Italian system. The statute, which has since expired, gave the Attorney General virtually no discretion about what to do. Once she had evidence that a high public official might have committed a crime, she had to ask for a Special Prosecutor. That provision helped make clear that the Attorney General would not favor important politicians. But recent events convinced Congress that there was too little discretion. Perhaps the French system provides a better model.

Ronald DWORKIN: All this suggests that though administrative discretion is often useful, it is also often troublesome and unsatisfactory. We have to face the question that Steve originally put to us. Not just about how prosecutorial officials should exercise discretion, but about how far the law should make politicians vulnerable to prosecutors. Have we gone too far in that direction?

Dieter GRIMM: I think that you suggested that, in this third category of ethical rules, the judges should not be involved. It tends to be instrumentalized. Was that not the point that you were trying to make?

Robert BADINTER: No, I do not want to hear that the judge should not or should. I look at the power of the judge, and I say: The prosecuting judges have power and, by exercising it, they hold almost a power of death or life over politicians. So many proscriptions—

going back to the example of your agricultural secretary—apply nowadays to all citizens, and particularly because of the media's interest in political figures, they are exposed to greater judicial risk. If you are a common citizen, not a star in business, but just a plain businessman and you have a problem with your income taxes, then you might be in trouble, you might incur lawyer's fees, and sometimes you might be prosecuted, but you can still carry on your business and go on. When it is over, you forget your troubles. But if you are a politician in the public's eye and you are accused of engaging in fraud on your income taxes, or of having received advantages of even minor importance, as the one mentioned about Juppé, then you risk being burnt like Joan of Arc in public by the media. It is a strange position in which judges find themselves. It is their duty to oversee prosecution power, but the result is destruction. That is a new phenomenon. Before, especially in France, and in other places too, the situation was simpler. As the judiciary was more or less controlled by the political power, if this had occurred to M. Juppé in the old days, nobody would have heard of it. It would just have been put in the closet and forgotten. Of course, if M. Juppé had killed his mistress, he would have been sent to criminal court. Remember the very famous case involving the wife of the Président du Conseil, M. Caillaux, before the First World War. She went to kill a newspaper journalist, the Directeur of the *Figaro,* because he was publishing the letters of the mistress of M. Caillaux in the *Figaro* every day.

Ronald DWORKIN: What a nice wife!

Robert BADINTER: But she was rewarded because she was acquitted. The jury let her go! Because it was passionate. It was right before the First World War, in July 1914, and strangely enough there was more space devoted in the newspapers to the Caillaux trial than to the murder of the Archduke of Austria, which led to the war. It was a jury of men and the defendant was a woman. And what did she defend? Her honor against a horrid mistress.

Nowadays, it is a very different situation, because if Mr. Caillaux would have, for unknown reasons, cheated the treasury, nothing would have happened. The press would not have known it and the Minister of Justice would have given instructions to the prosecutor not to prosecute.

Ronald DWORKIN: Do you really regret this change?

Robert BADINTER: By no means. But we live in a system in which just by initiating the investigation, you are killing the reputation of any politician, but not a common citizen.

Ronald DWORKIN: Robert, there are two distinct problems in what you have brought up. One is that the system can destroy a politician who is innocent. The second is that the system holds politicians to higher standards, so that a guilty politician is likely to suffer more than anyone else who had committed the same offense would. These are very different issues.

Robert BADINTER: No, they are held to higher standards because the consequences are higher. They will not receive a harsher sentence than others.

Ronald DWORKIN: But might they not also be prosecuted when another citizen would not be? If two people cheat on the income tax, one is a businessman who pays a fine and then continues his prosperous career, and the other is a politician whose career is finished. Now, many people think that it is as it should be, because to enter politics is to assume a special responsibility. In any case, this is a different problem from having laws on the books, laws that will inevitably trip up an honest politician, who might accept reimbursement of expenses for attending some meeting that the press decides was a bribe, for example. The public apparently wants such laws. It wants its officials vulnerable in this way. But there are grave dangers, not just of unfairness, but of turning able people away from public service altogether.

Robert BADINTER: There is a most remarkable passage in Tocqueville, in which he says, in 1832, something like "In aristocratic societies, you were born and then put in power by birth. People might find that unfair, but they did not resent the fact that you were in power. And they would see how you would use your power, but the fact that you were in power was not something against you, it was just chance." In democracies, the fact that the citizen grants another citizen power by election means that they consider him to be better than they are, and secretly the public resents it. Many think, "After all, why is he better than I am? Probably he has been chosen because he is a trickster, a cheater, maybe a crook, probably he wears a mask of fraud." The public likes this idea and the fact that the veil of honesty can be torn up. And so they wait and say, "Ah, we knew that if he was put in power, it is not because he is better than you or me, it is because he was a clever cheater and a crook." It is a very interesting remark because the consequence is that people are trying to scrutinize with a very suspicious eye anything that is said about politicians.

Ronald DWORKIN: The Greeks solved that problem, at least, when they elected by lottery!

Dieter GRIMM: It still remains the difference that the businessman does not represent anyone and does not have immediate power over others, whereas the politician does. He represents the people and he has the power to tell people how to behave. This justifies different treatment of politicians and other people. Of course, I expect everyone to comply with the law, but I may sanction others in a different way than I would sanction politicians. I think that this is not unreasonable.

Robert BADINTER: Yes, I would agree with that. But everyone should be equal in the eyes of the law, and the fact is that some people are less equal than others.

Antonio CASSESE: If I may go back for one second to the question of judicial scrutiny of the behavior of politicians, just let me give an example of the potential for judges or politicians to abuse their power by actually resorting to devious political means. In 1994, there was a G7 summit in Naples presided over by the then Prime Minister Berlusconi. It was devoted to economic matters, the problem of corruption, and so on. It was a two-day summit. The second day, all the newspapers carried the news that Berlusconi was under criminal investigation for corruption. There were allegations of bribery. Berlusconi said, "This prosecutor, Mr. Borrelli"—who is a well-known leftist and also likes the media and wants to be in the media—"could have waited one day, instead of destroying my image as the chairman of the G7 meeting in Naples. I am here with President Clinton, with Chirac, and so on, and he is attacking me." I think that he was right. You know what Borrelli, this chief prosecutor, said: "Well, before I sent officially a secret indictment to him (which, however, was immediately disclosed), I consulted with the head of state, and the head of state said, 'Well, you have this legal duty to proceed, I cannot stop you because of the principle of separation of powers.' The president of the Republic allegedly said: 'Go ahead, thank you for telling me that you are going to issue this formal indictment against Berlusconi.'" So Mr. Borrelli said, "I consulted with him and he gave me the green light." It is a way of politically manipulating criminal action and an abuse by the judiciary. As I say, Berlusconi was absolutely right. The prosecutor could have waited until two or three days after the summit. It is shattering for the Prime Minister of a country hosting a summit to be in the newspapers, accused of corruption.

This is the huge problem in our democracies: that prosecutors are like judges proper, like judges sitting in trials and *de facto* passing judgment on persons accused of crimes. They become prima donnas. One very good friend of mine, a famous Italian prosecutor, told me: "You know what happens to most of my colleagues, they open the newspaper only to see whether their name is in the newspaper. They are not even interested in politics or world events."

Stephen BREYER: Your example reflects three modern developments. The first is the tendency to create rules (such as the "you must prosecute" rule) and to force officials to justify their conduct through reference to those rules, whether or not that conduct independently makes sense. The second is to turn over to a prosecutor the power to destroy a political career. The third is the converse. Politicians may justify behavior that is immoral by pointing out that the behavior did not, in fact, violate any criminal law. The rule of criminal law thereby becomes a standard of proper behavior; a kind of *valeur judiciaire* becomes an ethical norm.

Robert BADINTER: On the subject of ethical behavior, the rules governing the Senate and the House of Representatives are formulated by those bodies themselves. They define their own misbehavior. They are closely supervised, are they not? There is a morality police inside the very halls of Congress.

Stephen BREYER: There is a Senate Committee and a House Committee that look into ethical matters. And there are instances in which it is claimed that those committees were too harsh, as well as instances in which they may have seemed too lenient. It is very hard to keep politics out of the Congress; and I would not claim we should try to do so.

Gil Carlos RODRIGUEZ IGLESIAS: The position of someone who becomes a justice of the Supreme Court of the United States, and who is subject to scrutiny, like Stephen was . . .

Robert BADINTER: There is a double standard whether one likes it or not. That means that the power of the judge, given the double standard, is somewhat greater as applied to politicians. That is a paradox, for the judges have not desired such power.

Dieter GRIMM: There is a difference. The social function of running a corporation does not depend on whether the person in charge complies with the law or not. He is running a business and has to follow economic rules. When he cheats on taxes, he should be punished for that. The social function of a politician depends on other people complying with the law, and he is no longer in a position to ask other people to comply with the law if he dispenses with the law himself. This, I think, makes the difference, and this difference justifies different standards.

Robert BADINTER: We are in agreement. That changes nothing in respect to the judge's power. It happens that the existence of the double standard . . .

Dieter GRIMM: When I hear "double standard," I always think of hypocrisy, unjustified . . .

Robert BADINTER: Let us just say that the objective circumstance is the following: The media is likely to pay more attention to a politician than to an ordinary citizen, and, consequently, the judge has greater power to affect the politician than the ordinary citizen.

Ronald DWORKIN: Robert, that strikes me as an odd way to put it. Many professions are held to higher standards than ordinary businessmen: accountants, for example, and lawyers and doctors. We do not say that, because there are special restrictions on lawyers or doctors, judges have more power over them. It is the public, not the judges, which has established certain special expectations for politicians, and in some instances has asked judges and prosecutors—and, in a different way, the press—to enforce those expectations.

Robert BADINTER: Rules and standards are tied up with the lawyer's profession. They are part and parcel of that profession. The unusual fact about the politician's situation is that he is held to a higher standard with respect to acts that are not part of his profession as politician, unlike the lawyer whom you mention. He may be held to that standard with respect to acts that took place even before he was nominated for office. He has greater exposure simply because he is now a politician.

Ronald DWORKIN: Dieter just made the point that we should distinguish among the expectations appropriate to a businessman, the somewhat higher expectations we should have for lawyers, and the still higher expectations for politicians.

Robert BADINTER: I am not making myself understood. You are a lawyer and then you become a politician. You may be prosecuted later, when you are politician, for what you did as a lawyer. Compared to ordinary lawyers who have not become politicians but who have done the same things, you will suffer much more. This is not linked with anything relating to the situation afterwards.

Ronald DWORKIN: I will pay, in various ways, because in offering myself as a politician, I claim, among many other things, that my past record fits me for that role. That may be unreasonable, but it apparently does not strike the public that way, and no one has to enter politics.

Robert BADINTER: Even so, it smacks of retroactivity. The fact is that you have judged a fellow by today's standards for mistakes he made yesterday. I am not now talking about the criminal law. I am talking about the consequences of the same act. That is where, as I said, there is an odor of retroactivity.

Ronald DWORKIN: That is a consequence of my choice to become a politician, not of the choice of the judge. . . .

Robert BADINTER: That is so.

Gil Carlos RODRIGUEZ IGLESIAS: The position of someone who becomes a Justice of the Supreme Court of the United States and who is subject to scrutiny like Steven was.

Dieter GRIMM: When you discover that, a few months before, he stole some silver spoons, I think . . .

Robert BADINTER: It is not quite what the politicians believe, that there are, for example, ferocious political witch hunts taking place in Italy, in Spain, in France, in Germany with Kohl. When you saw Starr pursuing Clinton, you thought he did so because it was Clinton, not because Clinton had committed what he was accused of doing. Rather, he was Clinton, and there is the odor of political incentive, that Starr did this because he was a Republican and sought Clinton's hide. But leaving this aside, in the very best of circumstances, the fact remains that the politician is more fragile vis-à-vis the judge. If you translate the matter into the language of power, the power of the judge vis-à-vis the politician is perceived as greater than vis-à-vis other citizens.

Stephen BREYER: In one sense, the businessman is in the same position as the politician. A criminal investigation might destroy the life of an ordinary businessman. The community in which he lives might turn on him. He may be unprepared for the reaction. He might even commit suicide. A politician may have a thicker skin and consider an investigation simply one of the risks of the profession.

There is also a sense in which the investigating prosecutor's power has not grown. The prosecutor is himself limited in what he can decide by the possibility that he himself will become the subject of commentary in the press. There is also a sense in which the prosecutor's power has grown. Society in the past may have had fewer written ethical rules, trusting more to the good sense of the people to decide whether, for example, a reduced apartment rent was, or was not, a serious ethical lapse. Today, we have more written rules. We try to decide in advance how to codify rules that will reflect our ethical sense. And application of those written rules consequently can surprise us.

Ronald DWORKIN: It is a question of what the law is.

Stephen BREYER: It is a question of how much one expects the criminal law to accomplish.

Antonio CASSESE: I wonder whether it is appropriate for judges to pass on ethical matters. I wonder whether an alternative solution might not be perhaps to set up what in France they call the *comité des sages*, or council of elders. I think, particularly with respect to prominent politicians, it is very bad to give so much power to judges. Whereas, in a *comité des sages*, you appoint wise people, old, highly respected politicians and, say, the President of the High Criminal Court or of the Court of Cassation. And then the *comité* takes into account not only legal considerations, but they do not have to apply the criminal code, and they come to their wise conclusion. You mentioned before a prime minister who paid very little rent, but is it a crime as long as he pays it back? In that particular case, the Paris prosecutor did not apply the law because, under the law, he should probably have initiated criminal proceedings. He was a wise man, he said, "On balance, there is no point in sending him to prison or in attacking that former prime minister only because he is now no longer in power." Probably one should think of alternative solutions.

Ronald DWORKIN: Isn't there a corresponding danger that such discretion opens the prosecutors themselves to political attack?

Stephen BREYER: But would we, in the United States, be able to find a *comité des sages*? When I was twenty-seven and worked in the Department of Justice, the Department would occasionally set up that kind of committee to give advice about beginning a case that might have serious economic consequences. But today, it would be far more difficult to set up such a committee without becoming subject to severe criticism. I think that today there is a greater feeling that law enforcement must be left to pursue its own course. Do you agree?

Antonio CASSESE: But you have less rigidity when you have a *comité des sages*. They do not have to apply the rigid criminal laws.

Ronald DWORKIN: But once again, less rigidity carries its own risks, including the risks of arbitrariness or favoritism or politics. Or, what is just as bad, the appearance of these vices. If one politician is, in effect, excused by a *comité des sages* because, though he broke the law, it was trivial, and another is prosecuted, there will be no lack of people who will say that what the second did was trivial too. Or that what the first did was not so trivial after all. Then the *sages* become themselves the targets and maybe they become too rigid themselves, out of self-protection. I think that there is less danger in judges administering laws.

Stephen BREYER: Of course, our Constitution was intended to create a *comité des sages*.

Ronald DWORKIN: Do you mean the Senate as a committee of sages?

Stephen BREYER: Yes.

Ronald DWORKIN: Originally, of course, senators were appointed and not elected. They were supposed to be beyond the reach of ordinary politics. But that became too inconsistent with the country's developing sense of democracy, and now they are elected and everything they do, conspicuously, including investigating other officials, is deeply political.

Stephen BREYER: There is a "noble tradition" of how the Senate, say, Senate hearings, are supposed to function. But the public is cynical.

Ronald DWORKIN: Politics seems to me to corrupt the internal aspect as well. In Clinton's impeachment hearings, there was not even the appearance of fairness in the facilities that the Republicans, who were in charge, gave the Democratic minority's staff. The Democrats got a tiny office and, when they asked for a Xerox machine, they were told that they did not need one. It is hard to see, in the impeachment story, much left of the old idea of the senators as politically independent statesmen.

Robert BADINTER: We have reached a conclusion. Ethical demands are greater for the public man and bear more serious judicial consequences.

Ronald DWORKIN: This discussion is in some ways independent of our larger conversation. We have been considering, overall, how the changing state of the law and society forces judges themselves, by a kind of internal constitutional logic, to assume a role of greater moral authority and judgment. The issues we are currently discussing are rather different and more limited: The greater judicial power over politicians is the inevitable and anticipated side effect of an independent public decision, apparently in all our countries, that politicians should be more subject to law, including criminal law, than before. Perhaps that is part of an even more general trend toward criminalization as a response to complexity. I do not mean it is not a large story in itself. But I think rather a different one.

Robert BADINTER: Along with that goes what Dieter GRIMM mentioned: the fact that we increase by law the field of action makes the one who holds the power to act more powerful.

Ronald DWORKIN: We see similar effects in the public's perfectly understandable desire to regulate industries that seem in themselves more and more unregulatable.

Robert BADINTER: That is true. Still, I would object that, when we consider the question of the media and the judges, the matter is not so simple. The Starr example is a caricature, but also the most striking. Did he investigate because the offense itself was intolerable or because, by investigating, he became famous? There is much to say about that matter. Do you prosecute because the crime is unbearable or because the prosecution will make you famous? Famous and eligible to enter politics? After all, we have seen judges who have subsequently entered politics.

Ronald DWORKIN: There is a terminological danger here, though I may be the only one who suffers from this. For you, the word "judge" includes a prosecutor; it embraces the whole judicial process. Not for us. Starr had been a judge, as it happens, and so he was called "Judge Starr." But that had nothing to do with his role as independent prosecutor.

Robert BADINTER: No, when we speak of judges, it is to avoid the term "magistrate."

Stephen BREYER: In the French system, a prosecutor is a kind of judge.

Robert BADINTER: But whatever the hand that holds the sword, it strikes the same wound.

4

International Criminal Justice

4.1. Presentation

President Antonio CASSESE

1. MAIN MERITS OF RECOURSE TO JUSTICE AS OPPOSED TO OTHER RESPONSES TO INTERNATIONAL CRIMES

1. A few words are fitting on the merits of the judicial response to the commission of international crimes (*e.g.*, war crimes, crimes against humanity, genocide, torture in times of peace, aggression, terrorism).

Justice is better than *revenge.* Revenge is undoubtedly a primitive form of justice, a private system of law enforcement. It has, however, an altogether different foundation from justice: an implacable logic of hatred and retaliation. Revenge can only be the last resort for persons who have been denied due process, as is shown by what occurred after World War I in the case of the Armenians (they took justice into their own hands to punish those whom they regarded as responsible for the genocide of Armenians that had occurred in 1915). Sakib Ahmic, one of the key witnesses in the *Kupreskic* case brought before the International Criminal Tribunal for the former Yugoslavia (ICTY), reportedly said in 1999: "My grandson is now three. If the murderers of the 12 members of my family are not punished, as they should be, it will be up to him, when he is twenty, to go out and kill them. Justice will thus be done."

Justice is better than *forgetting* through the granting of amnesties or simply letting crimes fall into oblivion. Forgetting beguiles future dictators or authoritarian leaders into relying on impunity. Hitler is reported to have said, when debating whether to proceed with his genocidal policies against the Jews: "Who, after all, speaks today of the annihilation of the Armenians?"[1] In addition, as was stated by V.

Jankélévitch (in his beautiful booklet *L'imprescriptible. Pardonner? Dans l'honneur et la dignité*) and repeated by E. Wiesel before a French court in the *Barbie* trial, forgetting means that the victims are murdered twice: first, when they are physically exterminated, and thereafter when they fall into oblivion. Furthermore, the memory of massacres and other atrocities is never really buried along with the victims. It always lingers and, if nothing is done to remedy the injustice, festers. A distinguished reporter from Belgrade, Julia Kokeva, who works for the Beta News Agency, recently said approximately the following:

> Crimes perpetrated in the former Yugoslavia have destroyed our past, are destroying our present and will destroy the future of next generations. Only truth can enable our society to heal. One is under a grave illusion if one believes that democracy and market economy may come about without the truth. They operate on a functional basis, and if denial and untruth are allowed to survive, democracy and market economy will not achieve anything; problems will remain. How could we live in a democracy if a former head of militias continues to be a living legend?

Instead, bringing alleged culprits to trial has at least these merits: (1) Trials establish individual responsibility over collective assignment of guilt (in the trials before the Yugoslavia Tribunal, it is clear from the testimony of almost all witnesses that members of each ethnic group tend to use disparaging terms when referring to *any member* of another group, lumping them together under a derogatory category: the Muslims are called "Turks," the Croats "Ustashis," and the Serbs "Chetniks"); (2) trials dissipate the call for revenge because, when the courts mete out the right punishment to the perpetrator, the victim's call for retribution is met; (3) by dint of dispensation of justice, victims are prepared to be reconciled with their erstwhile tormentors because they know that the latter have now paid for their misdeeds; (4) a reliable record of atrocities is established, so that future generations can remember and be made fully cognizant of what happened.

2. CRIMINAL JUSTICE BY NATIONAL COURTS

(i) Legal Grounds of Jurisdiction

2. The response of national courts to international crimes has long been disappointing. State courts have normally taken a "nationalistic" or "introverted," as opposed to "international," view. Indeed, it is on the strength of territoriality, or active or passive nationality, that traditionally states have brought alleged perpetrators of international crimes to trial before their courts. True, there exists a more advanced ground of jurisdiction, the so-called universality principle (also termed *forum deprehensionis*), whereby the state in which an accused is apprehended is empowered to bring him to trial, regardless of the *locus delicti commissi* (place of commission of the crime) or the nationality of the accused or of the victim. However, this principle has been accepted, at the level of customary international law, only with regard to piracy. At the level of treaty law, it has been upheld with regard to grave breaches of the 1949 Geneva Conventions and the First Additional Protocol of 1977, as well as with regard to torture, under the 1984 Torture Convention. These treaties, however, do not confine themselves to granting the power to prosecute and try the accused. They also oblige states to do so, or alternatively to extradite the defendant to a state concerned (the *aut judicare aut dedere* principle).

Although states tend to lay down a limited range of legal grounds of criminal jurisdiction in their legislation, one may well wonder whether they are nevertheless entitled under customary international law to exercise universality of jurisdiction over war crimes, crimes against humanity, aggression, torture, and terrorism. State practice does not provide much assistance. To date, crimes against humanity have been tried by national courts of states on whose territory the crime was committed, under the territoriality and possibly the passive (or passive and active) nationality principles (think, for example, of the *Barbie, Touvier,* and *Papon* cases). Alternatively, these crimes have been tried under special national legislation, such as that enacted in the United Kingdom, Canada, or Australia, in relation to a specific set of crimes, namely, those committed by Nazis during World War II, or they have been tried under legislation enacted to implement such international treaties as the 1984 UN Convention on Torture. It would appear that the only case in which a person accused of crimes against humanity has been tried in a state with which he had no links is *Eichmann* (in which Israel tried a senior Nazi figure). It is, however, particularly significant that no state concerned protested against that trial: neither the two German states, nor the countries on whose territory the acts of genocide planned or organized by Eichmann were committed, nor the states whose nationals were the victims of genocide. It would thus seem that these states did not challenge the principle enunciated in 1962 by the Supreme Court of Israel, whereby "the peculiarly universal character of these crimes [against humanity] vests in every state the authority to try and punish anyone who participated in their commission."[2]

The acceptance by states of the exercise of "universal" jurisdiction by Israel is in line with the general principle enunciated back in 1927 by the PCIJ (Permanent Court of International Justice) in the *Lotus* case: States are free to exercise their criminal jurisdiction over acts performed outside their territory whenever no specific international limitations (provided for either in treaties or in customary rules) restrict such freedom. Indeed, one fails to discern any customary or treaty limitation on the power of states to try to punish crimes against humanity and other crimes perpetrated abroad by foreigners against other foreigners.

More difficult is the question whether international rules impose on states *an obligation to prosecute and try* the authors of alleged crimes against humanity. Some commentators have given an affirmative answer. Their arguments, however, do not prove compelling. Although there do exist a few international treaties providing for so-called universal jurisdiction, it seems difficult to prove the emergence of a customary rule imposing an international obligation. State practice supporting a contention to this effect is lacking. In addition, no general international principle might be relied upon to warrant the proposition that such an obligation has materialized in the international community. At most, one could argue that, in those areas where treaties provide for such an obligation, a corresponding customary rule may have emerged.

(ii) Trends in State Practice

3. What happens in actual practice? The penal repression of violations of the laws of war (and, more generally, of international crimes) can be better assessed in its merits and shortcomings if considered in the light

of the fundamental distinction drawn by the great Dutch lawyer (and Judge on the Tokyo Tribunal) B. V. A. Röling between "individual" and "system" criminality.[3] The former encompasses crimes committed by combatants on their own initiative and for "selfish" reasons (*e.g.*, rape, looting, murder, and so on). The latter refers to crimes perpetrated on a large scale, chiefly to advance the war effort, at the request of, or at least with the encouragement or toleration of, the government authorities (*e.g.*, the killing of civilians to spread terror, the refusing of quarters, the use of prohibited weapons, the torture of captured enemies to obtain information, and so on). Normally "individual criminality" is repressed by the culprit's national authorities (army commanders do not like this sort of misbehavior, as it is bad for the morale of the troops and makes for a hostile enemy population). By contrast, "system criminality" is normally repressed only by international tribunals or by the national jurisdiction of the adversary. There are, of course, exceptions, such as the *Calley* case, "a typical example of system criminality" (Röling), urged upon the U.S. authorities by American and foreign public opinion.

By and large, repression of "individual criminality" is a more frequent occurrence than that of "system criminality," for the simple reason that the latter involves an appraisal and condemnation of a whole system of government, of misbehavior involving the highest authorities of a country.

It must be added that, strikingly, for about 40 years, the repressive system instituted by the 1949 Geneva Conventions was not put into practice. Only after the establishment of the ICTY (International Criminal Tribunal for the former Yugoslavia) and the ICTR (International Criminal Tribunal for Rwanda) did states commence to resort to it (think, for instance, of the *Jorgic* case in Germany and other cases brought before Danish and Swiss courts). In addition, as already pointed out, states have confined themselves to the more traditional criteria and, in practice, have instituted criminal proceedings only against alleged authors of crimes committed on their territory or against persons living on their territory and having acquired their nationality. Notable, and recent, exceptions are the *Pinochet* case (based on the 1984 Torture Convention) and the *Hissène Habré* case (brought before a court in Senegal, probably on the strength of the universality of jurisdiction principle).

3. PROSECUTION AND PUNISHMENT
BY INTERNATIONAL COURTS

(i) The Reasons Behind the Recent Strong Demand for International Criminal Justice

4. It is commonly known that, as early as 1919, after World War I, the victors agreed upon a few provisions of the peace treaty with Germany, signed at Versailles, in which they provided for the punishment of the major figures responsible for war crimes and went so far as to set down in Article 227 the responsibility of the German Emperor (Wilhelm II) for "the supreme offence against international morality and the sanctity of treaties." This, and subsequent attempts at justice, ended in failure, except for the Nuremberg and Tokyo Tribunals, with all their flaws.

A major breakthrough occurred in the early 1990s. Various factors led to the development of a new ethos in international society and a strong request for international criminal justice. Two factors in particular should be underscored.

First, the end of the Cold War proved to be of crucial importance. It had a threefold effect. For one thing, the animosity that had dominated international relations for almost half a century dissipated. In its wake, a new spirit of relative optimism emerged, stimulated by the following factors: (1) a clear reduction in the distrust and mutual suspicion that had frustrated friendly relations and cooperation between the Western and Eastern blocs; (2) the successor states to the USSR (the Russian Federation and the other members of the Confederation of Independent States) came to accept and respect some basic principles of international law; and (3) as a result, there emerged unprecedented agreement in the UN Security Council and increasing convergence in the views of the five permanent members, with the consequence that this institution became able to fulfill its functions more effectively. The second effect of the end of the Cold War was no less important. Despite the problems of that bleak period, the two power blocs had managed to guarantee a modicum of international order during the Cold War era. Each of the superpowers had acted as a sort of policeman and guarantor in its respective sphere of influence. The collapse of this model of international relations ushered in a wave of negative consequences. It entailed a fragmentation of the international community and intense disorder which, coupled with rising nationalism and fundamentalism, resulted in a spiraling of mostly internal armed conflicts, with much bloodshed and cruelty. The ensuing implosion of previously multi-ethnic societies led to gross violations of international humanitarian law on a scale comparable to those committed during World War II.

The second crucial factor was the increasing importance of the human rights doctrine. Its emphasis on the need to respect human dignity and, consequently, to punish all those who seriously attack such dignity prompted the quest for, or at least gave a robust impulse to, international criminal justice.

The third factor is the growing tendency of states to resort to international criminal justice as a diplomatic fallback whenever they are politically and militarily unable to settle important international crises. Often, if the UN collective security system fails to enforce international law or to cope forcefully with gross and large-scale atrocities, and if multi-lateral or bi-lateral diplomacy cannot help bring about a breakthrough, major powers tend to regard international criminal justice as the only avenue open to them to do something, or to prove to public opinion that they are not completely impotent. In short, international criminal justice is used as a political and diplomatic alibi.

(ii) International Trials: Main Merits

5. International tribunals enjoy a number of advantages over domestic courts, particularly those sitting in the territory of the state in which atrocities have been committed.

First of all, it is a fact that national courts are not inclined to institute proceedings for crimes that lack any territorial or national link with the state. Until 1994, when the establishment of the ICTY gave a great impetus to the prosecution and punishment of alleged war criminals, the criminal provisions of the 1949 Conventions had never been applied. National courts are still state-oriented and loath to search for, prosecute, and try foreigners who have committed crimes abroad against other foreigners. For them, the short-term objectives of national concerns seem still to prevail. This is also due in part to the failure of national parliaments to pass the necessary legislation granting courts universal jurisdiction over international crimes.

Second, as the crimes at issue are international, *i.e.,* serious breaches of international law, international courts are the most appropriate bodies to pronounce on them. They are in a better position to know and apply international law.

Third, international judges may be in a better position to be fully impartial and unbiased, or at any rate more even-handed than national judges who are caught up in the milieu in which the crime under trial was perpetrated. The punishment of alleged authors of international crimes by international tribunals normally meets with less resistance than national punishment, as it hurts national feelings much less.

Fourth, international courts can investigate crimes having ramifications in many countries more easily than national judges can. Often the witnesses reside in different countries, other evidence needs to be collected involving the cooperation of several states, and, in addition, special expertise is needed to handle the often tricky legal issues raised in the various national legislations involved.

Fifth, trials by international courts may ensure some sort of uniformity in the application of international law, whereas proceedings conducted before national courts may result in a great disparity both in the application of that law and the penalties given to those found guilty.

Finally, the holding of international trials is a sign of the will of the international community to break with the past, by punishing those who have deviated from acceptable standards of human behavior. In delivering punishment, the international community's purpose is not so much retribution as stigmatization of the deviant behavior, in the hope that this will have a modicum of deterrent effect.

(iii) The Crucial Issue of States' Cooperation with International Criminal Courts

6. Three major features of international criminal courts should be emphasized. First, they normally do not sit in the country where crimes falling under their jurisdiction have been perpetrated. They are located in a distant country or, at any rate, in a country not necessarily close to the scene of the crimes. In short, they are not the *forum delicti commissi*. As the Supreme Court of Israel stated in *Eichmann*, "normally the great majority of the witnesses and the greater part of the evidence are concentrated in . . . the state [where the crimes were committed] and [this] is therefore the most convenient place (*forum conveniens*) for the conduct of the trial." Second, these tribunals exercise jurisdiction directly over

individuals living in a sovereign state and subject to the exclusive juris-diction of such state. In addition, in most cases, these individuals, when perpetrating the alleged crime, acted *qua* state officials or at least at the instigation or with the support or endorsement or acquiescence of state authorities. In principle, international tribunals are therefore intended to cast aside the shield of sovereignty. However—and this is their third salient trait—they cannot in fact reach those individuals without going through national authorities. These courts do have the power to issue warrants for the seizure of evidence and for the search of premises, as well as subpoenas and arrest warrants. However, they cannot enforce the acts resulting from the exercise of those powers for lack of enforce-ment agents working under their authority and empowered to enter freely the territory of sovereign states and to exercise enforcement func-tions there, notably vis-à-vis individuals acting as state officials. This is the major stumbling block of these courts and tribunals. They lack an autonomous *police judiciaire* that overrides national authorities. They are like giants without arms and legs, who therefore need artificial limbs to walk and work. These artificial limbs are the state authorities. If the cooperation of states is not forthcoming, these tribunals are para-lyzed.

(iv) Main Problems Besetting International Criminal Proceedings

7. The crucial problem that international criminal courts must face has already been mentioned: the need for cooperation by states. As long as states either refuse outright to assist those courts in collecting evidence or arresting those indicted, or do not provide sufficient assistance, in-ternational criminal justice can hardly fulfill its role. This, of course, also applies to those cases, such as that of the ICTY, where assistance can be provided by a multilateral force established under the aegis of the UN (reference is, of course, made to the NATO forces operating in Bosnia and Herzegovina and, more recently, in Kosovo).

In addition to the need for international criminal courts to amal-gamate the various judges, each with a different cultural and legal background, the length of international criminal proceedings consti-tutes a serious problem. Lengthy trials primarily result from the adop-tion of the adversarial system, which requires that all the evidence be orally scrutinized through examination and cross-examination (whereas, in the inquisitorial system, the evidence is selected beforehand by the investigating judge). In addition, the protracted nature of proceedings is often exacerbated by the need to prove some legal "ingredients" of the crime (for instance, the existence of a widespread or systematic practice in the case of crimes against humanity) or by the need to look into the historical or social context of the crime. It should also be noted that the adversarial system was conceived of and adopted in most common law countries as a fairly exceptional alternative to the principal policy choice, namely, the avoidance of trial proceedings through plea-bargaining. In fact, on account of this feature, the adversarial model works sufficiently well in most common law countries. However, defendants tend not to plead guilty in international criminal proceedings, among other things because of the serious stigma attaching to international crimes. They, therefore, prefer to stand trial, in spite of the amount of time endured in the examination and cross-examination of witnesses, rendered at the international level even more intractable by language problems. (While at the national level all proceedings are normally conducted in one language, at least two, and more often even three languages, are used before international courts, with the consequence that all documents and exhibits need to be translated into various languages.) This factor, coupled with the need—already emphasized above—of upholding a typical feature of the inquisitorial system, namely, keeping the accused in custody, both in the pre-trial phase and during trial and appeal, makes for a situation that is hardly consistent with the right to "fair and expeditious trial" and the presumption of innocence accruing to any defendant.

4. DOES INTERNATIONAL CRIMINAL JUSTICE LACK LEGITIMACY OR MORAL OR PHILOSOPHICAL FOUNDATION?

8. It would seem that some authorities (allegedly H. Kissinger is one of them) believe that international criminal justice lacks any legitimacy or moral or philosophical justification. In my opinion, a different view can be soundly put forward.

An *ethical* justification has already been advanced above, in para. 1.

A *historical and political* basis can also be found for international criminal justice. First of all, this category of justice is clearly envisaged in some of the fundamental international instruments, such as the UN Charter (1945) and the Universal Declaration of Human Rights (1948). The former text, which actually constitutes the Constitution of the world community, lays down in Article 1 that one of the purposes of the organization is "to bring about by peaceful means, and in conformity with the *principles of justice* and international law, adjustment or settlement of international disputes or situations which might lead to a breach of the peace." True, this provision covers both interstate dispute settlement procedures and proceedings for administering criminal justice. True, it only deals with situations where a threat to the peace may arise, and not with situations that, although involving massacres or atrocities, do not pose a threat to international peace. The fact remains, however, that the UN Charter does envisage resort to justice as a justified means of settling grave situations. Thus, international criminal justice finds a firm and indisputable basis in the most important treaty of our times.

The same issue is taken into account in Article 28 of the Universal Declaration of Human Rights—no longer, however, from the viewpoint of interstate relations, but from that of the rights of individuals. This Article lays down that "[e]veryone is entitled to a social and international order in which the rights and freedoms set forth in this Declaration can be fully realized." This provision implies that any citizen of the world has a claim to an international legal system that safeguards and ensures his right to life, liberty, and security of person; his right not to be subjected to torture; his right not to be subjected to arbitrary arrest, detention, or exile; etc. Consequently, the international legal order must be fashioned so as to safeguard those rights and, in case of their violation, must provide the necessary and most adequate remedies. Obviously, among such remedies, dispensation of justice directed toward the prosecution and punishment of the perpetrators of those violations is the primary one.

We find here, again, the positing of a solid, albeit indirect, foundation of resort to international criminal justice. The aforementioned international instruments also offer the best *basis of legitimacy* of international courts. Unlike the Nuremberg and Tokyo Tribunals, which primarily represented, and gave voice to, the concerns and demands of the victors, at present, international criminal courts act *on behalf of the whole international community* (indeed, judges are elected by the UN General Assembly regardless of their nationality). These courts dispense justice and state the law (in actual fact, they "progressively develop" international humanitarian and criminal law) in the name and the interest of *mankind*.

I would contend that international criminal justice is also warranted *philosophically*. As this is an area where lack of expertise prompts me to tread gingerly, I shall confine myself to briefly mentioning some of the notions of justice propounded by two classical philosophers: Plato and Aristotle. According to the former, one of the concepts of justice is that "everybody must do what it falls to him to do" (*Republic*, 433b). Seen within the general context of Plato's philosophy, this means that everybody must behave in conformity with order as well as with the law that consecrates and sanctions order. Hence, justice ultimately means legality. A man is just when he behaves in conformity with the law. In consequence, any action contrary to law is not just and must be condemned and repressed. This is the notion of justice as order and law. However, both Plato (*Politics*, 295a) and Aristotle (*Ethics nichomachaea*, v.10.1137b) emphasized that the law may run counter to justice because it is general and abstract and may prove unable to take account of the unique circumstances of individual cases; hence, the need to temper *rigor juris* by moving from abstract justice to specific justice. This notion was later termed "equity," but can also signify application, by a judge, of the general law to a specific case, *i.e.*, judicial appreciation by a judge of the unique circumstances of a case in light of the law.

I would contend that international criminal justice is fully warranted by both notions of justice just set out.

5. INTERNATIONAL JUSTICE, DIPLOMACY, AND POLITICS

9. I have already noted above (para. 4) that one of the motivations underlying the present frequent recourse to international justice is the inability of diplomacy to settle international crises promptly and effectively.
The relations of criminal justice and diplomacy are fourfold.

First, in the present political constellation, when the Great Powers and the UN are unwilling (for lack of national or strategic interest, or political will) or unable to put an end to a serious political crisis involving bloodshed and atrocities, they tend to fall back on the establishment of a tribunal. They do so either while the crisis is under way (as in the case of the International Criminal Tribunal for the former Yugoslavia) or after the massacre has terminated, as a means to show that, even though they were unable or unwilling to put an immediate stop to genocide, they can at least contribute to the punishment of the culprits (this is, of course, the case of the International Criminal Tribunal for Rwanda). The Great Powers thus tend to use international criminal justice simply as a diplomatic tool, *i.e.*, as a way of putting pressure on the adversary, not unlike economic sanctions or the threat to resort to air strikes. They claim that the setting up of such tribunals has a deterrent effect, *i.e.*, they should discourage belligerents from perpetrating further massacres. However, to date, the failure of the Great Powers to provide the necessary financial wherewithal, enforcement powers, and other means to those tribunals as soon as they are set up has meant that no deterrent effect has come about. As a consequence, the tribunals' credibility has considerably suffered and the whole judicial exercise, as a diplomatic ploy to bring about changes in the behavior of the combatants, has proved pointless.

Second, international tribunals may only be set up as a result of diplomatic negotiations: Justice is the child of diplomacy.

Third, politicians and diplomats may, and in fact do, endeavor to condition (financially, politically, through psychological pressure, including failure to arrest some major indictees, etc.) the work of international courts.

Fourth, in its turn, international criminal justice may negatively impinge upon or even obstruct the diplomatic process by stripping possible negotiators of international legitimacy and thus removing them from the international political arena. (This actually happened in mid-1995 when the indictment of Karadzic and Mladic automatically entailed that they were not allowed to go to Dayton, Geneva, or other international gatherings, as the ICTY had immediately forwarded arrest warrants to all the relevant capital cities. The Russian Ambassador to The Hague rushed to contact the Tribunal's President to have the arrest warrants rescinded; of course, this attempt was of no avail. Something similar has recently happened to Milosevic and Milutinovic, who at present might play a significant role in diplomatic negotiations with the Great Powers, but are barred from doing so because of their status as indictees.)

In sum, international criminal courts, although they may have some limited impact on diplomacy, are by and large *strongly contingent upon and, in a way, subordinated to politics and diplomacy,* much more than any national court, including Supreme Courts.

6. CONCLUDING REMARKS: INTERNATIONAL CRIMINAL JUSTICE AND STATE SOVEREIGNTY

10. In spite of all its flaws and weaknesses, and in spite of the fact that it is often manipulated by diplomats and politicians for their own purposes, international criminal justice is of crucial importance in the present configuration of the world community. It shows that:

1. State officials may no longer hide behind their official functions when committing major crimes, but can be brought to justice and punished, if guilty, even if they were acting as heads of state, members of cabinet, or senior military officers. As was stated by the Nuremberg International Military Tribunals (IMT), "the very essence of the Charter [of the IMT] is that individuals have international duties that transcend the national obligations of obedience imposed by the individual state. He who violates the laws of war cannot obtain immunity while acting in pursuance of the authority of the state if the state in authorizing action moves outside its competence under international law."[4]

2. International courts may directly reach individuals living in sovereign states, sometimes without going through the intermediary of state authorities; while in the past international law and municipal legal systems constituted two distinct spheres of law, now international justice can pierce the *shield of state sovereignty,* directly penetrate national legal systems, and reach individuals living there.

3. Some values (*e.g.,* respect for human dignity; the right to life, security, and liberty; the right not to be tortured; etc.) have become so important in the world community that international rules have crystallized directly imposing on *all individuals of the world* the obligation to refrain from those actions [that impinge on those values]. Those who fail to abide by those rules, whatever their nationality or the place where the crimes were perpetrated, may (in principle) be brought to trial. There are now well-estab-

lished limits to the "omnipotence of the state": to quote the (then utopian) words uttered at Nuremberg by the British Chief Prosecutor, Sir Hartley Shawcross, "the individual human being, the ultimate unit of all law, is not disentitled to the protection of mankind when the state tramples upon his rights in a manner which outrages the conscience of mankind."[5]

4.2. International Criminal Justice

Discussion

Antonio CASSESE: I propose to focus on six issues that, to some extent, I did not discuss in my presentation. I will mainly focus on international judicial bodies and, in particular, criminal courts.

The first topic concerns the areas where clearly international judges do not and cannot play any role in the international community. There are huge areas of international law where they cannot do anything. I would call it "The silence of judges."

The second topic is why, in contrast, in other areas of international relations, international justice has recently become all the rage, particularly after the end of the Cold War. There are so many courts and judicial institutions mushrooming in this international community. I would call it "How international judges have become so important in the last few years."

The third area is whether the international tribunals (interstate tribunals or tribunals dealing with international crimes) have any basis of legitimacy. This is the issue raised by President Badinter, and I would call it "Do international judges possess legitimacy?"

The fourth issue is international courts, particularly international criminal courts, versus "truth and reconciliation commissions." As you may know, since 1974, 17 "truth and reconciliation commissions" have been set up in the international community—in Latin America, in Africa—quite a few African countries, Zimbabwe, Chad, for instance, Uganda, the first one was Uganda—and then, of course, the Philippines, and so on. It is really a crucial question to see to what extent one should opt for one avenue rather than the other one. This is really a basic moral, philosophical, and legal problem.

Another issue relates to the relationship between international courts and politicians. Special problems crop up for international courts, requiring judges or at least one judge, the President of the Tribunal, to play a political role that would be totally unacceptable and inadmissible at the national level. You have to grapple with politics and with politicians, and I wonder whether this is appropriate. There have been lots of critical remarks and critical comments about this.

The sixth and final issue is the role of international criminal courts in creating new law, I will say, acting as modern *praetores*, as the Roman *praetor*, who was allowed to create the law for a specific case. If the law had a gap, he was authorized in particular periods of Roman history to create a legal standard in order to cover that particular case. And this applies to international courts. So, the topic is "The role of international criminal court judges as modern *praetors*."

First of all, let us discuss the areas where the judges cannot have any say. There are huge areas of international law that are not amenable to international adjudication. Let me just give a few examples: first, international labor conventions, all the hundreds of conventions drafted under the auspices of the International Labor Organization (ILO) after 1919, when the ILO was set up in Geneva; second, the whole area of human rights at the world level (of course, I leave aside the regional level, the European Court of Human Rights in Strasbourg, and the Inter-American Court of Human Rights in San José, Costa Rica). At the world level, human rights cannot lead to international adjudication. A third area is the peaceful use of atomic energy and the possible manufacturing and/or use of chemical weapons. This area of modern weaponry is an area where you cannot have adjudication. The fourth big area of international law encompasses the hundreds of treaties and UN General Assembly resolutions on the protection of the environment or against pollution. A fifth area is international humanitarian law. This is a modern sort of label for what used to be called the "laws of warfare and neutrality." For these five, probably even more, branches or areas of international law, states have felt that judicial settlement of disputes is absolutely inappropriate, for reasons which I may quickly go through. In these areas, one should opt for permanent monitoring and, in particular, preventive institutional

action. There is no point in checking whether torture has been perpetrated somewhere because the victim has already suffered from
torture. It is more important to prevent torture, by setting up monitoring mechanisms that every year, on a constant basis, supervise
places where torture might be perpetrated and check beforehand
whether there are conditions that may lead to torture. But there are
also other reasons, say, in the case of chemical weapons: There is no
point in setting up a judicial body to decide whether a state has
breached the chemical convention prohibiting states to manufacture chemical weapons.

Robert BADINTER: Why not combine the two? Why not have both sur-
veillance and a judicial response if a violation of a legal obligation
should occur, say, through manufacture of chemical weapons or
putting atomic energy to use for purposes related to wars of aggression?

Antonio CASSESE: Formally speaking, in most of these treaties on the
four or five areas I have just mentioned, you also find a provision for
the judicial settlement of disputes. Normally, mention is made of either an arbitral court, or of an arbitral tribunal, or of the international court of justice. In fact, however, states have never submitted
any dispute to these judicial bodies in the areas that we are discussing. Politicians or diplomats have instead developed legal devices whereby you may issue a sanction. There is no point in saying,
"You are guilty of a breach of international law. You therefore incur
international responsibility." They feel that there is no point. It is
much better to say: "You must stop your misbehavior. If you do not,
we can take sanctions against you." The sanction very often is an
economic sanction. It turns to public opinion. This happens in particular in respect to the environment. States that are parties to some
treaties may decide that it is better to call it not a breach of international law, but *non-compliance,* so that they simply may decide to
impose sanctions, which may consist of withdrawing grants to a
poor country in order to do away with pollution, polluting factories,
and so on. So there are a lot of ways of putting pressure on states.

Dieter GRIMM: So your criterion is whether the states are willing to
submit certain questions. It is not a matter of principle that it does
not work.

Antonio CASSESE: Well, it is also because states have realized that, for
instance, in the area of human rights you do not have anymore—as

in the old Westphalian model, the old international community—the so-called synallagmatic relations, quid pro quo relations, or relations based on reciprocity. You have instead collective or community interests, collective obligations, and collective rights. As a consequence, there is no point in saying, "States may bring a case of genocide committed in a faraway country or before the International Court of Justice." There is no point. States are not using this legal power. Why? Because there is a lack of interest. Under the European Convention of Human Rights and under the UN Covenant of Civil and Political Rights, say, the French authorities are duty bound to treat in a particular way French citizens or whoever is living on French territory or is subject to French jurisdiction. But if the French authorities misbehave vis-à-vis French nationals, what other state is interested in bringing a case before the International Court of Justice or before the European Court of Human Rights? There is a total lack of interest. True, at the legal level, there is a legal entitlement. Any contracting state has a right to bring a case before the UN Committee for Human Rights (which is a quasi-jurisdictional body that actually does not issue any judgment, but may simply state that a particular country has violated the International Covenant). But, in fact, no other state has any practical interest whatsoever in bringing a case before this UN Committee in cases involving such violations. Italy would never sue, say, France, unless there are Italian nationals who are mishandled.

Ronald DWORKIN: I am not clear which is the cart and which the horse here. That is, if an international institution already existed with genuine power over states, then I think that the interest would develop. There would be a great interest in the United States to bring China before such a body. So are you talking just about how things have actually worked out?

Antonio CASSESE: Let me give you an example: say, genocide. You have the Genocide Convention, which was adopted in 1948 and which grants to any contracting state the power to bring a case of genocide before the International Court of Justice. Since it came into force, until, say, two or three years ago, no country whatsoever had ever brought a case of genocide before the International Court of Justice. So you have the legal potential for a case where a major issue may be brought before an international court or an interstate court, but actually all states refrain from doing so.

Ronald DWORKIN: But it had no real teeth. What could that court do that would make any difference in China?

Antonio CASSESE: The stigma. This is not a case of genocide, of course, but if the court were to find that a particular country, say, China, is responsible for genocide, it would not be a criminal case, it would be a case of state responsibility. This would be of tremendous political importance for legal opinion. China would be found responsible, would have to pay, and discontinue any acts of genocide. I mean that there is no sanction; the court can only say, "You have breached international law."

Robert BADINTER: But let me make a historical observation. You said that one nation has never prosecuted another. But, if I am not mistaken, some European nations, members of the Council of Europe, decided to call for prosecution of Greece, at the time of the Greek dictatorship, for having violated the Strasbourg Human Rights Convention.

Antonio CASSESE: Four Nordic countries, yes. This is the only case. There are one or two instances . . .

Robert BADINTER: Yes, but it does exist. Moreover, what does it matter? Must this exist at the world level if it already exists at a regional level? It is nonetheless, at the regional level, an international convention. Nations have joined it. And one nation may decide to ask the judicial system to say that another nation is systematically practicing torture. Of course, if an individual policeman strikes someone, say, within a police barracks, not by government order, but because he is sadistic, the matter does not interest the international community. But if one nation within the international community—and it need not be the world-wide community, perhaps only the Council of Europe—decides to prosecute another, it must be for the systematic use of torture. And they have done that at this stage, at least in Europe.

Moreover, if I remember correctly, I am not sure, there was a complaint filed by New Zealand or Australia in the United Nations Human Rights Commission, which claimed that Tahitian culture was threatened by atomic testing. The culture at issue was not current culture, but traditional historic culture. And it was threatened by the fact that they were being moved from one place—fellows who had always lived there—and taken to another place 100 kilometers away so that they would not risk exposure to the tests. And, if I am right, it was nations—Australia and New Zealand—that took action.

Thus, it is not exactly correct to say that nations do not do that. They have done it, when it is convenient for them or when they are aware of a massive invasion of human rights. As for China, I wonder if that would be possible. It already is, each year, the subject of a Human Rights Commission report.

Antonio CASSESE: But the UN Human Rights Commission is a political body.

Robert BADINTER: True, but it is basically a judicial approach.

Antonio CASSESE: No, it is only political. I have worked there for many years as one of the Italian delegates. I was the Italian representative, we got instructions from our capital city: "You vote like this." Once I quit, I said, "I cannot vote like this." I got instructions on Turkey. There was a report on genocide prepared by a wonderful African scholar who was a member of the Sub-Commission, and he said in one line of the introduction that, of course, one may remember the genocide of Armenians, perpetrated in 1915 by the Turks. I was formally instructed to ask that this line be dropped. I refrained from complying with the instructions. The line was eventually dropped because Turkey is such a key member of NATO that all NATO countries were very keen just to forget history.

Gil Carlos RODRIGUEZ IGLESIAS: There are several reasons why the special *rapporteur* for human rights issues in country X or in country Y is the object of political pressures in order to get phrases in or out of the report.

Antonio CASSESE: I can give you another example. We all know what was happening about the situation in Cambodia. A few years ago, I spoke with the Foreign Minister of a European country, a very progressive country keen on human rights. This man had been very active in the area of human rights. I asked, "Why didn't you take any action back in the eighties?" He said, "Well, I gather that in our foreign ministry the question was discussed. Some were pushing our country to institute proceedings before the International Court of Justice against Cambodia for genocide. At the last minute somebody said, 'Why should we poke our nose in affairs that happened thousands of miles away?' True, Cambodia has killed two million Cambodians, there was a massacre by the Khmer Rouge, and so on.

But why should we step in? Let us forget this, no action is worthwhile at the international level."

Robert BADINTER: At this point, a thought might help in respect to the subject that you are discussing. The tools that nations make to fight against massive violations of human rights—those tools—are one thing. Using those tools is quite another. It is one thing to say, "Ha! See how willing we are to fight against massive human rights violations." It is another thing to say to Putin that he is an evil murderer carrying on that kind of campaign in Chechnya. We shall find that contradiction throughout, a contradiction between stated rights, the mechanisms, and the will to use them.

Antonio CASSESE: My proposition is that, although states may and sometimes do provide for traditional adjudication in those areas of international law, for a lot of reasons, either legal reasons (because of a lack of legal entitlement or the existence of legal entitlement that is not supported by political interests in suing another state before an international court), or because of the loose character of international law (in particular, I am thinking of the environment where the international legislation is so loose because there are huge economic interests at stake), or for practical or political reasons, states do not rely on international adjudication. States tend to emphasize the role of monitoring, and this is a new area of international law. The UN prefers to tell states, "Send us a report every two years on the human rights situation in your country, and we will go through your report and make remarks." The UN Committee Against Torture, UNCAT, which is a very important body, receives every two years a report from all the contracting states. And the Committee goes through this report and, thanks of course to a lot of supporting material (they are fed in a way by Amnesty International, as well as NGOs, which are of tremendous importance), the Committee can ask questions. Recently, this happened to France. The question was whether or not inhuman or degrading conditions existed and what the authorities were putting in place to remedy the situation. This sort of monitoring on a permanent basis of state behavior is becoming more and more important.

This is therefore an area where I think it's appropriate to speak of *le silence des juges,* "the silence of judges." Let me just add one point. It is no coincidence that the first case brought before the

International Court of Justice relating to genocide was brought by Bosnia Herzegovina against Serbia, and Serbia put in a counter-claim, creating a second case: Serbia versus Bosnia Herzegovina. And then there was a third case, involving Croatia against Serbia Montenegro. But all this was politically motivated; this was only a way of using adjudication as a political tool.

My second issue relates to why in other areas we now actually have a mushrooming of international courts. There are so many courts and, all of a sudden, they have become so important. Well, I think that the main reason is because of the end of Cold War. As long as the Cold War was there, the world was divided up into blocs. There was no resort to international adjudication, not even by developing countries, because developing countries did not trust international legal standards. They said what we have heard so many times in the UN: "International law has been shaped by industrialized countries and by the major powers. It is not de-signed to meet our needs. So we do not trust international law. We also do not have good legal technicians. So we will never go before international courts." By contrast, the Great Powers were hesitant to go before international courts because there were areas that they thought were not appropriate for international courts. You remem-ber the case of *Nicaragua* v. *United States,* in which the court held that it had jurisdiction over the behavior of the U.S. in Nicaragua, including the role of Contras, of the CIA, and so on. The U.S. sim-ply decided to drop out, and this was, of course, in blatant viola-tion of international proceedings. Now, all of a sudden, you have so many courts. Why? As I say, this is, first of all, because of the end of the Cold War. It is also because (again I leave aside the re-gional level, in particular the European Court of Human Rights) international adjudication now has proved useful to politicians. Politicians may find that it is much better to hand over the hot po-tato to a court. Let me give you an example: the Aouzou strip case, Chad versus Libya. You may know that between Chad and Libya there is a huge desert. It is about a hundred thousand square kilo-meters of wonderful desert, which was occupied in the fifties by Libya. It was an armed occupation. Chad had always claimed that this desert belonged to it. It is not very clear why there was such a legal clash. People assume that at some point Gadhafi thought that the Aouzou strip was full of oil and/or uranium, which could be used for nuclear weapons. So Libya was thinking of exploiting the area in order to manufacture nuclear weapons. Probably, in the end, it became clear that it was so difficult that it was not economical to exploit that area for economic or military purposes. However, such strong nationalistic feelings had built up that Gadhafi thought that it was really difficult for him simply to give in to the request by Chad, strongly supported by France. In the end, to the general surprise, he accepted Chad's proposal to go before the International Court of Justice. It was very clear that he was hoping to simply say to the Libyan population, "Well, if we lose, it is because somebody else here, in The Hague, has decided that we should hand over this territory to another country." I remember that, at that stage, between 1989 and 1993 (in 1993, the International Court of Justice delivered its judgment), many people said, "Well, this will be quite a novel development in history if a country that is occupying with its armed forces a territory allegedly belonging to another country would withdraw his troops only because of an international judgment rendered by the International Court. It would be so new, so unusual." Moreover, states and courts tend to take into account the fact that they may lose face. Libya would have been in a position to say, "I do not care about The Hague." In this particular case, the court by a unanimous vote (minus the vote of the judge appointed by Libya) decided that that particular territory belonged to Chad. And Libya had to withdraw. Libya in a matter of a few months left, and now the Aouzou strip belongs to Chad. It was very clear that Gadhafi was simply delighted. He had no longer any economic or political or military interest in that territory, but he could not justify to public opinion in his country—well, public opinion or to his own tribe or whatever—that he would give in to another country, especially a poor country such as Chad.

So this is one of the reasons. It is a way out of a diplomatic and political quagmire and a way to avoid pressure from public opinion. There are quite a few cases demonstrating this.

Another case is the use of international adjudication as a political weapon. I have just given you the example of the cases alleging genocide brought by Bosnia versus Serbia and Croatia versus Serbia, now pending before the International Court of Justice. I presume that most members of the International Court of Justice are fed up with these cases. They might say: "This a political issue. We only have to pronounce judgment on legal issues."

Another reason is that courts do act at the international, and I would also say at the national, level, in lieu of governments, because of governments' inaction. Governments everywhere pursue short-term interests, and they do not want to interfere with crimes committed or violations committed by other countries. In this area, the European Court of Human Rights has played a major role with regard to torture in Turkey. You may know that Turkey has a wonderful Constitution and one of the most eloquent and clear provisions prohibits torture, which is quite unusual. Most European constitutions do not have any provision prohibiting torture in so many words. In Turkey, they have a whole state system with prosecutors, strong prosecutors and so on, but they do not do anything to prevent or redress torture. Therefore, faced with this lack of any judicial or political action by Turkey, the European Court of Human Rights has stepped in and said, "You have to do something."

I also think that courts may play a role as a way of legitimizing new governments. Again, this applies to the European Court of Human Rights. You may know that, before 15 or so countries from Eastern Europe decided to join the Council of Europe, the governments of Member States of the Council of Europe made it very clear that if those countries were to join, they would be duty-bound, first, to sign and ratify the European Convention of Human Rights and, second, to grant individuals the right to go before the Court, which was a huge step. These were two *sine qua non* conditions. The Member States said: "Otherwise we will not allow you to join our Council of Europe. Why? You want to be legitimized as democratic, but to do so you have to do something which is not in the statute of the Council of Europe." This is a new step. Again, the member governments were very good, I think, in saying, "In addition to ratifying the statutes of the Council of Europe, you also have to take these two supplementary steps." This was of course crucial for countries like Russia, Poland, Hungary, and so on. Previously, it was not automatic for individuals to go before the Court. States could go, and then a contracting state had to take a particular step, namely, to accept ad hoc the right of individuals to go before the Court. So it was something that was not automatic. But this was done.

Another reason, I think, for the major role now being played by international courts is again the lack of any action by national courts. Let me give you an example by referring to the 1949 Geneva Conventions, the famous four Geneva Conventions on the protection of war victims (the wounded, the sick, civilian populations, and shipwrecked persons). For the first time in world history, in 1949, a provision was added, which stated that each contracting state (now all members of the world community are contracting parties to those four conventions) has not only a power, but also a duty either to search for and prosecute individuals who may have committed grave breaches of the conventions or to extradite them (*aut judicare aut dedere*). It is a duty; it is a very stringent obligation. From 1951, when the four Conventions entered into force, until 1994, no case was ever brought before a national court. For instance, during the war in Vietnam, British, Italian, French, Canadian courts might have taken action against somebody—the Vietnamese from North Vietnam, or the Americans—allegedly guilty of a grave breach of the Conventions. (This means a gross violation, such as mistreatment of civilians or rape. There is a long list, a very detailed list, of so-called grave breaches.) Again, you have a wonderful legal instrument. You have the legal weapon available, but nobody makes use of that legal weapon. Why? Because national courts were not interested. Because of the nationalistic approach, and because of some difficulties in getting hold of the person. But this is what we now call the universal jurisdiction.

Dieter GRIMM: Who could have brought the case to a national court under these Conventions?

Antonio CASSESE: Any national authority.

Dieter GRIMM: So it was not the courts that were not interested, but the national authorities.

Antonio CASSESE: Actually, it was up to the prosecutors or the alleged victims to bring a case before national courts. For instance, as soon as you know that somebody who has committed a grave breach in Uganda is in your territory, and the police know that he is there, criminal proceedings should be instituted. Interpol works very well. Interpol knows; Interpol has a red list, and it is effective. If Interpol tells you, "I know that Mr. X is in your territory," then the prosecutor would have to take action and bring a case against that person before a national court. Neither the prosecutor nor the courts had ever taken any action until 1994. That year, all of a sudden, there were a few cases—Denmark, Austria, Sweden, Switzerland, and some attempts in France—against people who had committed, or who allegedly committed, crimes in Yugoslavia. Why? Because of the Yugoslavia Tribunal in The Hague. In a way, it acted as an incentive for national courts. All of a sudden, they woke up and said, "We have a wonderful weapon at our disposal. Why don't we use it? Why should we leave this job only to The Hague? Let us do something." And they started in Germany. The first case we had in The Hague was a case of Tadic, a man who was arrested in Germany. He was brought before the German courts. I remember that I said, "We do not have any indictee here in The Hague, but we have a wonderful UN prison that is totally empty." The German authorities, from the outset, were excellent in their cooperation with The Hague Tribunal. They said, "This is our case. We arrested this man, and he is accused of serious crimes. But if you prefer, we will hand over this case to you and we will give you the whole dossier concerning the investigations that we have carried out." So we started the whole action.

A final reason for resorting to international courts, in particular criminal courts, is the well-known *alibi*. It is an alibi for political impotence. This applied to the Tribunals for Yugoslavia and Rwanda. In Rwanda, crimes of genocide were committed in 1994. Neither the French, nor the Americans, nor the English, nor the Belgians did anything to stop the massacre. When Rwanda itself requested the establishment of an international tribunal, and the major powers also felt that it was appropriate, the tribunal was set up. As for Yugoslavia, it was clear from the outset that they had no military or political options open. Or, they felt they would not take any action at the military or political level. And therefore they decided to set up a tribunal. Of course, they knew that President Robert BADINTER had suggested the establishment of a tribunal. A proposal along the same lines was also put forward in the United States. But of course, the follow-up was given to this idea because of the absolute impotence of the Great Powers. When they set up the tribunal, there was no budget, there was nothing, zero. Not one penny.

Robert BADINTER: If I may, Antonio CASSESE knows that very well. I personally was involved in its creation, so I know how it occurred and why. And there I agree. We both know each other and we both very well know what happened.

At that time, I was President of the Arbitration Commission at the Peace Conference for former Yugoslavia. During the summer of 1992, the Western leaders considered the situation morally desperate. From a political perspective, crimes exist when they appear on television, and every day television showed the crimes against humanity that were then occurring in the heart of Europe 50 years after the end of World War II. The public was horrified, and the public arose with feelings of indignation. Leaders must take this kind of thing into account. And at the August 1992 conference, Carrington was present, and so was Butros-Ghali. We were perhaps five, no, more. Our view was that this could not be permitted to last. No one wanted to intervene militarily as it was too risky. Negotiation with the murderers was producing no results. The time had come at least to establish an international criminal court, so that we would know that, someday, somehow, with changes in political fortunes, we would not find those primarily responsible for these crimes benefiting from an amnesty, from pardons, living happily ever after, or honored by their communities. Rather, they would have to answer for their crimes.

The diplomats, adopting the traditional political approach, said that this was absolute nonsense, nonsense reflecting good humanitarian conscience, but still nonsense. Why? Because you cannot have fellows coming to a table to negotiate for peace, while simultaneously preparing courts to try them and cells to hold them. Peace must come first. Justice will follow.

We answered, "No." Rather, we must take a step toward assuring that justice will be meted out when conditions permit. Then I saw the political path taking shape within their thinking. At least creating a tribunal would appear as a step toward rendering justice and protecting rights—which public opinion so desperately demanded. The two men who insisted most firmly upon this point, and without whom it would never have taken place, were Butros-Ghali and Mitterrand.

The decision was made quickly. We were ready for it intellectually. For many years, we had been working on the project of creating an international criminal court. The juridical work was completely ready. But the political will, though strong, was also ambiguous. And that again illustrated for me something that I have found true many times in my life, that a person who has deep convictions different from those traditionally held and different from those of the majority must be ready. When he finds a door that is slightly open, he must push and rush through quickly. Opportunity does not knock twice. That is what happened in France when capital punishment was abolished. I consider it flowing from a chain of happily fortuitous circumstances. And it is just what happened in respect to the international criminal court.

Once the issue was decided, we went through hell trying to find the means to make the decision work. The entire history of the matter is extraordinary. The intellectual and legal work related to that tribunal is a great enterprise. The ebbs and flows of the political will: "We shall create it. No, we shall not use it. Yes, we must use it." That depended upon changes in political circumstances.

This story reflects a unique historical moment. The creation of this international criminal jurisdiction would leave its mark on the years since the end of the Cold War, years characterized by the ascension of the judge. Remember this. It was not victors, as in Nuremberg or Tokyo, who created the court. This time, it was the international community that decided upon a court. That court acts not in the name of winning nations wishing simultaneously for justice and revenge, but in the name of the international community. Thus, it is a great permanent step forward. And those who believe in this form of international justice must carry out a very difficult, permanently ongoing task.

And you have lived through this. We should not forget that a kind of fortuitous historical opportunity, seized upon and exploited by mad activists including you and me, my dear friend, led to the success of this creation. It did not involve a calm atmosphere, unlike the decision to create the great court over which President Rodriguez Iglesias presides, the Court of Justice of the European Community. That was quite a different matter.

Antonio CASSESE: Dumas was then the French Foreign Minister and was instrumental with Mr. BADINTER in setting up this tribunal. He once told me and other people that they were absolutely convinced in 1993, when the tribunal was set up, that it would never take off. And actually, when the judges met in November, on November 17, 1993, in The Hague, there were just three or four computers, four secretaries with short-term contracts (three-week contracts), no budget, and no headquarters. We were hosted, and the UN had to pay for four rooms in the International Court of Justice. At the end of the two-week meeting, I went to see the Secretary General of the Carnegie Foundation (you know the International Court of Justice building is owned by the Carnegie Foundation), and I asked, "Can we, when we meet again, come here?" He said, "Well, you know, some members of the International Court of Justice would resent your presence here. So you'd better look for another building." We had nothing, zero. It is therefore clear that the establishment of the Tribunal was really an absolute alibi. Let me remind you that at the outset of the Gulf War in 1990, Mrs. Thatcher said, "Immediately, before fighting, before engaging in a war against Saddam Hussein, we should think of establishing an international tribunal to bring this man to trial, because of the huge crimes he is committing." This was just after the invasion of Kuwait. And the Americans said that it was a good idea, but then they forgot. Why? Because the military action was effective. You see, whenever either the diplomatic action or the military action achieves major results, you simply forget about justice.

Let me just now wind up this section by quoting a wonderful sentence by a young man, the French journalist Pierre Hazan, whom I like very much. He is about to publish a book. He writes: "International justice is beginning to take root. It is becoming the site of a new utopia. It seeks, within the confines of a courtroom, to strangle the world's violence." It is a new utopia and an attempt to strangle violence in the world within the small space of a courtroom.

Now, let me move on very quickly to the issue of the legitimacy of international courts and tribunals. President BADINTER has said that judges in national legal systems are elected or appointed, or they get their job through a sort of democratic process. This is their source of legitimacy. What about international law? I would say that there is some legitimacy. First, the UN Charter, the world Constitution, and the Universal Declaration of Human Rights of 1948, do insist on the importance of resorting to justice. In the preamble of the UN Charter, there is even a short sentence that says that "the people of the world are hoping . . . to settle international disputes by applying international law, treaties, or customary law, and so on." This is a reference to judicial settlement.

Robert BADINTER: It always seemed to me that that involved differences between nations, not crimes committed by individuals in the name of a nation. It was disputes between nations, not those who commit crimes against humanity, which were brought before international courts.

Antonio CASSESE: This was the narrow approach taken by particular leaders, including President Roosevelt, who was actually behind the UN Charter: the idea of the four policemen who would police the world, the idea of a sort of governing body of the world. This was the narrow approach vis-à-vis peace. (You know, of course, the famous distinction between negative peace and positive peace—negative peace consisting of the absence of international armed conflicts, and positive peace being of course the realization of justice.) Real peace means that you change the conditions in the world so as to prevent resort to armed clashes. The UN Charter is based on the idea of negative peace, which means also, among other things, that only those disputes that may lead to international friction and armed conflicts are to be taken into account by the Security Council (this is the famous Chapter 6 of the Charter), whereas other disputes and criminal liability are left aside because these are of no relevance to the four policemen. However, some foundation can be found in some of these treaties.

What I would now like to emphasize is the selection process of judges. All these courts are made up of judges elected by assemblies, by democratic bodies. (To the best of my knowledge, the only court where judges are not appointed by a democratic process is the European Court of Justice because they are actually nominated by each government, which suggests one or two judges and, normally, the other countries agree.) In other courts, say, the International Court of Justice, judges are elected by the Security Council without veto power. There are only two cases where there is no veto power, one of the two cases being procedural questions; the other one is when judges are elected. A major power cannot veto somebody, say, from Costa Rica or from Libya. Eight votes are required out of 15 without any veto. Then the judges must be elected by the General Assembly. In the case of the International Criminal Tribunals for the former Yugoslavia and for Rwanda, judges are nominated by governments, then short-listed by the Security Council, and then elected by the General Assembly. Again, there is a democratic process, but any government of the world may nominate two people, one being a national of that country, another being a foreigner.

Stephen BREYER: Do they try for regional representation?

Antonio CASSESE: Yes, this is scrutinized by the Security Council, and I think it is quite appropriate because, first of all, they check whether the major areas of the world and whether common law and civil law countries are represented. They avoid having too many Europeans (they are right, there is no point for Yugoslavia to have many Europeans). Secondly, they check the judges' qualifications. Each judge must have a very good CV with solid experience either in international law or in criminal law, judicial experience, or diplomatic experience. The Security Council reviews all these requirements and short-lists some candidates.

Stephen BREYER: If the prosecutor wants to start an investigation, can a person seeking to stop the investigation appeal to a *chambre d'accusation*? In a civil law system with a *juge d'instruction*, one could do so. If one could appeal to such a *chambre*, and a North American judge were a member of that *chambre*, the appeal would act as a control on the behavior of the prosecutor. Perhaps that safeguard would help answer some of the North American critics of the court, who fear that the prosecutor will act irresponsibly.

Antonio CASSESE: The prosecutor has immense power; actually, he or she is the most important and powerful person in those tribunals. It is for this reason that the prosecutor is elected by the Security Council, where the major powers *de facto* wield immense authority. It was very clear during the appointment process of the last prosecutor that he or she could not be a national of a NATO country. We were told so in so many words by people in the Security Council. Why? Because Russia was against it, and it was siding with Serbia. Therefore, the Security Council unanimously appointed Madame Carla Del Ponte, who is a Swiss national.

Robert BADINTER: Before, the prosecutor was from Canada, which is a member of NATO. Could you explain that?

Antonio CASSESE: The first one was a South African, then a Canadian. People said that the Canadian was siding with NATO countries, and Russia was fed up at that stage. So they said, "We cannot accept somebody from NATO." We had one or two excellent candidates from NATO countries, but they could simply not make it. So, how can you check the prosecutor? Because, as I say, she can decide to indict an American pilot because of what happened in Kosovo, and so on, or a Russian, French, or Dutch general.

Stephen BREYER: But America worries about Americans!

Antonio CASSESE: She prepares an indictment, with a lot of supporting material, and the indictment must be submitted to a judge. The judge is either designated by the President of the Tribunal or, normally, and this is now the new sound practice, it is the on-duty judge who reviews the indictment.

Robert BADINTER: With respect to this subject, there have been modifications in the procedural rules of the international criminal court. The proceedings as originally determined followed the Anglo-Saxon model. But gaps in that model appeared so quickly in the criminal proceedings that they had to be modified. And it was modified, creating a mix. I find this fascinating, for I see in this process the future of common proceedings everywhere.

There is another very interesting phenomenon that has appeared over the past few years. People force a confrontation between a system and reality. They then decide that one aspect is excellent and another is no good. They may start with a particular traditional national system as a model, and they may eventually create a composite.

Ronald DWORKIN: Generally, whatever it is, they call it the third way.

Robert BADINTER: What is particularly remarkable is the process of creating a permanent, international criminal court, which has evolved over the last year. It is a remarkable composite of various systems.

Ronald DWORKIN: Tonio, you were about to give us the examples of this creation of the new procedure.

Antonio CASSESE: For instance, under the adversarial system—which was actually adopted when we drafted our code of criminal procedure—as we all know, the judge plays a minor role; he is just an arbitrator between two parties that fight each other and so on. And unlike the civil law judge, the judge in an adversarial system does not have a dossier, a file; he does not know anything, he has not seen the witness statements, and so he is really not master of the proceedings. Actually, normally they do not even ask questions. They simply settle procedural disputes and things like that. In our trial of Tadic, there were three judges from common law countries (it was presided over by Mrs. McDonald from America, a very good judge, and there was Sir Ninian Steven from Australia, and Judge Vohra from Malaysia). It was a typical American-style trial. We thought that it was very slow. And then, at that stage, I had become presiding judge of one of the trial chambers, and we had a very important case of rape. I said, "I am very naive and I do not have any judicial experience as a trial judge, but I do not see why I could not read the witness statements, and why we do not do so." My two colleagues agreed. They said, "Why not? If you insist on that, let's go ahead." We asked the prosecutor to pass on to us all the evidence that had been given to the defense counsel, and we got a huge dossier. We went through all the witness statements, so that when, say, the next day, Mr. X came to testify, I already had his two, three, or five statements, and I was in a position to say, "Mr. Prosecutor, you have asked him a sufficient number of questions. This particular topic is not so important. Let's move on to another question." And then, at the end, I would ask a lot of questions because the prosecutor had forgotten to go through the witness statements. In a way, we were interfering with the actions of the prosecutor and, of course, also with the activity of the defense. But we took an active role and, of course, we were extremely careful. We had to proceed gradually with the two parties to ensure that they were prepared to accept our new approach. "Why not?" they asked. Only with acceptance, with the consent of the two parties, could we proceed in this way. More judges then took an active role when we were adopting the rules of procedure, a rule which is quite new, whereby the court may call witnesses, or may request parties to call witnesses, which is quite unusual in common law procedure. The court there, as I say, has a very passive role. When we started calling witnesses, we said, "We want to hear this. Your witness mentioned in passing somebody else; we would like to hear that particular witness." At some point, there was a case involving Muslim victims and there were six indicted Croats in the box. Counsel for the Croats said, "We would like to call as witnesses some Muslims, but the Muslims who would have to testify on behalf of Croats, of course, in the view of their community would be regarded as traitors, because it would be disgraceful for a Muslim to go there to say that Croat indictee actually is a good man and that he had never committed any crime. How can we go about it?" We said, "For the sake of justice, we would call them not as defense witnesses, but as court witnesses."

So we started this new procedure of calling court witnesses. They would get an injunction from me saying that they must come to testify before the Court, not on behalf of the Croats, but for the sake of justice and truth. Again, this was a new way of approaching matters. We would also interfere in the cross-examination. We would limit the time, and we would say if the parties had too many witnesses on a minor fact, for instance, 20 witnesses on a very minor fact. In such cases, we would ask them, "Why don't you reduce the list of witnesses to, instead of 20, just 3?" At the outset, our whole procedure was American-style because the Americans, of course, being so good, were from the only country that had produced a wonderful document prepared by the Department of Justice, and we judges actually drafted our rules of procedure on the basis of that document. We were strongly influenced by the document because nobody else had prepared a similar document. At the outset, because of that document, there was a separation between the finding of guilt and sentencing. This meant two different stages, so that once you find that someone is guilty, it is then appropriate to decide on the sentence. In our civil law countries, there is no separation; you at the same time decide whether a person is guilty and, if so, how many years he will get in prison. We said, "Why don't we combine these two procedures?" The suggestion was accepted by our common law lawyers and, at that stage, the defense counsel started producing a lot of witnesses, character witnesses, not fact witnesses, saying, "This man who is in the box, he is a wonderful father." Dozens of character witnesses were repeating the same story, so we were wasting a lot of time. So we passed a new rule for character witnesses saying that you can produce in court one witness only: out of 25 witnesses, you may produce 24 affidavits and one witness alone whom you can call to testify. We will examine and cross-examine this particular witness, who testifies that this indictee is a wonderful man, is actually religious, loves children, and so on. Again, by using affidavits, we saved a lot of time. But again, this is against your system because, in America, you would never do so unless it is subject to examination or cross-examination.

Robert BADINTER: There is a law out there, which controls all justices in the world; it is time. Justices only have a few hours per day, and a few days per weeks to work. The American cross-examination system can only work because most of the cases are settled out of court or by plea-bargaining. When you are confronted with crimes against humanity, you cannot expect any plea-bargaining; you have to do it. The fact that you have no plea-bargaining possibilities makes it a necessity to save time, because you have to judge everybody.

Antonio CASSESE: We discussed this matter at great length. We have a guilty-plea system. We said, in cases of crimes against humanity, how can judges get involved in this horrible trade-off, saying, this man, although he committed atrocities, as in the case of Milosevic, Karadzic, or Tudjman, would not be prosecuted? We said that it is a dirty job, and we left it to the prosecutor; the prosecutor can do any bargaining, can strike a deal with the most horrible criminals, and we do not want to have any say. The prosecutor may decide not to prosecute somebody, or to prosecute him or her for a very minor crime. Why? Because he is prepared to tell a lot of things to the prosecutor about the big shots and the leaders. But we do not want to be involved in this process. Therefore, there is plea-bargaining, but without any judicial endorsement, because we thought it would be unacceptable for our moral conscience.

Ronald DWORKIN: It is hard to see how that modification could be thought of as unfair to the defense. Did you do anything in the other direction, where the reaction of an Anglo-Saxon way would be that the change is unfair to the defendant?

Antonio CASSESE: No. Any time we have always been keen to enhance the rights and the role of the defense counsel, we thought it was fair and appropriate, also because of the imbalance between the prosecution and defense. First of all, most defense counsel come from Yugoslavia and they are not used to the Anglo-Saxon system. We said that it was only fair for the defense counsel to call in some prominent British barristers or American attorneys so that they could spend, say, a week with them and learn from them how to cross-examine witnesses. The defense counsel are at a disadvantage vis-à-vis the prosecutor because the prosecutors are normally people from common law countries, or some excellent French prosecutor (some French prosecutors are first-rate). Defense counsel are generally at a disadvantage. They also do not have the financial means that the prosecutor has. The prosecutor now has about 600 people working for her. This means that each team of prosecutors is really made up of good prosecutors with a lot of experience.

Ronald DWORKIN: That is a good general principle, but the interest lies in following that principle by picking from two major traditions of protecting the accused.

Stephen BREYER: Written testimony, court-called witnesses, time limitations, and combining guilt and sentencing phases of the trial might or might not prove advantageous to the defense. My brief tutorial in the continental, "inquisitorial" system has taught me that the system has far more guarantees of fairness than common law lawyers tend to think. Its use in international human rights trials could prove to have certain advantages.

Robert BADINTER: These are very interesting problems, but we must move on to the issue of legitimacy of the judges. Who are these fellows? Where do they come from? Who are these cosmopolitan judges, as Mrs. Thatcher remarked when speaking of the Strasbourg judges?

Antonio CASSESE: Their legitimacy, in my opinion, cannot be called into question, first of all, because of the selection process of judges, which is quite democratic. The Russian candidate was put forward by Russia and Yeltsin in 1993, and he failed only because the Russians themselves felt (they told us later) that he was a poor candidate, not because he was Russian. At the outset, the Security Council was very keen to select people coming from four Muslim countries (Pakistan, Malaysia, Nigeria, and Egypt), though none of the judges themselves were Muslim. The Judge from Egypt is a Catholic, the one from Malaysia is a Hindu, the one from Nigeria was a Protestant, and the Judge from Pakistan was a Zoroastrian (only 20,000 Zoroastrians live in Pakistan, out of 150 million people). The Security Council was very keen to appoint people from other parts of the world, no Bosnians, no Croats, no Serbians, and even nobody whose religion might perhaps be seen as leading him to side with one party. I think that this is democratic legitimacy. I would also say that these judges apply not Yugoslav law, not American law, but a universal set of values and legal standards, and I think that again this props up the legitimacy.

Let me move, very quickly, to the two final issues, *les juges et la politique,* "judges and politics." This is unique for international criminal courts. International criminal courts do not have any *police judiciaire*; they do not have any enforcement agency at their disposal. They must rely upon national sovereign countries. Therefore, in a way, they have to come to some sort of deal or compromise with politicians. There is a metaphor that I have used many times, namely, that a criminal international tribunal is a sort of giant without legs and without arms, and he needs artificial limbs to act, to move, to walk, and to do anything. The artificial limbs are the national enforcement agencies or NATO armed forces. If we know that an indictee is in France, we have to ask the French authorities to arrest him and to hand him over to the international tribunal. That means that really, in a way, you heavily depend on national cooperation, and you have to come to some sort of deal. That is why the President of the Tribunal has got to go to New York and talk to the Security Council, which is a political body, and to the General Assembly, which again is a political body. The President also has got to go to Zagreb, Belgrade, and Sarajevo, and say, "Dear Minister, can you help me?" I went three times to see Mr. Matic, who was a cooperative foreign minister in Zagreb, and ask him in private to try to arrest some of the indictees. A judge in a national court would never do so; he would never go to a politician to ask for help to arrest people.

In addition, the prosecutor has got to get the support of the CIA and the American intelligence so that the evidence can be handed over. It is alleged that the Americans have everything, the crucial evidence on the wire-tapping implicating Milosevic, but they do not hand over that evidence. One day, NATO leaders decided to accept the request of our prosecutor to go and surround a building in Bosnia—now NATO is in Bosnia—so to play the role of police and seize about 200,000 pages of documents! It is so stated in one of the recent reports of the ICTY to the UN General Assembly. Tanks surrounded the whole building, all of a sudden, overnight, and troops seized all those documents.

Stephen BREYER: The fact that there was a "deal" does not sound promising.

Robert BADINTER: This is the heart of the matter. The court has not broken all its connections with the international political community. But, like the sorcerer's apprentice, it tries to escape the hands that were thought to control it. At that moment comes the clash. That is true. There is a continuous negotiation, but, still, the means remain in the hands of the nations.

Antonio CASSESE: In August or September 1995, after the arrest warrants were issued against Karadzic and Mladic, on a Sunday at one o'clock, the Russian ambassador phoned me. I was at the tribunal working as usual, and he said, "May I come urgently and talk to you?" He was a very nice man, a very good man. He came and he said, "I have got a very short cable from Moscow. The short cables are those that are really important. The short cable says to come here to see you and ask you to caution not to send and, indeed, to quash the arrest warrants for Karadzic and Mladic. I am acting under strict instructions from the foreign minister, and you should do so." I said, "I am so sorry, but I would never do so. I cannot do so for legal and political reasons and so on." I added: "Let us call Goldstone to see whether he agrees with me." And Goldstone said, "Of course, I agree with the President." The Russian ambassador said, "I am sorry. Let us keep this confidential." (I am afraid Goldstone, who used constantly to talk to the media, disclosed everything a week later. That is why I can tell you!) I told the Russian ambassador, "This is so bad for the image of Russia, that we should keep it between you, me, and Goldstone. Nobody else should know."

Stephen BREYER: Did the Russians say that they would not help the Tribunal unless it quashed the indictment against Karadzic?

Antonio CASSESE: The ambassador did not promise anything. He said, "For us, in Russia, in Moscow, it is really a blow that you have issued arrest warrants against those people, and we know that Karadzic can no longer go to Dayton." Then we said, "No, legally speaking, the prosecutor should request the judge to withdraw the arrest warrants, and the judge would be against it, so forget about it." So, from this example, you can see the pressure from the major powers on judges, and judges resisting those pressures.

Stephen BREYER: A civil law "inquisitorial" system has advantages. It controls the prosecutor, both through the professional training that it gives the prosecutor, and through the possibility of an appeal against the prosecutor to a *chambre d'accusation*. Since the key decision in your tribunal is the indictment decision (you want to be certain of guilt before indicting), this control over the prosecutor (apparently greater in a civil law, than in a common law, system) is particularly important. You might start with the civil law system, and modify it with common law approaches where necessary for fairness.

Antonio CASSESE: Again, I think that there is an issue that may be of some interest, but I will not spend much time on that. The issue is that international criminal courts in a way have to play a role that goes beyond the traditional role of the judge (the application and interpretation of existing law). Why is it so? Because international criminal law is extremely rudimentary, the precedents are very poor. If you read the Nuremberg judgment, you realize that it is really a rather poor judgment.

And actually, reading fairly well the French translation, I found a lot of discrepancies, because the French was rewritten by Donnedieu de Vabres, the great professor of criminal law at the Paris University, who could not accept some of the notions propounded by the other judges. There are changes, for instance, on the question of moral choice, the famous question of moral choice.

For instance, he was particularly unhappy with two issues: first, the question of *nullum crimen sine lege*, or the ban on *ex post facto* law. The judgment was drafted by the American and the English judges, who were very much in favor of saying that this was a new crime against humanity that had been acknowledged for the first time in the London Agreement of August 1945, which established the tribunal. They said, "So what? If it is a new crime, the *nullum crimen sine lege* is a moral maxim that must give in before stronger moral demands. It would be so appalling not to punish the horrible crimes committed by the Nazi leaders that we have, in a way, to prefer as a moral choice the punishment of a crime against humanity, a crime which was not provided for as a crime when it was committed." The French judge did not like it, and changed slightly, though not to a great extent, the French translation.[6] He wrote that these crimes against humanity actually were only a category of war crimes, and war crimes were already provided for long before, so that, in a way, he was not applying new law. He also took a different view on the important question of moral choice and the defense of superior orders. The Tribunal, in the text drafted by the majority in English, said, "Of course, a superior order is not a defense; the question is whether there is a moral choice." Then, Donnedieu de Vabres spelled out the argument and said, "It may be duress and, if you are under duress, it might be a defense."

So, you see, this is not a very good judgment. If you read all the judgments, the dozens and dozens of judgments handed down by the minor courts at Nuremberg, you realize that these are not first-rate judgments, at least as far as the legal reasoning is concerned.

All these cases were drafted mostly by American judges applying, to a large extent, American law. I think, probably, the only good precedent for international courts is the *Eichmann* case, the judgment delivered by the Supreme Court of Israel in 1962, which is a wonderful judgment written by great lawyers that sets out all the main major legal problems and does not just apply very quickly some general notions.

Today, international criminal courts are faced with areas of law that are full of gaps. Out of nothing—very few cases—you have to create a new law, and you have to say something new. So, again, the role of judges is increasingly important, particularly in the area of criminal law, where we normally tend to stick to the principle *nullum crimen sine lege,* but sometimes, you have to find a new principle. For instance, we had the Tadic case, where Tadic was acquitted by a trial chamber on a particular count because there was no evidence that he had taken part in the killing of five Muslims in a particular village. He was a member of a group, and there was no evidence that he had participated in the killing or that there was a criminal agreement with respect to the killing of those people. So he was acquitted because there was no evidence of direct responsibility. Then, at the appellate level, the court relied on the common law notion of a "common purpose"—which is to some extent unknown to our countries—where one should have reasonably expected, as a member of a sort of criminal gang, that some members of the gang may kill somebody, although the individual has not agreed on the killing and has no direct responsibility. The adoption of this principle, and the resulting category of crime, was a very important development. We were doubtful at the time. May we, in criminal law, use new notions and new principles? Does this practice infringe on the rights of the defendant? The defendant should know in advance under which category of crime he may be convicted so that he may adequately prepare.

Stephen BREYER: In a conspiracy, each member is criminally responsible for all that takes place.

Antonio CASSESE: In the case of robbery, where everybody knows from the outset that they are going to rob, and some people have guns and also kill some people. Under our law—in civil countries, in France, Germany, and Italy—everyone is responsible, even the person who was the look-out outside. He did not take part in the robbery or in the killing, but he is responsible for homicide, murder, robbery, and so on. That is very clear. The question is what happens when you have not agreed to use a weapon, when you have not seen that the other person is carrying a weapon, so that you have, in a way from the outset, no *mens rea* concerning murder, but only the intention to commit robbery.

Stephen BREYER: Responsibility lies for that which is foreseeable.

Antonio CASSESE: If it is foreseeable. Now, the question is, if you know that you are going to rob a place, a college where there is a dormitory with young girls, and you know and decide, "We will only break in and steal money and jewels and so on." On the other hand, you know that one of the members of the gang likes women and is a rapist. So you should expect rape because it is very predictable that he will, on top of the robbery, rape a girl. But is this is a common purpose or common design doctrine under English law?

Dieter GRIMM: I would just like to mention that, of course, in national courts, this problem also appears after revolutions or after changes of systems.

Robert BADINTER: Can you list some of the procedural advances that you have made as examples of the creative power of the judge?

Antonio CASSESE: Just one case, the *Furundzija* case, where the judgment was entered on torture and rape because the man had been accused both of torture and rape as two distinct crimes. The court decided to delve into these notions and elaborate on the concept of *jus cogens*; there were three or four pages on *jus cogens*. Now, *jus cogens* is that body of law that cannot be derogated from by countries or by states via treaties. Therefore, if a treaty is made by two countries derogating from a rule of *jus cogens,* that treaty is null and void. It is wonderful progress in international law. We said that torture is now enshrined in a norm of *jus cogens,* and then we tried to draw conclusions from this. For instance, if a country passes an amnesty law on torture, that law cannot be regarded as null and void, because a law can be only repealed by national parliament, but all the other countries are duty-bound not to give any legal effects to that law abroad. That way, we try to build up a new doctrine, and this was cited by the House of Lords three times, in *Pinochet,* for instance.

Anyway, there are some areas where major advances have been made, especially with respect to genocide and what is meant by *mens rea* in genocide. But I cannot spend too much time on this issue.

The last problem is the question of *international criminal courts versus truth and reconciliation commissions.* In some recent cases, a proposal has been made to establish both criminal courts and reconciliation commissions. Recently, a report prepared by Sir Ninian Steven, a leading Australian lawyer, suggested that for Cambodia. He suggested that both an international court should be set up for the genocide in Cambodia in the 1970s, and a truth and reconciliation commission. This is unique, because many countries create only truth and reconciliation commissions. I would make just two points.

First of all, a basic distinction must be drawn between the 16 existing truth and reconciliation commissions set up so far, and one, which is that in South Africa, which is quite unique. I think that Mandela and his group decided not to grant amnesty from the outset and not to drop prosecution. As you know, they said, "You can come before the Commission and testify and, at the end of your testimony and of the cross-examination by the Commission, which has judicial powers, we may decide either to grant you amnesty or to start prosecution, depending on the type of crime that you have committed and the extent to which you have disclosed the whole truth about your crimes." Therefore, as I said, two avenues were open. I think that this is what accounts for the tremendous success of this Commission. Only Botha, the former Prime Minister and later President, refused to testify, but he was then brought before a court. Nelson Mandela was extremely good, even in selecting members of the Commission, because at the outset, this was the power granted to him. He said that he wanted to consult with people and he collected suggestions and nominations by various bodies, including judicial bodies. In the end, he selected a group of outstanding people who were extremely independent, and this gave legitimacy to this Commission. Unlike this Commission in South Africa, in other countries in Africa, in Asia, and mostly Latin America, truth and reconciliation commissions are only keen to uncover the truth. They are not involved in any prosecution.

I would find three reasons for resorting to this device. First, the new political regime lacks the power to embark upon prosecution. This is the case in Chile; they simply cannot afford to prosecute and try the alleged offenders because of the position of the military and also of some members of the judiciary.

The second reason, I would say, is because the political contract that has produced democracy in these countries is predicated on a compromise between the old and the new regime, and this compromise precludes prosecution. Therefore, the establishment of these commissions is only possible because of this compromise. The old regime says, "Go ahead, find out how many people disappeared, or have been murdered or kidnapped." But in some cases in Latin America, they do not even name the alleged perpetrators. It is just a way of exposing what happened, of preparing a historical record for the future.

The third reason, I would say, is that the years of fratricidal civil war, normally between security forces and guerrillas, placed, I think, peace above justice through prosecution as a sort of national priority. People feel that the only way of achieving reconciliation is through this total healing process. To them, the healing process is more important than justice proper.

Now, I have a lot of doubts. A lot of people from American NGOs and from Serbia and Croatia suggested that a truth and reconciliation commission should be set up to gradually replace the Yugoslavia Tribunal. I feel that probably this is a way of watering down and probably forgetting about justice. I agree that justice cannot achieve reconciliation, probably only in some instances. I have said it so many times, and I know that it is a cliché, that not all Serbs are sinners, but only those four or five people. So we in a way absolve the whole group; we move away from collective responsibility to individual responsibility. Actually, they go on hating each other even after trial. The reconciliation is really peace in your soul and reconciliation for the victims of horrible crimes and for those who are put in prison for those crimes. This peace cannot be achieved, even for the victims who have suffered so much. But I would say that at least you have these advantages. First, there is the establishment of a thorough historical record. In a way, this was the major achievement in Nuremberg. In Nuremberg, although the judgment was so poor from a legal viewpoint, the historical record established by the court was very, very good, because it was based on evidence and on thorough cross-examination.

The second advantage, I would say, is retribution. Let us be very clear, I am speaking of retribution and the stigma placed on those who have committed the worst atrocities. And then, third, I would say again, citing the wonderful sentence by Jankélévitch, quoted by Elie Wiesel in the *Barbie* case. Before the court here in France, Jankélévitch said, "Let us not kill those people twice. You killed them the first time because you killed them physically, and the second time because you simply forgot about them. You forgot the victims' names, and you forgot what the perpetrators did." I think that this is very profoundly true. You should not kill them twice. You must at least remember who committed those atrocious crimes and the victims of those crimes.

I would say that these are the few advantages of criminal justice vis-à-vis truth and reconciliation commissions. On the other hand, I can see why in some Latin American countries it is absolutely impossible to set up tribunals.

Ronald DWORKIN: The last point is very important because this trend, which includes the *Pinochet* decision in London, may end by sharply restricting the ability of a particular country, like Chile or Argentina, to make a crucial decision for itself or to make a compromise that can prevent bloodshed. The choice is not just one between peace and seeking justice. It is often a choice between saving lives and serving a particular view of justice. When you pre-empt that choice at the international level by declaring that certain kinds of amnesty or forgiveness will not be respected internationally, you may be condemning people to death by making impossible a local decision that will end a civil war or a totalitarian regime. We can debate about whether justice includes retribution. I am less clear about that than perhaps you are. But when we celebrate the advances in international law that you describe, we have to accept that that there may be a cost in suffering and in human life.

Gil Carlos RODRIGUEZ IGLESIAS: Even from that perspective, international criminal justice is progressing. In the current state of international law, which gives universal jurisdiction to national courts, I think that the risk that you are mentioning is greater if national courts of other countries exercise that universal jurisdiction than if you have a specific international criminal court that certainly will be in a much better position from two points of view: first, to get evidence, because it is set up for that, and second, to take into consideration practical elements about political questions.

Ronald DWORKIN: You mean in the decision of whether to prosecute? If you have a rule established as a rule binding on that international tribunal, that it cannot respect certain local decisions to grant amnesty to a villain? The villain will be very aware of that, and much less likely to make a compromise that will bring a war to an end, or oppression to an end. How will that help?

Stephen BREYER: There is a role for plea-bargaining.

Ronald DWORKIN: But what would be the incentive to plea-bargain? Pinochet will know, or the Junta in Argentina will know, that they cannot enjoy the benefits of a certain deal. Perhaps, later, when a case arises someplace else, or in an international forum, there will be room for a bargain then. But that may not help now.

Stephen BREYER: Suppose that beforehand, say, in Colombia, it becomes important to assure military leaders that they will not later be put on trial before a human rights court in order to gain their agreement to call a halt to fighting. There should be a mechanism, say, through the UN, to work out an agreement in an appropriate case.

Robert BADINTER: Kofi Annan says that—because he knows the mandate of the United Nations, especially as the Secretary-General—nobody has the power to grant a bargaining agreement with criminals charged with crimes against humanity. Kofi Annan has no right to do that. The Security Council has no right to do it either.

Stephen BREYER: Do you think that it is progress or not progress?

Robert BADINTER: Progress, absolutely. I think that we are looking at a new world with a perspective based on the old order. If you want to have a new world with a rule of law, you cannot accept that tradition, a tradition not of bargaining, but of blackmail: "I shall keep on killing people and I shall retain power unless I have an amnesty or an assurance that I shall not be prosecuted." History says that no bloody dictator, indeed, no dictator at all, gives up power unless compelled to do so, unless he is forced out. No dictator leaves willingly. If he leaves, it is because he no longer can control the situation.

Stephen BREYER: There are soldiers who control certain areas of the country; there are deaths every day.

Robert BADINTER: And they say, "Tomorrow, if you grant us amnesty, we shall stop."

Stephen BREYER: The UN civil servants may believe that, by talking to both sides, there is a chance of reaching an agreement. But they also believe that the subject of amnesty will come up.

Robert BADINTER: It is not in the mandate of any negotiator, because you couldn't have that.

Stephen BREYER: Suppose a negotiator believes that, with the authority to discuss amnesty, he could start a discussion that would lead to peace.

Robert BADINTER: The negotiator operates under a mandate from the UN. He cannot possibly have the authority to grant an amnesty. Suppose the question came up during a discussion. Suppose someone said, "Okay, I am ready to surrender. Grant me amnesty. Give me an assurance that I shall not be prosecuted." The only possible response would be, "I do not have the authority to do so."

Stephen BREYER: I should like to ask a question. Is the status quo preferable? There are other possibilities. For example, the UN negotiator might be given the authority to discuss, but not to grant, an amnesty. He might have the authority only to make a recommendation.

Robert BADINTER: No, frankly speaking, I do not think that you could. You cannot change the Charter of the United Nations in this respect.

Ronald DWORKIN: There is a deep moral issue. On the one hand, as you say, to bargain with these people is already distasteful, and may be worse than distasteful. But you have to accept that, if you refuse to bargain, you are sentencing some people to misery and death. That is the price that insisting on purity requires. Perhaps the price should be paid. I am not ready to say that it should not. From the perspective of history, it may be better to pay that price now, for the sake of the rule of law in decades to come, and less suffering in the very long run. But we cannot ignore the price now, in the lives of human beings whose lives might otherwise be saved.

Robert BADINTER: We need not pose the question exactly that way. We have lived within a system where amnesty is possible, where a pardon at the national level is possible, and where the international community has not minded. The practice has always been to permit those who commit crimes against humanity, unless they are punished immediately, to live peaceful lives thereafter. They end up living happy lives. What exactly have been the results of this system as it is, up 'til now?

Ronald DWORKIN: Some people's lives have been saved.

Robert BADINTER: I do not believe it. Knowing that impunity can be granted, you go on fiercely practicing crime, like the Serbians did, because they always thought that nobody would take them up.

Ronald DWORKIN: Think of Argentina and Chile. You say no one gives up power willingly, but people give up power more quickly under some conditions than others. Of course, there are complex and perhaps intractable questions of psychology and human nature at issue here. Can we say that Pinochet would have been less likely to grasp dictatorial power, and abuse that power as he did, if he knew that at the end of the road there could be no effective amnesty for him no matter what happened? That sounds like an awfully speculative claim to me. Dictators do not think like that at the beginning. But is it likely that Pinochet surrendered power earlier because of the amnesty than he otherwise would? I think that the answer is yes. I see no reason to doubt that.

Robert BADINTER: Pinochet's regime was dying at the end. He could not keep himself in power much longer. But, I shall raise a more immediate issue that we have confronted these past few years, not years ago in the seventies, and not involving a dictator maintaining a dictatorship through dictatorial practices. It involves a matter that is fundamentally different, namely, the Yugoslav story that you have lived through. Suppose that you had been granted the powers that you actually needed to arrest Karadzic and Mladic. France did not play a brilliant role in the matter. We did not arrest Karadzic. Why not? Because (a) French soldiers might have been killed in action, and no French president wants to tell his fellow citizens that he has lost 10 men in action in order to arrest Karadzic; and (b) because of the continuously claimed fear that, if you arrest Karadzic, war will burst out again.

Antonio CASSESE: The Americans claim, and probably rightly so, that the French have some skeleton in the cupboard. They are alleged to have struck some political and military deals with Karadzic, back in 1992 and 1993. So, if arrested, he would have spilled the beans and said so many things.

Robert BADINTER: That is the kind of rumor that one power is always spreading about another. I could repeat worse rumors about others.

But it does not matter. I think that this reasoning was seriously wrong, and typically so. If Karadzic had been arrested, then the men in Belgrade would have known that they might be personally liable, which they did not believe. To this day, they do not really believe it. Mr. Milosevic and those beneath him would then have known that they were going to have to pay for their actions. Take a specific example. Suppose there had been a serious effort to arrest someone at the level of general or of colonel, someone who decided that a unit was free to take a village and then do what it wanted. If those men had, at the beginning of the Kosovo war, been arrested and surrendered to the tribunal, then those who became involved in crimes would have known that they would be held personally responsible for those crimes.

Robert BADINTER: But at the time they committed those crimes, there was not yet any international criminal court.

Antonio CASSESE: I am afraid I disagree. To my regret, it is very clear from past and present history that neither the prospect of an amnesty nor the prospect of being brought to trial for crimes against humanity diverts or dissuades generals or the military from committing atrocities. I agree with you, Ron. Actually, that prospect can push you into committing even more atrocities. I remember, for instance, when the Kosovo war started, the prosecutor, a Canadian former judge, Louise Arbour, decided to make public a secret indictment against Arkan. We judges knew that it had been kept secret for three years. She said, "I will disclose this indictment so that people who are now fighting under the orders of Arkan in Kosovo will know that they may be brought to trial because their boss is already regarded by me, the Chief Prosecutor, as one of the worst criminals in modern history." And yet those people in Kosovo went on committing atrocities, even more atrocities. So the Prosecutor's action was of no deterrent value. Neither amnesty nor the prospect of a criminal court has any deterrent effect on the commission of crimes. I agree with you that both solutions, both options, can push you to commit even more crimes. Because in any case, if I go on committing atrocities, even worse atrocities, I will be granted an amnesty or, in any case, I may be brought to trial. Let me just simply kill people and leave not one witness. Everybody should be killed. Everybody. If we have witnesses . . . For Sbrebenica, we found a key witness—a man who had been lying under a huge pile of corpses. He was a very poor man, a very old man. He described very vividly in court how he had managed to survive. He saw Mladic four times. When Mladic and the others disappeared, he came out. He was in the fourth layer of bodies. And then this poor man started shouting, "Is there anyone alive?" And of the thousands of people all dead, he found only one, who was wounded, and together, although they were wounded, they went away. But the purpose of criminals is to kill everybody. Sometimes, luckily, they make mistakes and leave one man alive. But they go to the bitter end. They try to kill as many as possible. *Si! si! si!* Sbrebenica was in July 1995. We were set up in November 1993. I remember, I was almost crying in The Hague. We were there, and we played no role whatsoever. They did not fear us.

Robert BADINTER: Because no means were granted to you.

Antonio CASSESE: They did not care, they did not care. They knew very well.

Robert BADINTER: But at that time neither would the promise of amnesty have changed their behavior.

Antonio CASSESE: No, that is why . . . You, I think, raised the right moral issue. We balance these two requirements. And I am afraid that there is no answer, because, in any case, they go on. In any case they will go on killing as many people as possible.

Ronald DWORKIN: The question becomes agonizing only when people see a genuine possibility of a deal in the offing. It may be a local deal, as in the South American cases, or it may be a deal with UN mediators, which Steve was talking about. It could arise in many ways. I think I see the moral reasons for a kind of rigidity, as a general rule, so that no such deals could be made. But surely there is a moral case for flexibility too.

Robert BADINTER: That is in the hands of the *procureur,* if any. But you cannot put out in the rule of law that the pardon will be granted regardless of the horror of the threat. You cannot.

Ronald DWORKIN: I am thinking about the power of the people most concerned to decide their own fates. It is about the power of the Argentinians or the Chileans or South Africans or other people who have suffered to say, "Yes, this is a deal, and we want it. We hate our dictators, but we see a way to end the dictatorship by forgoing retribution." Why isn't the decision whether that is right or wrong up to them? Should international law reply that it isn't up to them, that the fate of others in the future is at stake, that those with most at stake now cannot sacrifice the future for their own sakes? Perhaps. I am inclined, in fact, to think so. But the question is so hard, and it is so hard to have a confident opinion.

Dieter GRIMM: And I think that the way is to find a hypothetical balance for a certain period of time as to what will save more lives and what will sacrifice more lives. This balance can have a different result in each case. The *Schleyer* decision of the Federal Constitutional Court is an example. Schleyer, then head of the German industry, had been kidnapped by terrorists, who threatened to kill him if the government refused to release Ulrike Meinhoff and her companions. Schleyer's family sought an injunction by the Constitutional Court obliging the government to fulfill the conditions of the terrorists. The Court did not grant the injunction and based its judgment on the hypothetical balance. It argued that probably more people would lose their lives if the government had to comply with the demand of the terrorists. But in a case like the one we are discussing, the balance might have gone the other way. Of course, it remains a hypothetical balance. What would really have happened remains uncertain.

Gil Carlos RODRIGUEZ IGLESIAS: That is all highly political, but I do not think that you can go as far as to say that the evolution of international law is likely to give rise to more deaths and suffering in general. But I think that you are encountering the kind of problems that you always encounter at a purely national level, *i.e.*, problems of balance. I insist on one point: I think that, in an international jurisdiction like your court in The Hague, through the powers of the prosecutor, you might be in a better position to consider these problems than when actions are brought before national courts. I am sensitive to that because, as you know, my country is the chosen forum for proceedings against Pinochet, the leaders of the Junta of Argentina, and others. The evaluation of the impact of all these procedures, in Chile, Argentina, and Guatemala, is, of course, very controversial. In Chile, the whole case has had a very positive effect. It might turn out to strengthen the rule of law in Chile and to strengthen the power of the state to punish behavior that a few years ago seemed to escape any control. But the fact that it is precisely in Spain that the cases were brought is perceived by large portions of the population as judicial imperialism of a former colonial power. That does complicate things a bit. But then I think, from a political point of view, Felipe González was one of the few political leaders in Spain who utterly spoke against Spanish jurisdiction and said that this would be more appropriate for an international court to bring more legitimacy to the trial of Pinochet. This was not popular. He was reluctant to exercise Spanish jurisdiction because he thought that the case was only appropriate for Chilean or an international jurisdiction.

Robert BADINTER: But you could have extradited him and sent him back to Chile.

Gil Carlos RODRIGUEZ IGLESIAS: But Chile would have had to have been ready to take him.

Robert BADINTER: The Spanish could have waited until the extradition order had been prepared and then asked Chile if it wanted to try Pinochet. Here, we have one of the most serious problems of our time. We must never forget the victims in this affair. A crime against humanity is not a slogan. It is not a juridical concept. It refers to thousands of people who have been murdered or raped.

There comes a time when a dictator, such as Pinochet, says: "All right, no one wants me any more, or, at least a majority of the Chilean people do not want me. I am old and tired. Make me a senator for life, and put a clause in the Constitution that says I am immune from prosecution. That is the price you must pay for democracy. Add an amnesty for the Generals, etc."

A majority of the people of the new democratic Chilean nation accept this. You ask, why then should we contest it? But when you listen to the victims, the survivors, the families of those who were tortured by the Pinochet gang, they ask what right or title you have to prevent justice from taking place. How can you take justice and bury it under the table forever? What authorizes you to do that? Rule by democracy?

Ronald DWORKIN: We do not know. Doesn't it depend on what the people of the country as a whole—not just those who have suffered and want retribution but those who will suffer and want peace—decide? Isn't that democracy?

Robert BADINTER: Not in Pinochet's era. He was just staying in power, and that is all.

Ronald DWORKIN: But we are talking about a general principle. Whatever you think about the details of the Chilean case, there are surely cases—there will surely be cases—in which whether a dictator goes quietly depends on what deal he can strike for himself. We must imagine the voices of those who will beg for that deal because it will save lives. I do not mean, as I have now said too many times, that international law should make such deals impossible. But we must not pretend that it is an easy choice.

Stephen BREYER: Compromise is possible. You yourself believe that an international prosecutor (unlike an Italian prosecutor) should have the authority to decide whether a case is worth prosecuting. In the United States, a prosecutor can recommend a sentence to the judge. You could have the same kind of system in respect to amnesty. The UN negotiator could promise to recommend to the international court prosecutor that he honor an amnesty. In the United States, the prosecutor can promise to call a judge's attention to the matter and to recommend a particular sentence. The prosecutor does no more. The decision is made by the judge.

Robert BADINTER: That could be a power granted the international criminal court prosecutor, but that does not solve the basic problem. Does a majority have the right to say, "Let us turn the page of history no matter how bloody it is and forget about justice?"

Dieter GRIMM: It depends on how many more lives can be saved. I would not say that this is the only principle at stake. The rule of law is also a principle at stake, and I think that history tells that one can expand the scope for applying the rule of law gradually. I think that this is the message of what you told us, in a way.

Robert BADINTER: CASSESE, you cannot believe that using the instruments of justice could increase the risk of crimes?

Antonio CASSESE: Sometimes, yes.

Robert BADINTER: As when hostages are taken? When one who takes hostages turns to the police and says, "I shall kill them unless you give me a car and immunity"? Is that what you mean?

Antonio CASSESE: Yes.

Robert BADINTER: At such a moment, justice surrenders to crime.

Antonio CASSESE: I can tell you my experience in a Spanish prison, when I was president of the Council of Europe's Committee Against Torture, and we inspected prisons and police stations everywhere in Europe. I had a very nice talk with a tall man who had been sentenced to 250 years in prison. He was a killer, a murderer, a terrorist, and so on. And then he said, "Last week I killed a man here in the prison." I said, "What?" He said, "Yes, he's a sexual offender. He had raped his daughter and so on." And I asked, "But how did you manage?" He replied, "Well, I have nothing to lose. I can go on killing anybody in this prison, as long as I am able to do so, because I am being sentenced to 250 years in prison for my past murders." At some point, one has really nothing to lose, and so goes on killing. And he was able to kill somebody else.

Gil Carlos RODRIGUEZ IGLESIAS: I would like to insist that the problem that we are talking about is not exclusive to international justice. It is a general problem, and I think that it is very important to keep in mind that the problems of international criminal justice are mainly problems of lack of means and also the need to rely on the cooperation of the states, as Antonio CASSESE has stressed. Thus, international criminal justice is at a very early stage of its history and the issue is mainly a lack of efficiency rather than its alleged danger for the national processes of peace.

Robert BADINTER: What you are describing is not quite the problem. If we are to create an international criminal court, let us at least have the courage to give it the means necessary for it to act. Once such a decision has been made, one should not play a double hand, as happened to you at The Hague. We create the jurisdiction, but we control its exercise by keeping the evidence and the money from it. We prevent it from acting by not arresting people. Still, we say, "Aha! I have proved that I want those who commit crimes against humanity to be punished." That is what we have seen.

The first question, I believe, lies elsewhere. First, from a national perspective: Does a majority have the power to say, "It is over." Does the majority have the right to say that crimes against humanity, even genocide—crimes subject to no statute of limitations, crimes that you can always prosecute, crimes that the passage of time does not affect—will not be prosecuted? That is the first matter. We turn the page to help establish democracy. Of course, if we do so and another dictator emerges, the game will start all over again. But, that is still the first question. Can we accept an amnesty for crimes against humanity? After all, in Germany I never heard anyone say that we should forget about Nazi criminals after 10 years. No one has ever said such a thing, for it is simply too much that humanity . . .

Ronald DWORKIN: Because that was not how that war ended. That war ended with the Nazis not in a position to demand anything. But, of course, it is a question that historians will endlessly return to: whether the war had to end that way; whether, if the Allies had not demanded unconditional surrender, the war would have ended earlier; and whether the world would have been better off if it had. I suspect that there are no persuasive answers to those questions.

Robert BADINTER: Yes, but note. Some did say that the war could have ended sooner if a general pardon had been granted to Nazi war criminals, provided they got rid of Hitler. The answer was no. But what I mean without going to these extremes . . .

Ronald DWORKIN: I am not saying that unconditional surrender was the wrong policy, but only that it was a policy and that it represented a genuine choice.

Robert BADINTER: And that is the question. Will we admit that crimes against humanity need not be prosecuted because a democratic state has the right to grant an amnesty? That is a point.

Point two is the following: Once a new national assembly has granted an amnesty, should the international community, which has promised an international prosecution, impose its will upon the national community?

Ronald DWORKIN: And should it?

Robert BADINTER: Should it say to the legal authorities of the national community, "Okay, Pinochet will not be prosecuted in Chile, but Pinochet has committed crimes against humanity. And we do not care about your amnesty."

There it is. The two questions are distinct. The first question is preliminary. It is not of the same order. The second question is far more complex. It involves the relation between national and international sovereignties.

Ronald DWORKIN: The two questions are deeply connected. If we answer the second question in a particular way, then we all but answer the first question as well, though not entirely because a dictator could resolve never to go abroad or otherwise to put himself at risk of a foreign or international prosecution. But the threat of such a prosecution would still limit any local option of amnesty.

Robert BADINTER: You know that this sharp limitation does not exist at least for most crimes.

It is left to national justice. There is a boulevard open for those who have committed crimes against humanity.

Ronald DWORKIN: Yes, but we are discussing a movement which, as I took you to agree earlier, threatens to close down the boulevard. And some steps in that direction, as in the Pinochet decision, have already been taken. The question is whether we should try to encourage and intensify those steps.

Robert BADINTER: I shall speak bluntly. In my opinion, at this time, there is no possibility that those who now commit crimes against humanity will be punished internationally, except within the terms of the 1949 Convention and the international prohibition against torture. That is so for one simple reason. There is now no international tribunal for trials like the Tribunal for Yugoslavia. That Tribunal was created after the commission of crimes. A Security Council decision was needed to set it up: Chapter 7. In the Security Council, five members have a right of veto. Among them are the United States and China, each of which voted against the creation of an international criminal court. There is also Russia with the problem of Chechnya on its hands. It will never permit the creation of a new criminal court, not for Indonesia or anywhere else. There will not be any new ad hoc international criminal court created in the foreseeable future—because of the Russians.

Antonio CASSESE: They are now setting up a tribunal for Cambodia.

Robert BADINTER: They are creating a tribunal for Cambodia, but for matters that go back 30 years. I was talking about matters taking place today. As to that, no, for we have the example of Chechnya. I see no serious possibility at present that crimes committed today will be prosecuted. I speak of today's or tomorrow's crimes against humanity, not those committed in Cambodia where the regime has changed and the criminals are now for the most part old. That is because there will be no new international criminal court in the near future because of Chechnya and because the international criminal court lacks retroactive power. It will not be able to assert its legal authority until 60 nations have ratified the treaty. And the tribunal will not have the power to consider crimes committed before its legal authority takes effect. So, as long as ratification of the Treaty of Rome is delayed, only national jurisdictions in the places where the crimes are committed will be able to prosecute those who commit them. That is why I believe that we are in a period that is fortunate for those who commit crimes against humanity.

Of course, there is also a universal jurisdiction. I wanted to talk about it as well. It is not a good solution. It leaves the matter in the hands of activist national judges, or perhaps of judges who are not activists but who simply have an inclination one way or the other. There is no unified approach to the prosecution of even the most unheard-of crimes.

Nations sign treaties but they do not read them. They committed themselves to universal jurisdiction, or so they thought. Bologna! Now universal jurisdiction exists, but they do not want to respect it. They are unwilling to move backwards. They cannot do so. So here is the present state of the art: There is no ad hoc international jurisdiction in respect to crimes committed now. And the members of the UN Security Council are unwilling to create that jurisdiction in the foreseeable future. We will not be able to use the new international criminal court, for it will not have the right to look back, to consider crimes committed now. All that remains are those international conventions, which the nations signed but did not intend to apply.

The judges have read those conventions. They have discovered them and have said that the king is vulnerable. "Come here, Pinochet, you are exposed and vulnerable." And suddenly the public has discovered that that is so. He can be prosecuted. What a marvelous story. And, believe me, judicial activism is not going to stop. Thus, we are entering a period of a certain international anarchy, all in the cause of justice. It is extraordinary.

This does not advance us far in respect to the basic question under discussion, which is the conflict between an amnesty at the national level and the international legal order. That is an important and fundamental matter. You do have a very strong point. Why should foreign judges be able to enforce their own judgment contrary to the democratic will of a foreign nation? On the other hand, one might ask how a majority can set aside the demands of justice.

Antonio CASSESE: With all due respect, I do not agree with you about the Security Council. Actually, you may know that the Security Council—the five permanent members, including China and Russia—is keen to set up ad hoc tribunals, of course not about Chechnya, not about Indonesia, but other cases, Sierra Leone, for instance.

They are keen to do so precisely to undermine the authority and the credibility of the ICC, the International Criminal Court. Why? Because they do not like universal jurisdiction, or the thought of an international court that one day might deal with Chechnya or Tibet. But they do like a selective approach. They have taken a selective approach, and I am pretty sure they will go on doing so. David Scheffer, the U.S. ambassador at large for war crimes, suggested to the Security Council that it set up a tribunal to bring to trial Iraqi leaders, not necessarily Saddam Hussein, but other people who might be apprehended abroad. They do like the selective approach. The selective approach stands a chance of being taken again and again so that the Americans, just to clear their conscience, will say, "We are not in principle against the international criminal jurisdiction. We simply do not like this ICC. Let's go for ad hoc tribunals."

Robert BADINTER: But no! Here, you have two eminent members of the American community. The American Senate is dead set against all international jurisdiction. One should read what Senator Jesse Helms has written about Madame del Ponte in a congressional bill. He wrote, "A woman called del Ponte dares claim explanation from the American officers about their behavior." It is not about the International Criminal Court. Madame del Ponte is not the prosecutor of the International Criminal Court, which does not even exist yet. He does not want Americans on the witness stand. He is not saying, "Do not touch this issue." He means, "Do not ask them to come to the witness stand."

What about in cases where there has been American military intervention, as in most of the countries? The events in Cambodia are history now, and it was a communist regime that committed the crimes. Take the case of Iraq, for example. If you start investigating the crimes committed by the Iraqi regime, you will, by necessity, investigate the NATO intervention.

The response is very positive when you indict Milosevic, but when you want to call up on the witness stand a chief of staff of any army, then, as I have seen in France, the military says, "We are not used to answering such questions, and what we decide is fit for our soldiers. We refuse to go."

Antonio CASSESE: Only the French, the Americans, and the Brits have gone to The Hague and testified very well. Maybe sometimes they said, "Since I may disclose confidential information, or information covered by national security, I want to be heard in closed session, *in camera.*" But the French are the only ones who raised hell about the possibility of French soldiers testifying.

Robert BADINTER: Regarding Kosovo?

Antonio CASSESE: No, no, before Kosovo. The Americans do not resist, not as long as they are authorized by the Pentagon, and they normally are.

Robert BADINTER: May I remind you that, thanks to the efforts of a few fanatics, among whom I count myself, the President of the Republic was convinced that, in respect to the International Criminal Court, French judges would judge the French. Since French judges would judge French officials, there was no risk in making French officers subject to an international court. If a serious indictment was at issue, the case would be transferred to French authorities. Once the President understood that, he said okay. We modified the Constitution and we ratified the Treaty. We are the eighth country in the world to have ratified it. We are the second in Europe. The first was Italy. This is simply to say that explanations sometimes help.

If you explain to the American public that the only consequence of ratifying the Treaty of Rome is that cases involving Americans will be submitted to American jurisdictions, then . . . Of course, considering the proceedings in the Senate, this is a purely hypothetical matter, for the Senate will not ratify it. But I do not see what the problem is. You trust your own jurisdiction, don't you? So why is it a problem to say that the international court will act only if national courts refuse to act or there is a fraud? That is not true in respect to American jurisdictions.

Dieter GRIMM: Is that desirable? Every claim that one country can make can be made by other countries as well, and that would be the end of international criminal justice. Why are there privileged countries whose citizens are only tried by their own courts?

Antonio CASSESE: No, it's a basic rule.

Robert BADINTER: It is a rule applicable to everyone.

Antonio CASSESE: The court is auxiliary and complementary. If the nation is unwilling or unable (say, because of the collapse of the judicial system) to prosecute someone, then, and only then, can the ICC step in.

Stephen BREYER: Then why is the United States against it?

Ronald DWORKIN: If the national judges acquit, isn't that almost always, as a practical matter, the end?

Robert BADINTER: That is the end of the matter, even if the nation decides not to prosecute. We trust the judges.

Stephen BREYER: Isn't there any review?

Antonio CASSESE: Well, of course, there is a sort of power of scrutiny by the ICC, but not in the case of the U.S. where you have very serious court-martials. The tribunals are first-rate, and people take everything seriously.

Ronald DWORKIN: Even in court-martials?

Stephen BREYER: Are there defenses that American law, but not the Treaty, would provide?

Robert BADINTER: No, that is not the point. They are concerned about the preliminary proceedings. The matter has been depicted as follows: There will be leftists from all countries, say Amnesty International, who will provide the international court's independent prosecutor with false information about the behavior of our soldiers. Then the press will make a tremendous fuss about the Americans' activities. The press will write, "Ha. The international prosecutor is now investigating the behavior of the American military forces." (I have heard the French sing that song, so I can tell you about it.) The result is that American forces will be severely criticized. There will be an international press campaign against the American military forces. The soldiers will be handed over, for that is just what happens in such cases. Eventually, American courts will take care of the matter, but not without tremendous damage to America's reputation. Why should we expose ourselves to this kind of slander? There, that is the point.

Ronald DWORKIN: That I can understand.

Stephen BREYER: Perhaps if there were investigations of Americans in different parts of the world, and the results were perfectly acceptable to American opinion . . .

Robert BADINTER: Yes, but let us not wait and see how it operates. In the meantime, not only will we not ratify it, we also do not want others to ratify it. This is to say that the story of the International Criminal Court is a story of continuous international attacks.

Stephen BREYER: I reserve judgment. I would like to read the Treaty itself. When I read the treaty governing torture, I found that it defined "torture" in very broad terms, making internationally un-lawful police activity that might be commonly carried on—for ex-ample, putting strong psychological pressure upon a suspect with-out any physical interference. The United States entered a reserva-tion in respect to that definition. Perhaps it would be possible to narrow some of the definitions, thereby making the Treaty more ac-ceptable.

Antonio CASSESE: We have a treaty here on this particular point of na-tional, as opposed to international, jurisdiction. The court can only proceed and decide that the issue is admissible if it is proved that the state is unwilling or unable generally to carry out the investiga-tion or prosecution. The court cannot proceed if the state has inves-tigated a case over which it has jurisdiction and has decided not to prosecute the person concerned. It is very clear. It leaves to coun-tries broad discretion.

Robert BADINTER: No, the problem is more serious than that. The In-ternational Criminal Court does not have universal jurisdiction, nor does it fall within the aegis of the Security Council. Rather, that court's territorial jurisdiction is contiguous with the territories of the nations that have ratified it. And, for a matter to fall within that jurisdiction, either the crime must take place within those territo-ries or the perpetrators must be nationals of one of those nations. In other words, there is no threat to the United States.

Antonio CASSESE: Yes, there is. An American who commits a crime in France, a contracting party, may be brought before the International Criminal Court. This is the Americans' worry.

Robert BADINTER: Except in that kind of case. If he has committed a crime in France, he will be judged in France.

Antonio CASSESE: Of course. But if there is an extradition . . .

Robert BADINTER: The International Criminal Court does not have universal jurisdiction. Its jurisdiction is limited from the outset. The United States still says that it is not interested and that it does not want to ratify the Treaty. But it is also leading a campaign against ratification. That is what worries me. The United States is the world's leading power, and when it says it does not want some-thing, it has ways, in many instances, of preventing ratification.

It is just the opposite with respect to the European Union. The EU wants all the European nations to ratify the Treaty of Rome. And that will happen.

We shall continue, and we shall now discuss the non-criminal international judge.

Gil Carlos RODRIGUEZ IGLESIAS: Even if there are many differences between traditional international criminal justice and the international criminal justice that one might call "supra-national," there nonetheless are two common elements, which are linked to today's discussion. Keep in mind the fact that the traditional international justice system was designed to regulate differences among nations, while the new forms of justice that we see emerging do more. They involve new criminal justice institutions that apply the law very much in the way that national legal institutions traditionally have done. And that fact means that they constitute a new element in respect to the international community.

In large part, this phenomenon, in its many manifestations, reflects an important development in international law. The human person, and not only nations or international organizations, has become a subject of rights and obligations. And international courts can guarantee those rights and obligations. This new form of international justice has again focused attention upon the nature of state sovereignty as traditionally conceived. It has done so, not as a general matter, but, as Antonio CASSESE has pointed out, in particular contexts. These include human rights (even if only at a regional level), international crimes, and economic integration (and perhaps regional political integration).

The most recent and most spectacular manifestation of this phenomenon is international criminal justice. I shall comment on this matter only to the extent of pointing out that, in my view, international criminal justice, to a degree, constitutes a corollary, and a manifestation at the judicial level, of the development of international *jus cogens, i.e.,* of the development of obligatory norms from which nations may not depart and which primarily concern international crimes. I shall turn, however, to the phenomenon of international justice as it arises in the European Court of Human Rights and in the Court of Justice of the European Community.

Still, we must not forget that the supra-national model of justice is spreading throughout the world, even though it has not elsewhere developed as fully as within Europe. Thus, in the field of human rights, we should keep in mind the Inter-American Human Rights Court, which sits in San José, Costa Rica. It applies the 1969

American Convention on Human Rights, which took effect in 1978. It is enforced through a system similar to the former European system of human rights protection, a system based upon a commission and a court. We should also keep in mind the African Court for Human Rights and the Rights of Peoples. A 1998 agreement, which has not yet taken effect, provides for the creation of that court.

In the field of regional integration, I should mention the EFTA Court, created in 1994 by the European Economic Area Agreement. It is a twin of the ECJ (European Court of Justice) and also sits in Luxembourg. We should also recall the Andean Community Court, created in 1989, which sits in Quito, Ecuador. It was modeled after the ECJ. Its jurisdiction was enlarged in 1996, and it has already rendered nearly 200 decisions. They have principally involved interlocutory questions, particularly those raised by the Conseil d'Etat of Colombia.

I should similarly mention the Court for the Common Market of Eastern and Southern Africa. That Court, provisionally sitting in Lusaka, Zambia, has operated since 1998. And, I shall mention the Court for the West African Economic and Monetary Union. It sits in Ouagadougou, Burkina Faso. It began handing down decisions in 1998, and it is modeled after the ECJ.

Finally, I shall mention the Court of Justice for Central America. It works within the Central American Integration System, created in 1991 by the Tegucigalpa Protocol. It sits in Managua, it has been operational since 1994, and it has been granted large, heterogeneous, and ambitious jurisdictional authority.

The existence of these diverse courts shows that the supra-national model of justice is developing considerably. But I shall focus my remarks upon the two European courts. And I shall first consider the European Human Rights Court.

I wish to emphasize at the outset that the role, indeed the very nature, of the Court has been transformed in recent years, in that it has become a far more "supra-national" court than it was originally. When the Court was created, it shared with classical international courts two characteristic features. First, one had to exhaust all internal remedies before invoking the Court's jurisdiction. Second, the Court's procedures were not fixed.

Modification of this second feature has had revolutionary consequences. In an initial period, the Court developed the practice of permitting the victim of an alleged human rights violation to participate in a proceeding alongside the European Rights Commission, which, alone, was, formally speaking, a party. In a second period, in Protocol #9, the Court recognized the right of individuals to invoke the Court's jurisdiction, and it followed this up in Protocol #11 by making this right an essential element of the system.

A second decisive element in the evolution of the European Human Rights Court concerns the Court's own perception of its role as a guarantor of a "constitutional instrument of the European Public Order" in respect to human rights.

The result of these changes is that, abstracting from technicalities, the Strasbourg Court plays, in respect to human rights, the role of a court of appeals for decisions from national supreme and constitutional courts. Thus, for example, in respect to Spain (though the same is true elsewhere), one first seeks justice before an ordinary judge, then before the Constitutional Court, and finally at Strasbourg.

With respect to the ECJ, I should like to emphasize as a preliminary matter that it is generally conceded that the role that the ECJ has played in the Community has been from the beginning, and remains, a decisive role. But what is that role? In trying to synthesize the most important elements of the Court's contribution to the building of a Community legal order, I shall emphasize three aspects: first, guaranteeing fundamental economic liberty; next, developing fundamental principles of the Community's legal order; and, finally, the protection of fundamental rights.

As to the first point, I shall repeat that the Court has interpreted the fundamental economic freedoms in a way that is both anchored in the Treaty's terms and gives full effect to its provisions. It has prevented the Member States from deflecting the thrust of those liberties, and it has thereby decisively contributed to the effectiveness, first, of the Common Market and, then, of national markets.

The second element that I mentioned constitutes, in my opinion, the most decisive aspect, and, in a certain sense, the most activist aspect, of the Court's jurisprudence. It consists of the development of the fundamental principles of the Community's legal order. In fact, the Treaty itself does not expressly set forth the most characteristic of those principles. Rather, they were developed in the Court's own jurisprudence. The basic principles consist of (1) the principle of direct effect; (2) the principle of primacy; and (3) the principle of Member State responsibility for damages caused individuals by violations of Community law.

These principles rest upon a single fundamental decision, the 1963 case *Van Gend en Loos*. That decision enunciated the "direct effect" principle, while setting forth an argument that showed the existence of a critical jurisprudential choice. It was an occasion when a court found itself confronted with a fundamental choice. In that 1963 case, the Court made the choice that made the Community's legal order a legal order whose subjects are not only nations but also individual citizens. Over and above the strictly legal matter, this jurisprudential choice expressed a conception of the Community according to which it was not only a community of member states, but also a community of peoples and of citizens. In my opinion, this basic decision was based upon solid legal arguments and was in conformity with the spirit of the Treaty.

The third element that I said was particularly important consists of the jurisprudential development of protection through Community law of fundamental rights. That development is all the more remarkable because the Treaty says nothing specifically about the protection of basic rights, which are at most indirectly referred to in the Preamble. Now, the Court jurisprudence has incorporated within Community law the substance of the European Human Rights Convention, as well as fundamental rights protected by the national constitutions of the Member States. The Court did so by considering general principles.

Alongside granting protection to fundamental rights as they are ordinarily understood, the Court has also interpreted fundamental economic liberties in a way that protects individual personal rights, assimilating them, in a sense, to fundamental rights. This amounts to a great transformation, for the Treaty conceived of economic liberties (*i.e.*, the freedom of circulation of goods, of services, of workers, of investment, of economic creation) largely in terms of rational economic policy. The same is true of the principle of non-discrimination between men and women, a matter originally written into the Treaty to make certain that the same constraints would apply to businesses from different Member States. Thus, the Court has transformed what was originally, in the

Treaty's logic, a functionally economic matter into a source of personal individual rights connected with fundamental rights.

Finally, we should remember in this context that the notion of the European citizen, expressly established after the Maastricht Treaty, was already latent in the Court's jurisprudence, insofar as the Court had extended its broad concept of fundamental economic liberty into the area of the application of the principle of non-discrimination by reason of nationality.

The Court has been able to play this role because of its institutional position and its jurisdictional authority. Compared to classic international jurisdictional authority, there is an essential difference: Its jurisdictional authority is obligatory; there is no need to obtain any supplementary consent from Member States.

I also believe that an essential aspect of the explanation of the success of the Community's jurisdictional system lies in the cooperation between the ECJ and national jurisdictions. In effect, we have built a judicial system that, even without text, is based upon the principle of subsidiarity. We have made sure that ordinary judges in national jurisdictions are the ones who ordinarily apply Community law and who protect the rights of citizens. We have reserved to the ECJ the kind of jurisdictional authority that national judges cannot exercise. One could not, for example, ask national judges to consider the lawfulness of the acts of Community institutions. One could not ask national courts to declare that Member States have failed to live up to their Community obligations. The Court has given the means, through the device of interlocutory questions, to interpret Community law. This guarantees decentralized application of Community law through national courts, while respecting the need for a uniform interpretation, and, hence, the equality of rights among citizens who seek to have their rights protected by judges from different countries.

The role of that national judge, defined in the Treaty, has also developed naturally in light of the three principles I mentioned: direct effect, primacy, and responsibility. The Court set forth these principles, but national judges have applied them. Indeed, it is national judges who protect a citizen's rights through the application of the "direct effect" principle. They are the ones who are faced with the direct conflicts between national rules and Community rules and who must resolve those conflicts in favor of Community law. They are the ones who must declare that a member state has violated Community law and require it to indemnify an individual.

Underlying the jurisprudence that sets forth these different principles, one can find the principle, set forth more or less explicitly depending upon the case, of granting effective protection to the rights of individuals through Community law. That principle has led the Court to ask much of the national judge, in the name of effectively protecting the rights of the parties. If necessary, national judges must even set aside their own system's basic jurisdiction-protecting rules to the extent that those rules would end up limiting the protections accorded the rights of the parties. The most spectacular aspect of these demands for protecting effective jurisdiction is contained in the jurisprudence concerning provisional jurisdictional protection. It concerns the *Factortame* case,[7] in which the Court, responding to questions from the House of Lords, said that, even if national law does not permit a court to provide provisional protection from a law of Parliament, a national judge can, and must, grant that protection as a matter of Community law. It is interesting to note that this jurisprudence concerning provisional protection, which some considered a kind of constitutional revolution in the United Kingdom, was introduced by the House of Lords. I want to emphasize that the Court's jurisprudence has contributed to the expansion of judicial power and to effective jurisdictional protection in the Member States.

Finally, I should like to raise the question of the ECHR's and the ECJ's jurisdictional legitimacy. Are there specific problems of legitimacy that exist in respect to those Courts that do not exist in respect to national courts? First, is there a difference in this regard between the ECHR and the ECJ? With respect to this point, I do not agree that the ECHR has greater legitimacy than the ECJ because the members of the former are chosen by the parliamentary assembly of the Council of Europe (on the basis of lists proposed by Member States), while the members of the ECJ are chosen by the governments of the Member States. I should like to point out that we are chosen by the governments of the Member States acting together as a group. It is true, however, that, in practice, a judge proposed by one government is not turned down by the others. But, in principle, that possibility exists.

Regardless, I do not think that the different selection methods create any differences in respect to legitimacy. And that is not simply because many people mix up the Strasbourg Court with the Luxembourg Court. Even if they did not mix them up, it would seem to me, experts aside, that ordinary people have no idea how the judges at either Strasbourg or Luxembourg are selected. Nor even in judicial circles does the method of selection, in my opinion, have much of an impact on the perception of the legitimacy of one, or the other, Court.

As to legitimacy, both the ECHR and the ECJ enjoy widespread acceptance. That acceptance rests, in part, upon a purely juridical consideration, namely, that the authority of the Courts rests upon treaties that have granted it to them. It also rests, in part, upon the credibility that they have gained and which has ended up with widespread acceptance of their authority. This acceptance is confirmed by the fact that the authority of both Courts has been confirmed and enlarged on many occasions. In respect to the ECJ, this has taken place when the treaties have been modified in different ways during the last few years; the same has taken place in respect to the ECHR in light of Protocol #11.

I would also like to emphasize not only that the Luxembourg Court has seen the legitimacy of its authority widely accepted, but also that it has proved an important legitimating factor in respect to the entire Community edifice, insofar as a juridical kind of legitimacy can make up for the absence of direct democratic legitimacy (and I insist upon using the adjective "direct"). In this respect, I should like also to observe—going beyond the bounds of the judicial arena—that, in my opinion, even if an essentially juridical kind of legitimacy might have proved sufficient for the Community at the time when it was functionally integrating, the extension of the EU's authority to affect the lives of its citizens now demands a supplement of direct democratic legitimacy.

Stephen BREYER: You can read somewhat similar things in the letters of John Marshall. He thought it necessary that the Court act with the means at its disposal. Others among the Founding Fathers thought not. But it was necessary.

Dieter GRIMM: With regard to legitimacy, one can formulate as a general rule that the legitimacy of courts, as opposed to the legitimacy of other governmental branches, depends only to a very small degree on the way that judges get into office. The legitimacy of courts depends much more on their independence from those who nominate, appoint, or elect them, and, of course, it depends on whether courts succeed in demonstrating that they decide according to the law and not according to judges' personal interests or beliefs. Therefore, the question of the democratic legitimacy of judges is not of such importance if these other two requirements are guaranteed.

Stephen BREYER: Consider the following account: The people of our countries want (1) protection of fundamental rights, (2) a reasonably free market, and (3) a degree of integration among nations in order better to achieve economic and social prosperity. Judicial institutions can help them achieve these objectives: First, judges and courts are experts in applying basic principles to concrete cases. Second, judges know how to apply them in light of both justice and common sense (*pace* Ronnie). Third, judges also know how to develop the basic principles slowly. They begin with what is obvious, such as Articles 30 and 36 of the Treaty of Rome. After several years, they interpret the Articles as applying to every possible kind of obstacle to the free flow of commerce. And they adjust the legal web that they weave as different circumstances come to pass, for example, new conflicts among nations or institutions.

If people have these sorts of objectives, and if courts have these sorts of characteristics, why not give judges the power better to achieve the objectives?

Robert BADINTER: This is just a remark about the notion of "choice." I do not believe that there was a choice. Or, perhaps I should say that necessity dictates the choice. You cannot build something like the Community (as it was) or the Union (as it now is) without a regulating body any more than you could have the United States of America, a federation, without a Supreme Court. You need that mechanism or it will not work. What was not foreseen in advance was what the members would make of the Court. They could keep a very low profile or they could become activists. That was not predetermined. That is what is interesting. At the outset, the political choice is not voluntary, it is necessary. Afterwards, the European Community recognizes the wisdom of the action. But it is at this point that the match is played. This is where we hear references to the sorcerer's apprentice. That is because, sometimes, more likely in Strasbourg than in Luxembourg, the nation states must come to terms with domestic public opinion. When a European nation is condemned for torture, whether it be the U.K. with respect to prisoners in Ireland or France with respect to what happens at police headquarters, that nation receives a public blow. That is what happens, and it is moving to see it.

Stephen BREYER: Again, you can read some of what you have said in John Marshall's letters. He understood the need for judicial power.

Robert BADINTER: As a matter of comparative law research, someone should look at the original debates at the time a court was created, consider the founders' intentions, and then see what happened 50 or 100 years later.

Dieter GRIMM: May I just add one element that can explain the success of some courts, certainly of the European Court, but also of the American Supreme Court? The landmark decisions you mentioned, which shaped the European Community, *Van Gend en Loos* and the others, were made in politically unspectacular cases and without public notice. The third one was different, because the Court had already gained much attention. But these landmark decisions, whether you classify them as choice or not, did not emerge from highly visible political controversies. When the controversy came up, the law had already been established.

Ronald DWORKIN: Two ideas have emerged from our discussion that may seem in tension with each other. The first is that judges are creating an entire new international jurisprudence, and the second is that the legitimacy of what judges do depends on the plausibility of the claim that they are applying existing standards, not inventing new ones. The tension between these two suggestions is evident, and the danger is that, in combination, they mean that judicial legitimacy depends on a lie, which we cannot accept. So we should take seriously a different idea of legitimacy: that it depends not on pre-existing standards, but on the method through which judges develop new standards and new sources of standards. Even if we accept that in an important sense judges make law, that is, they can claim legitimacy for what they do because it is based on a certain kind of reasoning that is different from the reasoning of other political institutions, we can describe this, for constitutional courts within nations, as reasoning from the ideal of democracy. Majority rule is fair only when certain conditions are met, and it is the job of constitutional judges to explore what these conditions are, and how principles protecting them can be seen as embedded in the nation's culture and constitution. But can we make sense of this argument internationally? It is certainly easier to see how judges can appeal to conceptions of democracy embedded in the history and practice of particular nations. The challenge of this session is to see how far we can make the same kinds of arguments, to ground the legitimacy of judicial innovation, across nations with somewhat different histories, practices, and cultures.

Gil Carlos RODRIGUEZ IGLESIAS: I think that your idea is very important: legitimacy through methods. And I believe that this applies to all courts, but not necessarily in the same degree.

In the European Court, the concern with explaining the methods and with giving reasons in order to justify its own legitimacy to develop legal principles is something relatively new. My impression is that this concern has been growing more and more in the last 20 years. Probably, it was not necessary before because the legitimacy of the Court, which was supported by the experts in Community law, was not frequently challenged. Of course, occasionally it was. I remember Professor Duverger writing in *Le Monde* that the Court practiced a *léniniste* interpretation of the law.

Nowadays, European law is no more a matter for "European" specialists because it has an impact on most legal specialties. Thus, many jurists who do not specialize in European law have to deal with the case law of the Court in their area, and they tend to be critical. For instance, specialists in labor law or tax law are often very critical of the case law of the Court in these areas.

But, of course, there is also criticism on the development, by the case law, of basic principles. I myself have special experience with the principle of state liability, having been the judge *rapporteur* in the leading cases of *Francovich* in 1991,[8] and *Brasserie du Pêcheur/Factortame III*, in 1996.[9]

In *Francovich*, the Court declared for the first time that it is a principle of Community law that the Member States are obliged to make good on losses and damages caused to individuals by breaches of Community law for which the Member States can be held responsible. There was some criticism about the brief reasoning of this judgment and, in particular, about the lack of any explanation on the competence of the Court to develop such a principle.

A few years later, in *Brasserie du Pêcheur and Factortame III*, the Court had the opportunity, on the basis of specific and detailed questions referred by the German Bundesgerichtshof and the English High Court, not only to develop and refine the scope of the principle of state liability, but also to address the question of its own competence. Actually, in those cases, at least two governments submitted that the Court was not competent to develop a general principle of state responsibility (whereas other governments took a different position). On this point, the Court stressed that the existence and the scope of such a liability was a question of Treaty interpretation, for which it was competent. And, it held: "Since the Treaty contains no provision expressly and specifically governing the consequences of breaches of Community law by member states, it is for the Court, in pursuance of the task conferred on it by Article 164 of the Treaty of ensuring that in the interpretation and application of the Treaty the law is observed, to rule on such a question in accordance with generally accepted methods of interpretation, in particular by reference to the fundamental principles of the Community legal system and, where necessary, general principles common to the legal systems of the member states."[10]

Now, coming back to a more general perspective, I think that it is interesting to notice that the most activist decisions of the Court have been accepted and even confirmed by Treaty amendment or by practice. Thus, the decision of the Court on the *locus standi* of the European Parliament was, so to speak, constitutionalized in the Treaty of Maastricht. So was the case law of the Court on the protection of fundamental rights. And the principles of direct effect and primacy have been consistently considered as basic elements of the *acquis communautaire*, which new member states have to accept. In fact, when the United Kingdom acceded to the Community, the European Communities Act was adopted in order to be able to accept and to implement the principles of direct effect and primacy of Community law notwithstanding the doctrine of sovereignty of Parliament.

By the way, when Euroskeptics complain about these principles being the result of judicial activism, it has to be recalled that the existence and the scope of such principles were well known and present at the time of the accession of the United Kingdom.

Robert BADINTER: What you say about the U.K. is true. At this stage, I should like to return to the earlier discussion of how an international court, the International Criminal Court, could carry the day in light of the many who would benefit from an amnesty or of a nation's democratic determination that it wants to "turn the page." We asked ourselves what was possible or impossible, and that, I think, is a key problem in respect to the International Criminal Court.

If you look at Strasbourg or Luxembourg, you find international jurisdictions with primacy over national law. There is the heart of the problem. The determinations of international judges trump member state law because the treaty that they interpret and apply trumps national law.

The legal situation of the International Criminal Court is not fundamentally different. There is always a treaty that gives authority to a jurisdiction. Since the treaty is superior to national law, international judges trump national judges and national law. It is no different in respect to a crime against humanity. It is no different. It is just that the interests are more heated and the decisions more difficult to accept. If Luxembourg has succeeded more easily than the Strasbourg Court in giving rise to less resentment, it is simply because the problems that they deal with seem more technical. When they handed down their great decisions in the 1960s and 1970s about primacy, incorporation, and direct effect, only specialists, legal seminars, and law reviews were interested. Only afterwards, with the emergence of a stronger European Union, did the public begin to recognize their implications.

The matter in Strasbourg was different, because the decisions concern more controversial matters and the Court intrudes, not upon economic principles or economic interests, but upon the classic domain of the state itself. Strasbourg strikes at the state itself and upon its most important territory: democratic legitimacy related to the state's respect for human rights. The tension of the dialectic that we have discussed—national law and sovereignty faced with a superior international legal legitimacy—is here at its peak.

The most complex intellectual problem lies in the nation's delegation of its sovereignty through a treaty to international judges.

The judge, the sorcerer's apprentice, takes that power and causes the international law to develop, to the public's general satisfaction and despite the feeling of those who are responsible at a national level that power is being taken from their hands. The story is extraordinary, for justice is no longer being rendered in the name of the state, but against its will.

Ronald DWORKIN: We must distinguish between two issues, though they both concern legitimacy. The first is the issue that you have mainly been talking about just now, which is the legitimacy of an international organization whose officials are appointed by, and are continually responsible to, the member nations of the organization. The second is the legitimacy of international judges who are not responsible to any national or even any other international organization. Such judges claim continuing independence from national or even international control. What then makes their power legitimate? It is not an answer to that second question that we have reasons, in treaty and history, for establishing the primacy of international over domestic law. The question is: Who makes international law, and under what title? Judges plainly do play a role in the development of international standards. But why is that legitimate? The more visible the creative power of an international judiciary becomes, the more pressing the question of legitimacy.

Antonio CASSESE: I agree with Dieter that, in a way, the legitimacy of international courts does rest on the independence and credibility of judges. They have to build up their own credibility, but I would also add that they have to use some sort of judicial wisdom. An international court must be extremely careful in proceeding slowly so as not to raise objections on the part of sovereign countries. You are confronted with sovereign countries, and you have to gradually build up a system that actually erodes state sovereignty. Let me give you two examples. The European Court of Human Rights was confronted from the outset with a huge problem: whether or not it could issue interim measures, and these interim measures could be of great importance in the case of expulsions. For instance, France, Italy, or Germany could decide to expel a Moroccan, who then goes to his own country or to Turkey and claims before a national court: "If I go back there, I will be killed or tortured because I am a political opponent." The man then goes to Strasbourg and requests an interim measure. In international judicial practice, it is normally stated in the legal literature, by judges, and by the International Court of Justice that, unless the state in the treaty establishing a court explicitly provides for the power of the court to issue binding interim measures, the court has no power to do so. In Strasbourg, they said, "All right, we do not have any rule in our Treaty. Let us then adopt such a rule in our rule of procedure, without saying that our interim measures are binding." It was very shrewd. Then they started saying, "When there is an urgent problem, such as when this man may be killed when he is sent back to Algeria or Morocco, let us do something and gradually convince states that they should, in a way, bow to our decisions." The judges do not have any provision, even in the new Protocol #11, stating that the Court has this power. They do not need such a provision, because I know that only in 1 case out of 400 or 500 cases of interim measures did the state say that the Court lacked this power and that the state was not bound by the Court's decision of yours. This was Sweden.

Ronald DWORKIN: And they sent the person back?

Antonio CASSESE: They sent him back, but then later on, the Court said, "You were right, because his life was not in peril."

Ronald DWORKIN: Fascinating!

Antonio CASSESE: Actually, I spoke with the various judges. They said, "As soon as we have a problem, the Registrar, on behalf of the President, phones the authorities of the country, saying, 'We are about to send you by fax an order with interim measures, could you please stay the expulsion of Mr. X?' All states comply." So you see how they proceed in a subtle way, and they do not need to have provisions formally stating their use of authority. Another very short example relates to the International Criminal Tribunal for the former Yugoslavia and the clash between judges and politics. As I said yesterday, this Tribunal is impotent as long as either states; NATO; countries such as France, the U.S.A., and the U.K.; or the Security Council (the Security Council has the power to adopt sanctions against a state that blatantly violates its obligation) do not take action. Article 29 of the Tribunal's Statute provides that all states of the world, including Switzerland, are duty-bound to comply with orders, arrest warrants, and decisions issued by the tribunal. We have had cases where states repeatedly do not comply, and the question that cropped up was: What are we going to do? We cannot impose on the Security Council the obligation to take action. Then the Tribunal came up with a very innovative and imaginative solution. It stated: "We do not have any power to ask a political body, such as the Security Council, to issue sanctions. However, we may decide to issue a judicial finding saying that the Tribunal, as a judicial body, states that, for instance, the Federal Republic of Yugoslavia is grossly violating its obligation under Article 29. This is a judicial finding, based on judicial reasoning, on the evidence provided by the prosecutor, scrutinized by judges, and with the stamp of the President of the Tribunal. The Hague Tribunal then sends this judicial finding to the Security Council, which then may decide whether or not to take action. The Security Council is a political body; it is up to the Security Council to base its decision on political reasons. However, what the Security Council cannot do is to challenge the judicial finding by the Tribunal." This is the first time that it has ever been said that the Security Council has in a way some margin of discretion, but only on whether or not to take sanctions; it cannot say that the Tribunal is wrong.

We found a subtle way of saying, "We cannot trespass on your powers. We are a judicial body, and you are a political body. However, we can move the law a bit further." We were expecting an uproar on the part of the Security Council, but there was silence. They accepted it. It is very interesting. So, you see how you can move on. I would say that it was judicial cunning.

Stephen BREYER: There is no need to use the pejorative phrase "judicial cunning." You could as easily call it "judicial statesmanship." He who wills the end must will the means. The end, willed by 90 percent of the public, is the protection of basic human rights. If the public must decide, by vote, how or whether to protect those rights in each situation each time, it will often not protect them, defeating its own basic end. The public, understanding this, creates an institution—courts—to which it gives the task of protecting those rights. It also wants a judge who is honest, reasonably intelligent, possessing common sense, and who has some understanding of the millions of citizens to whom he is, in a certain sense, responsible. Then, the role of judicial statesmanship is for that judge to achieve the ultimate end within the public's expectations and understandings about the working of the judicial enterprise. In the civil system, judges must fill in the gap in the codes; in the common law system, judges work at the "frontier" of the law. But they are similar. John

Marshall knew how to work at that frontier, but within established understandings of judicial practice. He built the Court, expanded its possibilities, and thereby helped to achieve the public's basic objective. "Statesmanship" is needed even after a court is well established, for in a democracy power ultimately flows from the people.

Ronald DWORKIN: There is rarely a decision that is dictated by "good sense," that is, that every sensible person will recognize is the right decision. In every important case, there are arguments both ways; the people who lose feel that their interests have been ignored or slighted. The problem of legitimacy is the problem of what justification can be offered, if that is what they think, to them. That is why I bridle when I hear lawyers or judges talking about "good sense." We have to admit that reasonable people of good sense can disagree, and that there won't be a "knock-down" argument that convinces all sides. That is why I find certain expressions judges use by way of apparent explanation for what they have decided, like "that works," or "that is common sense," rather offensive because they pretend that what is hard and controversial is not. I doubt that we disagree about that.

Stephen BREYER: You think the phrases "common sense" or "good sense" lack meaning, but you admit that they are not entirely empty. I am a little more suspicious than you of the phrase "good argument," because I read and hear so many "good arguments."

Ronald DWORKIN: My problem with the phrases "good sense" or "that works" may come from my experience at Oxford. We have great arguments in the Senior Common Room, and all of a sudden we get tired, and smell the food coming for lunch, and someone then says, "I think that we have got it just about right," and everybody else says, "Yes, we now have it just about right," and then we eat. I do not claim that there is only one good argument in a hard case. Quite the contrary. But what judges owe us is an argument that meets two conditions. First, they have to believe it; they must offer it in good faith *as* an argument. Second, it has to connect what they do in a particular case with something more general and basic. Of course, in the end, what argument a judge finds convincing will depend on that judge's more general attitudes and convictions, and no one can demonstrate to those who do not share these attitudes and convictions that they are inescapably right. But they must seem right, after open argument and serious reflection, to those who rely on them. That form of sincerity is an indispensable condition of judicial legitimacy. You do not have to convince others that your argument is the best one. That will often be impossible. But you should be able to convince them—and, of course, it should be true—that after the deepest reflection that the circumstances permit it seems the best one to you. Other institutions are under no comparable obligation to try to find and present such arguments. They can say, "We represent the will of the people," or "We represent the compromise that will satisfy people and will not interfere too much with anybody's deepest interests." But we do not want our judges to talk or think that way.

Dieter GRIMM: I really think that there is a bridge. When I say that the courts have to at least create the impression that they do not decide politically, this can only be done through reasoning. There must be an element of generalization, so that even the loser may admit that the court followed a sound principle, although he may still think that it should not have been applied in his case.

Ronald DWORKIN: Right. You need not deny that your decision is original. But you should do what you can to show that your decision is, in the sense that we have been trying to specify, a decision of principle.

Dieter GRIMM: Ron, in your previous statement, you asked us to distinguish between two levels. On the first level, the power is given to these institutions by a democratic act. On the second level, the exercise of that power can no longer be controlled democratically. Is there any difference in principle between the international and the national level, when on the national level it comes to constitutional adjudication? I ask this question because the same remarks were uttered in our systems, where constitutional adjudication is not as old as it is in your country. I do not think that there is any difference in principle, but I think that there is a difference in circumstances and that this difference in circumstances has something to do with the fact that national courts act in a much tighter framework of one legal culture, which allows many things but not everything, whereas the legal culture and the net of court decision and critical reactions, both academic and by the public, is not that dense on the international level, so that the problem of control becomes a more difficult one. But in principle, I do not see a difference.

Stephen BREYER: There is another difference. The process of selecting judges is farther removed from the people.

Robert BADINTER: This is a crucial question. Among the key questions about the legitimacy of the judge is the recognition by the people who are judged that those are their judges. That is why the process of nomination is so important and should be so carefully conducted, because afterwards, as you say, there is no way of controlling the judges. In international jurisdictions, it is far more striking because the powers exercised on the state, I would say, are greater than by the national judges, except for the constitutional judges. But what is the relationship between the citizens of state and this international body of judges? Remember Madame Thatcher's reference to *les juges cosmopolites*; the "cosmopolitan judges" did not have anymore a nationality, they just were cosmopolitan.

Ronald DWORKIN: There is no greater term of contempt for her, I suppose.

Robert BADINTER: Monsieur Le Pen also uses the word. When you go back to the traditional xenophobic and anti-Semitic literature of the thirties in Europe, the word "cosmopolitan" was always used. The word "cosmopolitan" means non-national, anti-national, or foreign. I will return to this. The point is that the decision seems to come from the sky. You do not even know who these judges are, and they are above the decisions of your own representatives. Nevertheless, it has worked.

Gil Carlos RODRIGUEZ IGLESIAS: I was one of the "cosmopolitan" judges that Lady Thatcher referred to. And I am also a professor, which, in her view, seems also to be a sin. I think that she said once in the House of Lords: "What can you expect from a Court including professors with no previous judicial experience?" But I have heard that, when Margaret Thatcher was Prime Minister, she said that she would only accept the possibility for Member States to maintain national provisions in derogation of common rules adopted by qualified majority in order to preserve higher standards of protection of the environment, or other major interests, on the condition that such a unilateral action would be subjected to the judicial control of the European Court of Justice (in spite of its "cosmopolitan" judges, I would like to add).

Ronald DWORKIN: A crucial problem arises when we move from national to international constitutional adjudication. Within a national culture, judges can draw on a history and tradition. They can say with sense, even if only controversially in particular cases, that they are applying principles embedded in a common history and practice. That claim is much more problematic when you move from a particular nation to a region and, of course, still more so when you try to make claims about the jurisprudence of the world. You may find principles that you can claim to be embedded in everyone's history, but these are likely, if at all plausible, to be very abstract. We are more likely to find these principles of very wide application in the criminal law, because when life and liberty are at stake, rather than only property, principles of fairness seem to have a much wider currency. It seems more plausible, even if not fully accurate, to appeal to what British lawyers call principles of natural justice that all cultures accept. But when we turn to principles about individual rights—to free speech, for example—or about economic freedom or the equality of political status, these seem much more culture-sensitive. That seems to me the greatest challenge that the idea of a truly international civil law faces.

Stephen BREYER: The American public has had a much smaller role in selecting a judge of an international court than a judge of a domestic court. That means that a judge of an international court has a greater obligation to stick to the heartland of that judge's written mandate. The more that judge deals with obvious instances of serious human rights violations, the more likely a consensus of the public of many nations will support that judge's activities. When they depart from that basic task, they may lead the public to lose faith—like the French public in the aristocracy after Crecy—and look for other ways to do the basic job. The more debatable the "human rights" violations that they adjudicate, the more difficult for the court to remain legitimate among those publics that had little voice in selecting the judges or voting for the specific laws that they apply.

NOTES

1. Kevork B. Bordakjian, "Hitler and the Armenian Genocide" (1985).

2. *Atty Gen. of Israel* v. *Eichmann,* 36 I.L.R. 277, 287 (Isr. Sup. Ct. 1962).

3. See generally, A Cassese and B. V. A. Röling, "The Tokyo Trial and Beyond."

4. *United States et al.* v. *Goring et al.*, 1 International Military Tribunal, Trial of the Major War Criminals 223 (1947).

5. Concluding Speeches by the Prosecution, 19 The Trial of German Major War Criminals, Proceedings of the International Military Tribunal Sitting at Nuremberg, 433 (1948).

6. Compare *Trial of the Major War Criminals before the International Military Tribunal* (1947) with *Procès des Grands Criminels de Guerre devant le Tribunal Militaire International* (1947).

7. *Regina* v. *Secretary of State for Transport, ex parte: Factortame Ltd.* (1990) ECR I-2433 (Ruling).

8. *Francovich and others* v. *Italian Republic* (1991) ECR I-5357 (Court of Justice).

9. *Brasserie du Pêcheur SA* v. *Bundesrepublik Deutschland* and *The Queen* v. *Secretary for Transport, ex parte: Factortame Ltd. and others* (1996) ECR I-1029 (Court of Justice).

10. *Brasserie du Pêcheur and Factortame III* (1996) ECR I-1029, paragraph 2.

5

The Infernal Couple

Justice and the Media in the Information Age

5.1. Presentation

President Robert Badinter

In contemporary democracies dominated by communication, the relationship between justice (the third power) and the media (the fourth—or the first—power) is complex and ambiguous.

I. COMPLEXITIES

Traditionally, freedom of opinion and of expression is considered a fundamental right of a constitutional dimension. Constitutional courts and international jurisdictions are willing to apply this principle. When faced with attacks or threats, the media consequently find protection in the courts.

However, those who believe that the media have violated their rights to privacy, honor, reputation, dignity, personality, etc., also look to judges for protection. Making public information of a confidential nature, whether it concerns national defense or finance or industry, also can lead to judicial proceedings. Similarly, racist or revisionist propaganda can lead to court action. In such cases, the judge seems to be not the protector of the media, but ultimately their censor. Whether the one role or the other is at issue, whether it sanctions or protects the media, justice seems to hold the superior position.

II. AMBIGUITY

The traditional interaction between the media and judges (where the media represents a subject of judicial decisionmaking) has been singularly modified in our contemporary information society.

The judiciary, in effect, is only an institution with the mission of deciding litigation or sanctioning violations of law. Judicial matters, including the procedures themselves, are just so many episodes of social life that attract the public's attention and, hence, that of the media. Judicial matters, particularly great criminal cases or those involving public personalities, are broadly followed by the media. At the same time, questions that the judge must consider and decide include a number of contemporary ethical problems about, for instance, artificial procreation, the environment, or abortion. It is thus inevitable that the media will become particularly interested in judges' decisions and will give them widespread publicity. Since the information diffused goes beyond a single instance and includes commentary, the judge suddenly finds himself the subject of a media critique. Thereby, the power relationships in an information society are insidiously transformed. The media are thus in a position of critical power, though not of authority, in relation to judges. And they can similarly influence the course of justice, in an indirect but effective manner.

I would add to this commentary on how the media influence justice the fact that, in our age of celebrity stardom, certain magistrates, either through function or vocation, have achieved a media star status of the greatest magnitude. They are, for the most part, prosecuting magistrates. *Procureurs* or *juges d'instruction* have taken on in the media the roles of modern sheriffs courageously confronting the forces of evil. Now, these magistrates find it greatly tempting to be led on by their desire for celebrity rather than by their concern for objectivity. I am thinking of the prosecutor Di Pietri, the prosecutor Starr, certain French and Spanish *juges d'instruction,* and others whose connections with the media reveal back-and-forth exchanges. They practice a policy of intense communication in order, they say, to put the media at the service of justice. Through the publicity that their actions receive, they prevent any effort to silence them or to slow down their prosecutions, either through political or economic pressure. Sometimes, however, one feels that they also put justice at the service of the media, by giving them confidential information. Whatever the causes and effects, the judge's independence, the key to judicial ethics, must be rethought in light of the media and the related attraction of publicity.

The matter is so much the more important because judicial time and media time do not coincide. Justice works according to strict procedural rules, those of the legal process. It unfolds prudently and often slowly. The media are comprised of commercial enterprises competing in the information marketplace. No sooner is news known than it must be published for fear of being scooped by the competition. Now, there is nothing more damaging to the reputation of a private person, even more of a public person, than the announcement that his affairs are undergoing judicial scrutiny. How, in the information society, are we going to reconcile the need to protect the person with the need for transparency? This problem, while not a new one, is posed to the judge in terms not previously known in this age of the Internet.

5.2. The Infernal Couple
Justice and the Media in the Information Age

Discussion

Robert BADINTER: The problem of the connection between the judge and the media is fundamental in societies as media-driven as ours. That problem, in my opinion, has taken on a new dimension. When the written press was dominant, relationships between the media and the judge were far easier. There was not then the complete and total media pressure that dominates society today.

With respect to judge/media relationships, there are first what I will call classical relationships. These are dialectical relationships, continuous but almost contradictory. At the outset, there is the principle, and I speak of our democratic societies, of free expression and opinion. Read the *Declaration of the Rights of Man*, for example. This is one of our most precious rights. Everyone agrees about that. It defines the first relationship between judge and the media. From the very moment that the legislator begins to define conditions for exercising the freedom of expression and opinion, inevitably questions arise about possible limitations on that freedom in light of other constitutional principles, such as the protection of the individual's personality or privacy, or other more general rights related to national security or the struggle against racism. Hence, you have a principle, freedom of the press, and other principles that end up legally limiting the field within which press freedom may operate.

In this respect, note that the media find, by virtue of the relationship with judges, protection from the grasp of a political power that is only too ready to try to control the media, particularly in our age of audio-visual technology. The media go to the judge, whom they expect to protect the right to free expression. That is particularly true for the constitutional or international judge, for I recall that in this field there is very important case law from the Strasbourg Court. This is the first aspect of the problem: the protection of the media and of freedom of expression by the judge.

The second relationship is different. It concerns those who believe themselves harmed or threatened by press freedom and by press excesses. They include those who believe that the press has attacked their private lives or ruined their reputations, or the state itself, which believes that, say, military secrets or information about atomic installations have been stolen. At that moment, they will seek from the judge protection against the media.

At the first stage, it was the media who came to the judge to seek protection; at the second stage, it is private citizens or the state who seek the judges' protection. But in both cases, and this to me is the interesting point, the judge is in a superior position, a position of power, vis-à-vis the media. Is the judge going to find, as we so often see at Strasbourg, that freedom of expression is one of the most fundamental rights of all—one that we should touch only with trembling hands, as Portalis put it? Will the European media and European journalists find as much protection at the ECHR as is found in the American First Amendment? Or will they find less protection? All that is part of the first question. But whatever the answers, it is the judge who will decide.

As to the second question, judges find before them those who want them to condemn the press, and they may well do so. Then they are treated differently. The "good judge" then becomes the "bad judge." The treatment is different. The "good judge" is the judge who says, "Yes." The "bad judge" is the judge who says, "No."

I want to point out that, in both cases, the judge is in a privileged situation in regard to the media. I recall a passage in which the ECHR (our basic reference tool) proved very protective of freedom of expression. In its first major case, it held against the U.K. in the *Sunday Times* case in 1979. The Court also held against the Swiss, the Austrians, the Germans, and the French too. In their preambles, the Strasbourg judges always say how important these rights are. In a recent decision (a 1997 case from Germany, I think), the Court wrote that it is in the interest of a democratic society to assure and to maintain press freedom as much as it is possible to do so. You all know the dialectic. Freedom of expression can be restricted, but necessity must be shown. In sum, the judges are more pro-press than pro–anything else. There are some salient cases involving racist propaganda, which one might talk about. I find, in respect to those cases, involving fine efforts to fight against racist propaganda, that the Court has made decisions that were much resented by the countries involved.

Ronald DWORKIN: But there has been no decision outlawing, for example, the "Auschwitz Lie" legislation, has there?

Robert BADINTER: I am not aware of any decision about revisionism. But there is one similar example that I should mention because it took a rather remarkable path. A journalist in Denmark, a country with a strong civil liberties tradition, interviewed two anti-Semitic, xenophobic skinhead leaders on TV. During the interview, he pushed them, and they spoke about xenophobic themes, setting forth racist and xenophobic propaganda. Their prosecution followed.

A Danish law forbids racist propaganda and public manifestations of racial hatred. This had appeared on TV. So not only the two skinheads, but also the journalist, were all convicted and sentenced. It was held that his questions, and his having brought the skinheads to the interview, made him one of the authors of the racist propaganda. The case went to the Strasbourg Court. The Court decided that they could not be convicted, nor could they be sentenced, because of freedom of expression.

The Danish Supreme Court resented that decision. It, in effect, said, "Why should others give us lessons in morality? We are Danish. We are a moral people. We have a tradition of freedom. We simply do not want to have people come here and preach xenophobia and racism on television. Please do not tell us that the limitation that we have consequently imposed upon free speech was unnecessary."

This is interesting, for it shows that resentment sometimes comes from judges who resent the actions of other judges, rather than from politicians who simply resent international judges. I have always said to our Strasbourg friends, "Be careful." When procedural technicalities or the due process of law are at issue, it is expected that you will be precise, demanding, and punctilious. When moral standards are at issue and the matter comes from a national supreme, or constitutional, court, you should not say that you have superior wisdom about what to do about a person who indulges in anti-Semitic or racist propaganda. The Strasbourg judges went a little too far. The Danish judges followed the thrust of their own law, its jurisprudence, and the views of the Danish people. They determined that all were in agreement. But the Strasbourg judges were simply following the trend of their own First Amendment views. When I take all the decisions into account, I think that the Strasbourg judges went further in the free press direction than the national judges, who were more prudent. It is a difficult, one-of-a-kind case.

The Danes strongly criticized the Strasbourg decision. I also want to point out that there is a distinction in respect to press freedom between the written press and broadcasting. You are free to print, but you are not totally free to use the airwaves.

But there is another, more interesting tendency that runs the other way. It arises out of what one might call *la force des choses*, the "momentum of things" or the pressure of events. That is a magnificent phrase of Saint-Just, Robespierre's friend, who wrote near the end of the Terror, just before it collapsed, that "la force des choses nous a menés plus loin que nous ne pensions aller," that is, "The pressure of events took us further than we had intended to go." That is an understatement, but a magnificent phrase.

Lovely things have been written about the freedom of the press. We are a society characterized by transparency and publicity. Some might call it exhibitionism, but it does not matter. This society, which sometimes the French call *la société de spectacle*, or the society of "theatrical events," finds the media ever more interested in the judicial scene. In a sense, this interest has always been present in that people were always interested in criminal trials, etc. But now, the interest is greater and more direct. The media want to keep judicial events within the public eye. That leads them to provide commentary on a judicial decision. And doing so requires comment, not only upon the decision, but also upon the person who made the decision, and the role that each party played in bringing it about. In this way, the judicial process becomes a form of theatrical event with protagonists, among them the judge.

In this situation, the situation that we are now in, it is the media who have the upper hand, who supervise the judge, and not the other way 'round, as in the first example. That is so because all human beings, when placed in the public eye, change their behavior. What the impact of the judge's decision will be not simply upon society, but also in terms of the media's reaction, is unfortunately a matter that is often taken into account. That means that the media also regulate judicial activity by saying things like "This is a good judgment," or "This is a poor judge," or "These judges are fools."

You, as the judge, take the high road; you ride the white horse, and you put on your fine armor. But matters are not so simple. Not every judge is immune to flattery or criticism. Each of us can find examples, and the media have understood that. Let me add another factor, which is that the relationship is highly complex and dialectic. Taking judges and the media together, we find what I call the "infernal couple." We see them every day in France, that "couple from hell." They are, in our over-exposed information society, an alliance formed among a judge, a prosecutor, and a major media player. And when I say "alliance," I mean it. It is deliberate. The major media players want a politician's hide, proceedings begin, and the wheels are set in motion. In our democracy, it is difficult to mount any resistance to this process.

Ronald DWORKIN: The Starr with two "r's," not one. You complain about the star system as well, but this is the Starr system (with two "r's") that you are referring to.

Robert BADINTER: You are right. There is the star system with one "r," and the Starr system with two "r's". That provided us with an extraordinary illustration. In Italy, I believe that the connection between a prosecutor and the Italian press, a newspaper in particular, changed the nature of the whole proceeding. There are many examples. Even in a democracy as mature as England's we find revelations about private lives. Remember the number of ministers who resigned because their private lives were exposed.

This illustrates how the existence of a judicial procedure does not suffice. If the person conducting the investigation has the will, he can achieve his objective by delivering material to the press. At that instant the fundamental principle, the presumption of innocence, is tossed out the window. It no longer exists.

This change in circumstances matters. We have here a situation tied to the development of the *société de spectacle* and the society of hyper-information and, at the same time, to the growth in the power of the judge. After all, the judge or the prosecutor is not always innocent. The prosecutor may say, "I can do nothing. After all, he is who he is, or she is who she is, and the press is interested in them. I just treat them like any other citizen." But that is not always true. There is a temptation to be a star. And if you are tempted to become a star (or Starr), then you will work with the media. You will give the media what you should not give them. I am thinking in particular of Roland Dumas. You could read before the judge heard the matter just what questions would be asked and what documents they would concern. That is not chance; it reflects a deliberate decision. At the same time, the judge is glorified as a man of great courage who will unhesitatingly challenge the rich and the famous.

The next step will take place when the media, society's premier power, and the judge, its second power, confront each other. After having heaped praise upon judges (which is not the tradition in my country) during the last 20 years, particularly the last 10, the media will turn against the judges, who will not bow to their will. The judges who make decisions that the press does not like will be torn to pieces. That is the next step.

Why the "infernal couple"? Because it is not quite the same as the marvelous lines of Paul Valery in *The Diary of M. Teste*: "I am much loved, I am much hated; we have grown old together." Rather, for the "infernal couple," it is: "We are much loved, we have lived together, and now we are hated." That will be the beginning of a new story that I am not sure we shall not have opportunity to witness.

In any case, all this is brand new. I shall conclude by saying that, at the present moment (since we are talking about the growth of the judge's powers and the ascension of the judge in contemporary society), there is a kind of complex. You recall the military-industrial complex, the Pentagon and defense industries that Eisenhower denounced. If I am right, there is a new complex in our society, and it is too powerful. The complex is the "infernal couple," the juridico-media complex, the alliance between the judges and the media. It is our newest strike force. It is an all-powerful force in current society, at least from the perspective of the person prosecuted. The media work in real time. They must have news immediately. The infernal hunting-down must make the daily headlines.

Here is a subject that I believe calls for keen reflection. It is the birth of a new power in a democracy, the alliance of the judge and the media.

Ronald DWORKIN: We need to talk about two issues. One is the question of hate speech. I think that I understand the special offense that would be given to the people of Denmark by the broadcast that you described, but in my view, the two racists, and not just the journalist, ought to have gone to Strasbourg, and the judges there would have been right to say that they must all be protected against any kind of condemnation. What gives a democratic majority the moral standing to impose its will on dissenting minorities? That is a standing—and extremely difficult—question of political theory, but one thing seems plain to me. The majority has no legitimate power over individuals unless those individuals have been given the opportunity to put what they believe, no matter how offensive, to the majority in hopes of convincing it. The majority wishes to prohibit actual discrimination against Jews—for example, in employment—and its moral title to do so depends on its having given the appalling racists a chance to speak out. It cannot otherwise claim that its opinion has won out in fair politics. Of course, that principle, like any principle, has limits, and if there was a genuine possibility that irreversible fascism would take hold in Denmark if anti-Semitic rhetoric was permitted, a terrible question would be raised. But that was not the fear that motivated the Danish court: It was infuriated by the content of the speech, not terrified of its consequences. It decided that the speech was too offensive, not too dangerous. If I am right that the moral legitimacy of a democracy depends upon giving everyone subject to its dominion, even racists, the opportunity to attract their own support, offense is the price that we must pay for legitimacy, and surely it is a price worth paying.

Robert BADINTER: There were dissenting opinions in the Strasbourg Court. It was by no means a unanimous decision.

Ronald DWORKIN: The second point that I shall mention is the one that you raised near the end, which is the attention that the press now pays to the judiciary. In my view, the media attention to Starr was beneficial to fairness and to democracy. The attention in the end badly damaged him: He had expectations of a political or judicial career that I think have been extinguished, although we may never know. The press's reports of the brutal initial interrogation of Monica Lewinsky, for example, outraged the public, which was an entirely good thing.

Robert BADINTER: I would like to say that the result is not necessarily what was intended. Do you think that Starr did not want to use the press to destroy Clinton? I was told that he hated the Clinton family, that he planned to use the media to destroy them, and that he expected that result.

Ronald DWORKIN: I do not know Mr. Starr, and I do not know how much he hates the Clintons. Did he want to use the press for his own advantage? Of course, he did. But he did not succeed. I want to make a more general and, I hope, provocative point, however. On the whole, in spite of fairly obvious shortcomings and dangers, the trend that you describe—the increased media attention to the judicial process in all its manifestations, from the actions of a prosecuting attorney to the decisions of the Supreme Court—is a good thing and something to be encouraged. You raise questions, as you have throughout all our discussions, which connect the contemporary phenomenon of the increasing role and power of the judiciary to more general questions about political morality. So let us consider the issue of judicial publicity in that light. Steve at some point described the black robe as a metaphor for an ideal of opacity: that the public should be encouraged to think of the judiciary as a Delphic institution that from time to time delivers judgments that must be accepted as the pronouncement of an institution whose anonymity encourages respect. I prefer a different ideal: transparency. We cannot expect the public any longer to think (if reflective members of the public ever did think) that what judges do is independent of their own personal convictions. We should put our hope in a different idea: that the judges should explain what their underlying convictions of principle are, and how these are organized into overall constitutional approaches and philosophies, and then invite the journalists and the public to discuss their decisions and opinions as controversial but honest exercises of political principle, exercises that the wider public can understand and criticize, and not be shocked by the connection between a judge's general ideology and his particular opinions, but informed by that connection. That model of transparency has one great advantage over the model of opacity: honesty. I think that it has another: that people may come to see that the authority of a judge is derivative not from hidden craft or from representation, but from good-faith argument. Of course, there is a down side: Judges who are candid are more vulnerable to the irresponsible and ignorant criticism of an irresponsible and ignorant press. In the United States, and I expect soon enough elsewhere, opacity provides no shield against that ignorance and irresponsibility anyway. The American public knows about 5-to-4 decisions dominated by conservative justices. They do not know, except by way of mendacious slogans, whether the conservatism has a principled base and, if so, what it is. I cannot think that we would be worse off, with all the attendant dangers, if we accepted an obligation to encourage a public discussion, at all levels of sophistication, of that issue. What means should judges use to encourage transparency? There is much room for debate about details—about cameras in the courtroom, for example. But we should debate the details with a sense that the public demand for more information about who judges are and what they think and do is both inexorable and justified. Of course, most of the press is still ill equipped to do that. But we must hope and aim to improve that. I do not know whether *Le Monde,* for example, has trained constitutional lawyers among its reporters.

Robert BADINTER: It has good constitutional experts.

Ronald DWORKIN: So I end with this rose-colored suggestion. Since you cannot, and have no right, to discourage the press's attention to your growing powers, you should aim to make them partners instead of obstacles. This is easier said than done.

Stephen BREYER: If all journalists covered the courts like the *New York Times* reporter covers the Supreme Court, there would be no problem. But they do not. In any event, the press is necessary to maintain the public's confidence that the judges are honest. In the United States, we must fill out elaborate disclosure forms reporting every penny received by ourselves, our spouses, and our minor children. The press typically prints whatever they learn from these very extensive reports and, in particular, whatever assets the judge may own. And they will emphasize any mistake that they find.

When I was nominated to the Supreme Court, some journalist used a computer to match every share of stock that I had ever owned with the names of every litigant in every case that I had ever heard. There were, of course, thousands. They found one instance where the names matched, but luckily I had found the conflict at the time it came up many years before and had taken appropriate action.

Indeed, the *Washington Post* assigned reporters to investigate my life in San Francisco and to sift through all my government expenses over the preceding years. They found an instance where I had accidentally charged the government $200 extra for a judicial trip to Puerto Rico because the ticket included a side-trip to Nevis, which was personal. I repaid the government, and the newspaper wrote a story about it.

At that same time, the press discovered that some judges had failed to report expenses paid them by a conservative economic group to attend a seminar about the environment. I am reasonably sure that this failure was accidental. The public does not realize that the reporting requirements involve thousands of lines of information, and expenses can sometimes be accidentally overlooked.

The upshot is that no judge likes this system. But, in today's world, it is a necessary system.

Ronald DWORKIN: Which part do you disagree with?

Stephen BREYER: Part of the press is less responsible. I am concerned about what will happen if court proceedings, particularly criminal proceedings, are regularly shown on television. Antoine Garapon recently wrote an interesting book on this subject. Will television turn a court proceeding into a "story," with a villain and a hero? The public, which is not made up of lawyers, will want to do so, because people inevitably are more interested in people than in ideas or institutions like courts that must be concerned about general rules extending well beyond the "human story" taking place in a particular courtroom at a particular time. The television public may not understand the formal, ceremonial, or institutional functions of the courts, and therefore (unlike readers of the press, which tries to interpret what occurs) misunderstand what is taking place.

Robert BADINTER: Yes, but in a second I shall go farther. The true answer, I believe, to what Ronald said is the structural incompatibility of judicial and media approaches. During our discussions, we have seen the importance of fair procedure and of "due process of law" in a democracy. Nothing like that exists in respect to the media. There is no "due process of the press." Remember that the one thing that the press never mentions is the law of profits. Steve does not use his decisions to make money, I hope.

Ronald DWORKIN: He made $200 on a trip to Nevis!

Robert BADINTER: The final object of the political process is political decisionmaking. The final object of the judicial process is, we hope, fair decisionmaking. The final object of the media is not truth; it is money. At the end of the day, the media have to earn money.

Ronald DWORKIN: Robert, we can rail against the sea, but my point is, you cannot stop it!

Robert BADINTER: The result is terrible. Why? Because the law of profit in the marketplace requires making more money than the next person. In order to get the public's attention—and that is what produces money—you have to sell stories. And you have to do so working at a rhythm that is not like that of the judiciary. Put injustice to the side. Consider the classical three unities. They require not only unity of place and subject; they require unity of time. It is time, dear Proust, time that is not the same. Structurally speaking, judicial time is not the same as media time. If you are in the media, you must be the first to announce a front-page event: "Dumas is corrupt." If you wait until tomorrow or the day after, the matter is forgotten. The judge, on the other hand, must take certain necessary steps. There are investigations, certain precautions, and respect for rules of procedure. That is why proceedings in a court of justice will never match those in the court of public opinion. The rule as to the latter is: The first who publishes, wins. You cannot say this is progress. I would call it threatening.

Ronald DWORKIN: Everything you say is true but you cannot honorably restrict or restrain the press. We should start with that stark fact, and then see what alternatives there in fact are.

Dieter GRIMM: Within the media, you can create non-commercial islands, so to speak, in which the media operate, but not necessarily under what you call the law of profit, but the laws of professional journalism. This is, for instance in TV . . .

Robert BADINTER: Television looks to audience ratings. They have to justify to the proprietors that the public is watching them, because the rating is the key for advertising, which depends on whether or not you have an audience.

Ronald DWORKIN: Some American television programs—the best news programs on public television—are not so terribly bad. But most legal reporting is deplorable, I agree. Judges do not make it better by withdrawing institutionally—by discouraging dissenting opinions that journalists will seize on, for example. The only thing that they can do, so far as I can now see, is to try to redirect attention, away from personality and background, which journalists find easy to report, and toward argument, toward intellectual disagreement, which journalists now find so hard. Judges could help by writing more lucid, less legalistic opinions that bring principle and disagreements over principle more to the surface. That would, I suspect, help a good deal.

Robert BADINTER: The answer is a very simple one. Structural trends being what they are, you cannot do much. But what remedy there is lies in the hands of the judge, who can help to untangle matters. The way it works is as follows: In respect to judicial cases, press treatment does not match judicial treatment. The only remedy for an unfortunate person whom the press persecutes is in the judge's hands. The victim will go to the judge. The judge can say, "Media, you have gone too far. What you are doing has nothing to do with press freedom. It is slander, pure and simple. Or, it is false information, pure and simple. I shall penalize you."

Then the press will raise hell. It will shout: "Freedom of the press." That is why I say that the next step in our drama is confrontation between the judge and the press. That is why I speak of the "infernal couple." It is because they shift from love to hate. And that is what will happen. The press now uses the justice system. When the time comes, the justice system will confront the power of the press. You will see how the press then will treat the judges.

Gil Carlos RODRIGUEZ IGLESIAS: I should like to say something about that. I believe that the greatest challenge for the justice system is to face up to the power of the media in an appropriate way. It is a problem with which we have to live. As Ronald said, it is an enormous problem, and the problem will not go away. It is terribly difficult for a judge to protect victims of the press and other media both because of the media's power and their corporate solidarity. Here's an anecdote: In Spain, a journalist was sentenced to two years in prison because he published the fact that certain individuals were helping the police in the struggle against terrorism. The ETA then killed those individuals. The journalist fled the country. The media then unanimously baptized that journalist "the first political exile of the Spanish democracy"—because he had been criminally prosecuted.

There is also the more general problem, that of media pressure affecting the content of judicial decisions. The judge's ethical values provide the only way out. There is no other answer. Then there is a very practical problem, an essential one: that of creating a policy that will help the media understand judicial decisions and provide accurate information.

Robert BADINTER: It is necessary to help the media understand decisions such as those of the Luxembourg Court. There has to be an in-house specialist who will provide it.

Gil Carlos RODRIGUEZ IGLESIAS: Certainly. But an evolution of judicial thinking is also necessary. I can tell you that, when we began the distribution of press releases at the Luxembourg Court, it was difficult to convince some of my colleagues that any more was involved than simply sticking a few things together. It is necessary to simplify. It is necessary to depart from judicial objectivity. Otherwise, it is difficult to understand the judgment. Many judges find that difficult to admit.

Dieter GRIMM: I have five comments. First, had the Danish case come to the German Constitutional Court, I am pretty sure that we would have reversed the judgment of the criminal court, provided that the journalist did not identify himself with what the two guys said. It certainly makes a difference whether he interviewed them in the role of a mediator or whether he identified with the content of their statements. But as far as I remember the case, he did not do so.

Second, judges exercise public power, and so they must be submitted to public control. This is the job of the press and of TV. The question can only be: "What are the limits for the media?"

I find it somewhat misleading to speak in a very comprehensive way of the press because my experience, at least with respect to democratic countries, is that there are various organs, and when you are criticized by one side, you are normally praised by the other side and vice versa. So this is not just one voice—it is not the same—when no alternative views or opinions can be uttered.

Antonio CASSESE: Except, let me just say, if you are criticized for having ruled against a journalist, then there is unanimity.

Dieter GRIMM: Even in such a case, I have a different experience. In the last few years, when, because of increased competition, profit became more important for the media, we rendered some decisions that placed very clear limits on the media. These were heavily criticized by some organs and they were warmly welcome by others. So, even in this case, I do not see this complete front of a single opinion.

The next remark goes back to my experiences with cases that received very much public criticism. The most important, of course, was the crucifix case. What was the experience? The important newspapers and the public TV stations have specialized journalists in Karlsruhe, from whom you get very fair reporting. This does not mean non-critical reporting; rather, the description of what has been decided and a description of what the reasons were are usually very accurate. Sometimes, there may be insufficient comprehension of a judgment, but usually it is very fair.

Third, whether they like the decision or not, when they criticize the court, the media are doing their job. Now, in cases of this sort, there is a second round. The second round consists of other journalists rushing out and trying to get statements from politicians. So they get hold of the Minister of Defense and say, for instance in the "soldiers are murderers" case: "The Constitutional Court has just decided that soldiers are murderers." That is, of course, not what the court decided. They ask the politician: "What do you think about this?" In such cases, the Minister of Defense does not say: "Let me first have a look at this decision and then I will tell you," because then the press will write "Minister of Defense abandons soldiers." So he reacts immediately and says: "This is an outrage. It is beyond my understanding. We need other judges." He says something of that sort. During this second round, the reporting gets disconnected from the case. The subsequent reporting is on a fictitious judgment. But for the public, it is difficult to see this. The public takes the reporting for the fact. The problem is that courts are not in a position to react; it is almost impossible. Probably the only thing that they can do is issue a communiqué saying that the reporting is incorrect. But this does not have the effect of a statement that has authority to end the debate. It is just an argument among others. But again, this is only the case—at least in my experience—in very few and very heated, and very emotionally received cases. It is not the normal course of events.

Finally, as to TV in the courts. TV reports on trials do not merely report on what is going on. They tend to change the procedure itself and to change the behavior of the actors. Therefore, TV is still excluded from the courtroom in Germany. Cameras can get in before the trial begins and during the breaks, but there is no opportunity to film the procedure itself. So what they are doing now is trying to play court. They play court in the way that you mentioned. They play it with extreme cases and they engage professional judges who play the judge in this fictitious case. But what they show is a different story. As you said, they do not show what is really going on in a court. They make it a spectacle that has very little to do with the court or the case itself.

Anyway, this is not a special problem for the judiciary. The same is true for the economy. Businessmen are dissatisfied with media reports on their matters. The same is true for physicians, hospitals, etc. We live in a society where different systems specialize in different functions and actors operate under a certain code. The judges do it, the economy does it, the health system does it, and the press does it too. It operates under a certain code, and the code of the press is: Is this interesting or boring, new or old? We cannot change this code unless we completely change our society. We have to realize that judicial systems are not exempt from these conditions. We operate under a code that other systems do not like at all. Trade and industry do not like at all that we do not take into account how our judgments affect the export prospects of companies, but we cannot take these factors into account.

This is the way that modern society functions, and we have only three ways out—three ways to cure the over-spilling effects at least to a small degree. One of these ways, of course, with regard to the media is law. And we can see that, in different legal settings, the effects are different. The second means is structure. One can establish a structure where not the whole media system has to function according to the law of profit, but where a non-commercial sector exists and is strengthened. And the last means is, of course, education. People must be prepared early enough to use the media critically.

Antonio CASSESE: I have two small points to make. First of all, at The Hague, from the outset, it was decided unanimously by all judges to broadcast every minute of our proceedings and it works very, very well. It is free so that everybody everywhere in the world can watch on TV how the proceedings unfold. And it operates with only a delay of twenty minutes because the prosecutor or the defense counsel or even the judges may sometimes mention a name that should not be disclosed. So, we check within twenty minutes whether something must be deleted to protect the victims or witnesses. We have five cameras that film live, and it works very well. There is no problem. This is just for purposes of information.

Let me just add that, before deciding to go public, there was a poll among the judges and other people working in the courtroom. They were asked: "Does it make any difference to you that you are being watched? Does it matter that your face and the face of the judges and the witnesses and the defense counsel and the prosecutor are on TV? Does it make any difference?" The reply was: "No, it does not make any difference." You get used to it in a matter of a few minutes. You do not change your behavior, and you do not speak differently. Not the prosecutor, not the defense counsel, and not the judges. Of course, we have to protect the witness so there may be times when we distort voices or images, and so on. But, otherwise, as long as you protect the victim or the witness, there is no problem. I think that it is a very healthy system because there is absolute transparency. I think that this is important probably also because this is an international court sitting far away from the place that the crimes were committed, at The Hague, whereas in the U.S., in a local community, this would have a huge echo, a huge impact.

My second point may be a bit more important. I just want to take up what Ronnie said before about the Danish case. If I understood you correctly, you mean to say that, in a true democracy, freedom of expression must go so far as to allow anybody to say what he thinks about say Jews, blacks, and so on. I agree that it should be allowed in a true democracy. People should be allowed to say what they think, for instance, that all blacks are lazy and stupid and so on. These silly and despicable utterances should not be punished. But we have to have a limit. Do you think that the limit should be that as soon as it moves from that to incitement to commit a crime, for instance, if you say, "Because of that, we have to beat up all blacks," then the judge should intervene?

Ronald DWORKIN: Yes, we have to draw a line between protected speech and incitement, and the argument I made about democratic legitimacy is helpful in seeing, in general, what the distinction is about, even though there are, of course, hard border-line cases. But in England now, you do not have to go anywhere near incitement to commit a crime. All you have to do is utter a racial insult. So the disagreement is not about whether violence or incitement must be tolerated. It is about whether deep, serious, horrible offense must be tolerated. It is horrible when the collective memory of a community includes the most savage atrocities, and bad people, for their own ends, want to open the wounds again. And here we divide: I think that there are some kinds of harm, including that one, which we must suffer in order to protect the moral standing and legitimacy of coercive government.

Robert BADINTER: My answer lies in the distinction between censorship and responsibility. To censor, *i.e.,* to forbid or to refuse to permit the distribution of a text is despotic and signals the end of free expression. At the same time, there is no freedom without responsibility, which accompanies the exercise of that freedom. One who, with regard to a particular community, say, the black community, says on television before millions of viewers, "Blacks are a group of do-nothings whom we take care of with our social security budgets, and who cost us a fortune," seriously insults black people and stirs up racial hatred. So, if one does that—and this is not a matter of censorship but of responsibility—the black community has good grounds for saying: "You have insulted the black community, you have provided incentives for racial hatred, and you are liable for what you have done."

6

The Judge Confronts Himself as Judge

6.1. Presentation

President Gil Carlos Rodriguez Iglesias

BASIC CANVAS FOR REFLECTION

The expansion, diversification, and politicizing of the judge's field of activity and the economic and technical complexity of the matters submitted to him.

The discussion points sketched below under the heading "The Judge Confronts Himself as Judge," that is to say, the judge's perception of his or her own role, are not simply the fruits of simple introspection. They flow from the observation and analysis of the reality of the judicial phenomenon in contemporary society. That observation and analysis takes place within the limits defined by the observer's own position. Those limits, like all such limits, make any perspective of reality no more than a partial one. Here, that perspective must carry the weight of my own judicial experience, which, in my case, is that of a member of a rather special kind of court, the Court of Justice of the European Communities.

The canvas for reflection is the objective determination of a perceived modification in the judge's role—away from the traditional model of "oracle of the law." That modification reveals itself in the expansion, the diversification, and the politicizing of the judge's field of activity, as well as in the growing technical and economic complexity of the problems that are submitted to him. I shall mention a few of the many diverse factors that have brought about this change—though I certainly recognize, in doing so, that they are only partial aspects of the same phenomenon:

- The reinforcement of the "rule of law";
- The expansion and reinforcement of individual rights as against power;
- Increased demand for effective jurisdictional protection;
- Reduction in jurisdictional immunities, in other words, domains taken out of the area of judicial supervision;
- The development of constitutional jurisdiction in the broad sense, *i.e.*, the submission by every power to the authority of a court along with the conditions for exercising that authority;
- The proliferation of litigation, including that related to economic crimes in a free market economy;
- Growth in litigation about family rights and financial relations, related to the liberalization of customs and the instability of family ties.

ACTIVISM VS. JUDICIAL RESTRAINT: APPLICATION OF THE LAW, DEVELOPMENT OF THE LAW, AND CREATION OF THE LAW

This second point concerns the fascinating matter of the "normative" or "creative" nature of judicial activity. How does the judge perceive what he does? How do others perceive her activity? In this respect, judicial activism and judicial restraint constitute two attitudinal models, which, in my view, are not mutually exclusive.

I am aware that my approach strongly reflects my own experience within a court that is often considered activist. That Court indeed considers itself "activist" in the sense that it sees itself as a driving force of integration rather than simply as a guardian of the law. And it has believed that its interpretation of the law would be influenced by the objectives of advancing European integration and increasing the Community's authority.

Yet I consider the "activist" label erroneous, for the objective of European integration is itself set forth in the treaties. To favor this objective by means of a purposive interpretation of the treaties and of Community law is an obligation for the Court that arises out of its role of assuring respect for the law.

I shall begin my reflections with a very simple observation: The judge's basic job is the application of the law, both written law and general legal principles. Now, it is obvious that the correct interpretation of a written text is often a matter of debate, open to judicial choice. That circumstance is yet more evident where the application of general principles is at issue.

The essential question is that of knowing in different circumstances *the degree* to which a judge has freedom to choose. In this respect, the position of a judge within a hierarchy, where parties can obtain supervision through appeals, differs from that of a judge on a supreme court. The latter is not subject to any judicial supervision; indeed, such a judge is supposed to develop a jurisprudence, or case law, that, even if it does not bind, will at least orient the ordinary judges.

In many cases, applying the law essentially amounts to a technical operation that leaves the judge with little leeway in interpreting the rules. Nonetheless, every judge, particularly one in a supreme or a constitutional court, is sometimes confronted with jurisprudential options that not do not simply offer an opportunity, but impose an obligation, to choose. The choice among such options can contribute to the development of the law. And such choices often have important social and, hence, political consequences.

The requirement that judges set forth the reasons for their decisions along with the objective existence of a generally shared judicial framework of reference limit jurisprudential "creativity" to the point where it is difficult to determine whether a judge's choices really had a discretionary character. Nonetheless, there is a certain margin of choice within which a judge has the option of choosing among different possibilities. The judge's operations within this margin may reflect opportunistic considerations, but they may also reflect the judge's perception of the judge's own legitimate role in helping the law to evolve.

I am convinced that every supreme court judge is again and again confronted with choices involving an important jurisprudential development about which he will ask himself: Is this choice *reasonable,* or is it not? Is this choice *juridically acceptable,* or is it not? By "juridically acceptable," I mean properly based upon objective law and generally accepted methods of interpretation. Is it "legitimate" for a judge to take this particular jurisprudential step in this way? Or, to the contrary, in taking it does a judge step outside the judicial role and encroach upon the legislator's domain or, ultimately, that of the constituting power?

The ECJ's jurisprudence provides a particularly interesting example—one that puts this kind of reflection explicitly, though succinctly. In effect, the Court had to face the question of whether it was legitimate for Parliament to act in a way that the treaties did not foresee, and which, through interpretation of the relevant texts, they could not be said to have recognized implicitly. In a judgment handed down on September 27, 1988, in the *Comitologie* case,[1] the Court emphasized that the applicable texts did not authorize it actively to legitimate the European Parliament's power to annul. Two years later, in a judgment handed down on May 29, 1990, in the *Chernobyl* case,[2] the Court faced the same problem and said that the absence in the treaties of a provision that foresaw the European Parliament's right to annul amounted to a "procedural lacuna." It added that this kind of lacuna could not trump the fundamental interest in maintaining and respecting the institutional equilibrium that the treaties define. Thus, the Court, in 1990, considered that it could, through this jurisprudential route, actively legitimate European Parliamentary authority of the very kind that, in 1988, it had decided "the applicable texts" did not permit it to legitimate—which texts had not changed in the interim.

I should like also to refer to another example drawn from the ECJ's jurisprudence, the July 13, 1990 decision in the *Zvartveld* case.[3] The case arose out of a criminal proceeding in the Netherlands involving fraud connected with the coming into effect of Community fishing rules. The Dutch judge sent the ECJ what amounted to a request for interlocutory legal assistance. The judge asked the Court to order the Commission to send its inspectors' reports written about the Netherlands over a two- or three-year period, to send the names of its inspectors, and to authorize the inspectors to testify as witnesses. The Commission had concluded that it could not respond to the request because it could not be justified under the European Community protocol on privileges and immunities, which did not foresee the possibility of the Court's authorization of the transmission of documents at issue in a case or the testimony of Community employees.

The ECJ found the Dutch judge's request appropriate. The Court ordered the Commission to send the judge a list of all the reports at issue, to indicate any reasons (of a kind that might show a need to avoid hindering the functioning or independence of the Community) compelling enough to justify a refusal to transmit certain reports to the national judge, and to transmit the others immediately. It added that the

Commission should authorize its employees to testify as witnesses in the absence of compelling reasons showing the need to safeguard Community interests that might justify refusal. Finally, the Court said that it had the authority to examine any reasons that the Commission asserted were sufficiently compelling to justify its refusal to transmit documents or to authorize its employees to testify.

This ruling is important here in that there was no specific legal basis setting forth the Court's authority or the procedure. Nonetheless, the Court's judicial action, in my view, was very well received in that it reaffirmed and reinforced the principle of the rule of law.

SUBJECTIVE ELEMENTS IN THE EXERCISE OF THE JUDICIAL FUNCTION: IDEOLOGY AND THE VALUES OF THE JUDGE

Justice's very vocation is to be objective. Thus the words chosen as a title for this part of my paper might be thought provocative. But it is evident that here, as in all human activities, subjective factors play a certain role. Certainly, that role is small when, as is normally the case, applying the law amounts to an exercise that is basically technical. But when judicial decisions involve broader choices, subjective factors may become very important.

Aharon Barak, the President of the Supreme Court of Israel, in his important work *Judicial Discretion,* expressed in what I consider magisterial terms the importance of subjective elements:

> A decisive component in the determination of the reasonableness of the choice is the judge's personal experience: his education, his personality, and his emotional makeup. There are judges who are more cautious and judges who are less cautious. There are judges whom a certain argument influences more than other judges. There are judges who insist on a heavy burden of proof before they will deviate from the existing law, and judges who are satisfied with a light burden of proof in deviating from existing law. There are judges who are more impressed by the writings of authors, scholars, and other judges, and there are judges whom these impress less. Every judge has a complex human experience that influences his approach to life and therefore also his approach to law. A judge who experienced the

Weimar Republic will not have the same attitude toward the activity of undemocratic political parties as someone who did not experience it. There are judges for whom security considerations count much more than for other judges. There are judges for whom considerations of freedom of expression count much more than for other judges. There are judges whose personality makeup demands order and discipline, and as a result they also insist upon organic growth and ordered development of the law. There are judges whose personality makeup causes them to take interinstitutional considerations into account to a lesser or to a greater degree. All these considerations—and many others—determine the judge's personality and his human experience. One cannot ignore this factor. It seems that we would not want to operate in a system in which this factor did not carry substantial weight.[4]

When the judicial choice involves questions that touch upon great social debates and ideology, the judges' religious or secular convictions, their *Weltanschauung*, becomes particularly important. Such subjects as abortion or gender equality (*e.g.*, quotas, and affirmative action) are paradigmatic examples. I shall provide another literal quotation:

These new issues, the product of the entrenchment of guarantees of individual rights, tend to transform the courtroom. No longer is it a place where parties come to have their private disputes determined, private in the sense that, although a government or its instrumentality may be party to the dispute, the dispute will concern the right or obligation, usually material and self-interested, of some individual or corporation. Instead, the dispute will be in the area of human values, broad social issues seen by the parties as of deep moral significance, going to the root character of the society. Racial discrimination, unequal treatment of particular classes, religious observance—these are the sort of issues that may arise, bred by a bill of rights and having to be decided one way or another by the judges who have to interpret and apply the broad text of the constitutional guarantees. These new issues are not only of their nature highly emotive; the rival contentions will often be non-negotiable. The parties espousing such issues may be doing so quite disinterestedly, a deep-seated sense of moral right being involved rather than any question of material gain or loss. Matters of high principle, passionately adhered to, will be at stake, often on both sides. Because such issues "are usually seen in absolute terms, as matters of right and wrong, those who dispute over them are seldom inclined to compromise their differences." . . . The true burden lies not in the work-load involved, a relatively minor matter, but in the responsibilities to be assumed when a court enters the field of social policy making.[5]

The essential question posed when judges are to make decisions based upon values is that of determining the frame of reference for identifying those values. Few would disagree with the need first to refer to the judicial system itself to the extent that, either expressly or implicitly, it incorporates certain values (for example, human rights in general, expressly recognized human rights, fundamental constitutional values, and so forth).

The problem becomes more difficult when judges must adapt their legal interpretations to a new context embodying new values or in which new values are in the process of emerging. To what extent, then, should the judge simply rely upon existing values dominant in society or favor emerging values? When contradictory values are in competition, how can the judge choose among them? Whatever the theoretical responses to this question may be, experience reveals that, in such matters, the personal convictions of the judge have considerable importance.

THE LEGITIMACY OF JUDICIAL POWER

The essential terms of the debate about the legitimacy of judicial power may be synthesized in two fundamental questions: First, what is the source of the judge's legitimacy? Second, what are its connections with other powers that a direct democracy may legitimately exercise?

I see the essential matter as coming down to two arguments:

First, judicial power may be legitimized by its independence and obedience to law ("functional" legitimacy), as a counterbalance to political power based upon democratic legitimacy.[6] This argument begins with the recognition of the "rule of law" as a supreme value to the extent that it stands as the only guarantee against the citizen being crushed by "power." The rule of law thus represents a value that is superior to that of democracy, which can function only under the law's control. The argument implies the subordination of the legislative power to the hierarchic superiority of constitutional rules and fundamental legal principles. In order fully to carry out his role as a counterweight to the "dictatorship of the majority," the judge must have a "functional" legitimacy that flows from the combination of the principles of independence and submission to law. Through training, recruitment methods, and status, the judge must be made capable of acting with full independence and responding in an enlightened way to the demands of obedience to law.

A different view, one to which I adhere, sees the rule of law as a constitutive element of a well-established democratic system. In this view, the power that is given to the judge implies that he too (without interfering with his independence or professional abilities) enjoys a certain democratic legitimacy.

The debate about the source of judicial power necessarily has implications for the ways in which the judge's selection and the judge's status are understood. To explain this matter further, I shall have to distinguish between "ordinary" judges and constitutional judges. As far as "ordinary" judges are concerned, we should note the existence of two distinct models. On the one hand, there is the model of the judicial career quite similar to a bureaucratic career. It includes recruitment at a young age through competitive examination and, at least to some extent, training within the career itself. On the other hand, there is the Anglo-Saxon professional model. As found in the United States, it is a more open model, including, at the recruitment stage, intervention by other political authorities and sometimes direct intervention by the electors themselves.

The form the judicial system takes as an organ of government is crucial. In a career system, in particular, the conditions and guarantees that affect promotions and the exercise of disciplinary power are of determinative importance. The need to reinforce independence underlies developments in certain nations (for example, Italy, Spain, Portugal, and France to a certain extent) related to the specific system of governance of the judicial power. The discussions about that governance well illustrate the different prevailing concepts about the legitimacy of judicial power. In this respect, the discussion about the composition of the Consejo General del Poder Judicial in Spain, and the Constitutional Tribunal's decree 108/1986 about legislation regulating the methods for selection of members of the Consejo,[7] are particularly representative.

As far as the recruitment of constitutional judges is concerned, the purely "professional" judicial model is excluded—whether we speak of the United States or of the European nations that have systems of constitutional supervision. Selection procedures are varied, but they share the characteristic of intervention by political bodies.

Finally, we should consider one other matter that merits debate. How long should the terms of constitutional judges be? In this respect, we might compare the American model, with its term of service for life, with the most commonly found European model, which is a mandate for a limited term either with or without the possibility of renewal.

INDEPENDENCE AND RESPONSIBILITY

Independence is without any doubt a judicial characteristic "par excellence." I shall not try to define this notion. Rather, I shall try to make it better understood (though incompletely) from several perspectives, which I shall express in the following propositions:

First, independence is connected with the impartiality that the judge must bear in respect to the litigants before him. Independence is a precondition for that impartiality. And it is consequently important not only from the point of view of substance, but also from the point of view of appearances. We all know that, in respect to impartiality, the demands of appearances go far. Recall the importance that ECJ's jurisprudence attaches to appearances, as well as the House of Lords' decision setting aside the first judgment in the *Pinochet* case because of Lord Hoffman's ties with Amnesty International.[8]

From the point of view of substance, the judge's independence must be assured vis-à-vis the different powers that exist in society—political powers, economic powers, as well as all sorts of pressure groups. Its major concern is to prevent the judge from being unduly influenced by the Executive Power—which can have particularly formidable means of influencing the judge insofar as it has the ability to affect the course of a judge's career.

Statutes may confer upon judges certain guarantees. Non-transferability (at least during the period of the judge's term, when that term is limited), selection conditions, and, finally, promotion conditions are the most important guarantees needed to assure the judge's independence, from the point of view both of substance and of appearance.

The need to guarantee the judge's independence is difficult to reconcile with the adoption of a proper system of judicial responsibility. What kind of a system of responsibility should one have with respect to judges? Mario Cappelletti has established a typology:[9] political responsibility; social or public responsibility; the state's juridical responsibility for damages flowing from judicial acts; and finally, the personal responsibility of the judge, which might be criminal, civil, or disciplinary.

A judge's personal responsibility, whether it be civil (where a certain measure of personal responsibility is recognized for judicial acts) or criminal, can normally be brought into question only before a judicial body. Public opinion often finds something akin to corporate solidarity in the judicial nature of this procedure for deciding a judge's responsibility. And the same is true in respect to judicial disciplinary procedures.

The personal responsibility of a constitutional judge is of a political kind in that its activation seeks to determine whether the judge's behavior is, or is not, incompatible with his function, and whether, if so, the judge's functions must be taken from him. I should add that the political nature of this responsibility is either more or less explicit depending upon whether the relevant decision is made by a political body (for example, in the American or British systems, through parliamentary impeachment) or by the constitutional authority itself. If the former, there is a risk to judicial independence. If the latter, there is a risk of corporate solidarity.

By way of example, I would note the risk of corporate solidarity inherent in the system that the ECJ Statute sets forth. (Happily so far there has been no need to activate that system.) The text of Article 6 of the Statute provides that "the judges can be relieved of their functions or deprived of their pension rights or of other benefits only if, *in the unanimous opinion of the judges and the advocates general of the Court,* they no longer satisfy the requisite conditions or obligations related to their responsibilities. The party in interest will not participate in the deliberations."

Probably when constitutional judges are appointed for life, as in the Supreme Court of the United States, it is necessary to accept the risks connected with intervention by a political body. But when judges serve a limited term, as in the ECJ, it is necessary to accept the risk of corporate solidarity so as not to put independence at issue.

I shall put to the side those situations in which criminal or political responsibility is at issue—situations which, happily, are extraordinary.

In other situations, the kind of responsibility that is most effective in the supervision of judicial activity, particularly the activity of constitutional courts, is what is called public or social responsibility. That kind of responsibility, and I shall emphasize this point, concerns not individual judges, but courts as such, even if there is a difference in this respect between courts where judges have the right to express their individual opinions and those that act solely through collegial decision.

In fact, for constitutional courts to carry out their mission, they must have credibility and social acceptance, both of the court as such and of its decisions. Obviously, there need not be a social consensus about the correctness of every decision, but rather about the legitimacy of the decisions taken as a whole. In this respect, the insistence that reasons be given for a judicial decision, along with criticism of the court's doctrine, both from legal circles on the one hand and from political, economic, and social circles on the other, seem to me to constitute important means for supervision, even though they do not amount to an organized form of supervision and do not lead to a formal body of material setting forth the judges' responsibilities.

As a final remark, I should like to add that independence is a matter that depends upon the judge's state of mind. What is important is the judge's independence from the judge himself. May I remind you of a few words of the late Judge Constantinos Kakouris, which he spoke at the time of his retirement from our Court: "It is difficult, but noble, to set aside one's own beliefs and one's own sentiments, in order to reconstruct oneself as a constitutional Community—a judge who is independent, even in respect to himself. Judges from every country in every period have lived through cases where they have had to split their personalities in two, at the moment of exercising their mission." And Constantinos Kakouris illustrated these remarks by recalling one of the seven wise men of ancient Greece, who, in his role as judge, had voted to convict his friend, all the while weeping at his friend's fate.

6.2. The Judge Confronts Himself as Judge

Discussion

Gil Carlos RODRIGUEZ IGLESIAS: I shall now make some observations about the problem of applying the law, the creation of law, the legitimacy of judges, the conditions of judicial selection and the judges' status, and problems of independence and responsibility.

At the outset, with respect to the question of activism and the question whether a judge is creating law or applying law, you will find several observations in my presentation. I believe that we would all agree that the judge's basic job is to apply the law. Normally, a judge must apply written law, but the job also requires the application and elaboration of general legal principles. In any event, even when written texts are at issue, it is undeniable that interpretation is often a controversial matter. Were that not so, we would not have litigation. And often interpretation leaves the judge with options in certain instances, and the judge must make a judicial choice. This margin of choice expands as one moves away from written texts and toward the application of general principles.

Clearly, we are often confronted with options, sometimes important options that involve the law's development. And we must choose among them. Sometimes, the choice is between the law's development and respect for that which is already in place. But an option is not always of that sort. I believe that sometimes there are options that lead to the development of the law, whichever way one goes. For example, I believe that the option the ECJ took in its 1963 *Van Gend en Loos* case was much the more "revolutionary" option. But the other option—the option not taken, the option that would have excluded the possibility that individuals could directly call upon the norms of a treaty formally addressed to Member States— would have had equally important social consequences.

My next observation is that the demand for the reasons upon which a judicial decision rests along with the objective existence of a jurisprudential frame of reference generally accepted among judges are both elements that condition and limit jurisprudential creativity. Those limitations, in my view, make it inexact to consider the judge's choices as if they were entirely free or discretionary. There are certain generally accepted methods. Judicial choices, even where there is a large margin of discretion, are different in kind from legislative choices. Nonetheless, there is a margin of choice that permits the judge to choose among different possibilities. And the judge, when operating within that margin of choice, can, depending upon the case, work with considerations based upon jurisprudential concepts or with opportunistic concerns. It is there that the problem of the judge's perception of social needs to which the judge's decision must respond arises.

I have indicated that, in my experience—and I believe you share that experience—a judge is often confronted with circumstances in which he or she must decide: First, does a certain jurisprudential development seem reasonable? Is it a good or a bad thing to take a jurisprudential step in that direction? Second, could such a jurisprudential step be taken in a way consistent with a jurisprudential methodology that is generally recognized as acceptable? Third (although these three elements cannot always be easily separated in practice), is the taking of that step legitimate or is it not? Is the jurisprudential development a legitimate thing to do, or does it represent an intolerable interference into the sphere that properly belongs to the legislator, or even to the constituent powers? I have lived through this kind of situation many times at the Court of Justice. And there, as in all constitutional jurisdictions, we have a collegial atmosphere and collective discussions, which provide a very important moderating element.

As particularly significant examples, I refer to two well-known ECJ judgments. They are spectacular because, dating respectively from September 27, 1988, and May 22, 1990, they are separated by less than two years, but they are contradictory. (There was certainly change in the Court's composition, but I do not believe that this fact was decisive.) The problem was that, in terms of the Treaty's text, the European Parliament did not have the direct authority to attack the actions of other institutions by annulling them. In both cases, the Parliament resorted to annulment because, in its view, the legal basis upon which a particular action rested reflected a misunderstanding of Parliament's prerogatives. The Parliament believed that its intervention into the legislative process would have been different if the actions in question had rested upon a legal basis that it believed was proper.

In the first case, the Court arrived at the following conclusion: It flows from all the preceding developments that the texts as they presently read do not permit the Court to recognize that the European Parliament has the authority to act through annulment. The Court examined the Parliament's arguments. And it said: "You have very good arguments, but the text of the Treaty is the text of the Treaty. It does not allow us to recognize in Parliament the authority to act in this way."

Two years later, in the *Chernobyl* case, what did the Court do? The Court proceeded to analyze the different ways through which existing law guaranteed protection for the European Parliament's jurisdictional authority. And the Court concluded that they were not sufficient. The Court noted that the European Parliament's prerogatives constituted an element of the institutional balance that the Treaty had created. Then, the Court took the step that it had believed itself unable to take in the earlier case. It said: "The Court, charged by the Treaties with overseeing the law when it interprets and applies them, must consequently be able to assure the maintenance of institutional equilibrium. And the Court must be able to supervise jurisdiction related to Parliament's prerogatives, when Parliament asks the Court to do so through a legal route adapted to securing that end." The Court continued: "The absence in the Treaties of any provisions foreseeing Parliament's power to resort to annulment may constitute a procedural lacuna. Such a lacuna cannot prevail over the fundamental interest connected with the maintenance and respect of the institutional equilibrium defined by the European Community's constitutive treaties." We have here the principle of institutional equilibrium, an affirmation of the constitutional role of the Court, and then a conclusion that contradicts its decision made only two years earlier. Two years later, without any change in text, the Court rules that institutional equilibrium demands actively legitimating what the Parliament has done.

I participated in both decisions. Without giving away deliberative secrets, I can tell you that each time there was much discussion about perceptions of limits upon the Court's role. On the one hand, it was clear that the European Parliament needed the jurisdictional protection and that the need translated into a need for jurisdictional supervision of institutional equilibrium. It was equally clear that the Treaty's provisions did not confer upon the Parliament the power to act through annulment. Are we then supposed to eliminate that lacuna? Would doing so amount to intruding upon a domain exclusively reserved to the constituent powers? Or would we fail in our duties as Community constitutional judges if we do not fill in the lacuna?

Within two years, the Court changed its mind about this matter. It is interesting to note that, on the first occasion, Advocate General Darmon recommended the activist choice, as did Advocate General van Gerven, on the second occasion. And we took his advice even though doing so amounted to a spectacular U-turn.

In my view, the *Chernobyl* decision amounts to the most startling instance of judicial activism in the Court's history, to the extent that it clearly departs from the texts. Now, it is interesting to note that, several years later, this activist decision was welcomed. When the Maastricht Treaty was concluded, the treaties that create the Community were modified so that they recognized the authority of the European Parliament to take necessary measures to protect its prerogatives, conforming to the Court's jurisprudence.

Stephen BREYER: You thought it necessary that the Parliament have the authority to annul certain actions of the Commission?

Robert BADINTER: In the first case, you did not have the power to help the Parliament, and in the second case you found that power. The first beneficiary of this development was the Parliament; the second beneficiary was the Court. The Court gave itself the power to help an institution better carry out its role. The Court gave itself the power to do that before the treaties did so, before Maastricht gave it that power. It is the Court that extended its own authority to the benefit of an equilibrium that the Court considered implicit in the treaties. Even so, it is the Court that created its own power.

Gil Carlos RODRIGUEZ IGLESIAS: Yes. But I should like to emphasize that it was an exceptional matter. Indeed, if there is one area in which the Court is reticent about being "activist," it is that of its own authority. It seems to me that we are aware that our authority flows from the Treaty. And it would be particularly debatable if the Court attributed to itself, through interpretation, powers that were not conferred upon it, even implicitly, by the Treaty.

Consider, by contrast, the matter of the adjudication of complaints by individuals. As we know, individuals can complain only in respect to actions aimed at them as beneficiaries or which at least concern them directly and individually. The Court certainly has developed a jurisprudence that takes account of the demands of the

principle of effective jurisdictional protection. But it has not modified the system that the Treaty put into place in respect to justicia-
bility. In the case of actively legitimating the Parliament's powers,
it did just that and explained how that was so.

Stephen BREYER: The Court changed its mind about the possibility of
finding a Parliamentary authority necessary and legitimate given
the Treaty's silence. Perhaps it is less extraordinary for courts in a
civil law system to change their minds because the force of precedent is less powerful.

Gil Carlos RODRIGUEZ IGLESIAS: It is true that our decisions do not
have the precedential value that those in a common law system
enjoy. That said, the Court does refer systematically to its own jurisprudence, which it is not in the habit of changing. Moreover, at
the time of the cases I was speaking about, it was yet a much more
exceptional thing to do.

In fact, I have noticed, in this respect, a remarkable evolution.
When I came to the Court in 1986, its jurisprudence was sacred. You
did not modify it. And if one made a tiny change, one presented it
as a nuance or one found a difference in the case, distinguishing the
former case. Later in the 1990s, after the *Chernobyl* case, there were
important and explicit turn-arounds in the jurisprudence. These
were instances in which we decided the contrary of what had gone
before, while expressly emphasizing that it was a matter of recon-
sidering the earlier jurisprudence or even using the formula, "contrary to what was previously held." I shall mention, as well-known
examples, the decisions in *HAG II* and *Keck and Mithouard*. I believe
that the Court's attitude today is much more open to changes in its
jurisprudence, even if they remain exceptional.

Ronald DWORKIN: Was it thought necessary to have the other institution ratify the second decision?

Gil Carlos RODRIGUEZ IGLESIAS: A few years later, in the Maastricht
Treaty, the Member States amended the Treaty. And now they have
expressly given the Parliament, under the conditions that we have
recognized in the judgment, the *locus standi* to challenge the legality of acts of other institutions.

Ronald DWORKIN: Suppose your decision had been accepted as an interpretation. Then it would not have been necessary to change the
Treaty?

Gil Carlos RODRIGUEZ IGLESIAS: I do not think that it would have been necessary to change the Treaty. Indeed, after our judgment in *Chernobyl*, nobody challenged the *locus standi* that the Court had recognized with respect to the European Parliament. But, the Maastricht Treaty introduced a change in order to "codify," so to speak, the jurisprudence of the Court.

Ronald DWORKIN: It was a codification—that is, it did not suggest any general sentiment that what you had done needed a change because it was not quite legitimate until the Treaty had been changed?

Gil Carlos RODRIGUEZ IGLESIAS: No, no, I do not think so. I think that it is like—there are several cases—our case law on the fundamental rights, which has always been, to a certain extent, codified in Article 6 of the Treaty on European Union in the same terms. Reference was made to international instruments, in particular the European Convention of Human Rights, and to the common constitutional principles of the Member States—so I do not think that it showed any concern about legitimacy. On the contrary, they said, "Well, since we are changing the Treaty anyway, it would be good to put it *expressis verbis* in the Treaty," but not because it would otherwise have been illegitimate.

Stephen BREYER: The first time that the Parliament sued the Commission, you held that the Parliament could not obtain what it wanted because the Treaty was silent. The second time, you held the opposite, despite the silence, because the Parliament's demand was necessary to maintain the "institutional balance." It sounds as if you believe that the Treaty charges the courts with keeping the institutional balance, including the power to create new procedures where necessary to do so.

Robert BADINTER: That is correct. And I should like to emphasize the words "you create." You create what is not in the Treaty so that the Treaty will work better. But the creation itself is striking. Why is this example particularly striking? Because you, Stephen, belong to an old and great institution rooted in the Constitution of the United States and born with the United States. But there is no European State. These are judges from different states who are imposing upon the political powers in those states an equilibrium in respect to European institutions that those states had previously neither considered nor accepted. This is not the same thing as when an old, well-integrated Court says, "Here it is." Rather, here these "cosmo-politan" judges say, "But the Treaty permits us to do this." After-wards, that is found to be perfectly fine and there is ratification. But what is it that is being ratified? The creation of a Treaty interpreta-tion by judges? At that moment, the Treaty is supreme, for who could deny it? There is, uniquely, a new Treaty provision. There is, in my view, no more striking example of "judicial imperialism," for these are judges who can point to no sovereign authority.

Antonio CASSESE: Do you mind if I ask Steve a question? Would you, in your Court, have applied the "implied powers" doctrine in such a case? This American doctrine has played a significant role and, to some extent, has been applied by courts of continental Europe. This is perhaps the best legal tool when you have no power.

Stephen BREYER: The question of "institutional balance" comes up in different legal contexts. Federal courts often review the actions of federal administrative agencies at the request of a person "ad-versely affected" by the action. We were recently asked by Congress to review an administrative decision. One could consider our hold-ing (that Congress lacked "standing" to obtain that court review) as based upon the need to maintain "institutional balance." We too will change our decisions, on occasion, but we find it easier to change a recent precedent because the public is less likely to have relied upon it yet.

Robert BADINTER: Jurisprudence is like wine. It improves with age.

Dieter GRIMM: It seems to me that almost everything in cases like these depends on the level of abstraction that you choose. The higher the level of abstraction is, the more it becomes possible in methodolog-ical terms. If you choose, say, the equilibrium among the institu-tions as a criterion, very much becomes possible. One level below, it would be very different. When you enter the level of abstraction of separation of powers in general, disconnected from the special way the separation is organized in the United States Constitution, more becomes possible for the judge to do.

Ronald DWORKIN: Do you have any opinion on the correct level of ab-straction?

Robert BADINTER: I have a single question on this point. Can you think of any example of a supreme court that has retreated—that is to say, after having extending its authority, it says, "No, after all, I did not have the right to that authority. I shall give it up"? Are there such examples? You see how this is the inverse. One begins with "I can," and follows with "I cannot." Are there such examples in American jurisprudence?

Stephen BREYER: The courts do say, sometimes, that they lack the power to review certain decisions of other branches of government. The Court held, for example, in *Heckler* v. *Chaney*,[10] that courts could not review the decision of an agency (the Food and Drug Administration) *not* to take action against a certain, allegedly mislabeled, drug. A contrary decision would have given the courts more power; the Court's actual holding gave the courts less power. Still, it was an unusual case.

Antonio CASSESE: I have read somewhere, but I would have to check again, that a French court (I do not know if it was the Cour de Cassation) held that Article 55 of the Constitution, which provides that international treaties trump domestic law, cannot be applied. That would amount to an enormous retreat. But I would have to verify that.

Robert BADINTER: Yes, but that was not an abandoning of authority; it was a sharing of authority. That involved a consideration of the authority, under the French Constitution, of French supreme courts in respect to international treaties. I was thinking of something different. That was a case where, as here, the Court says, "I shall regulate matters to re-establish an equilibrium," but with the inverse consequence. I have never seen that kind of retreat. I have always seen an advance, sometimes in the form of a consolidation; sometimes the form changes, but always one advances. A judicial retreat, say, like Napoleon's from Russia? That I have never seen.

Dieter GRIMM: We have an interesting example of retreat in Germany. Basically, I agree that almost every new interpretation is a broader interpretation so that the side effect is an enlargement of the power of the court. But we have an interesting example where the Court limited its power whereas the drafters of the Constitution amended the Constitution in order to make clear that, in their understanding, the Constitution had a different meaning. It was a federal matter. In the field of concurring legislative powers, the states are permitted to legislate as long and insofar as the federal legislature has not taken over the matter. However, the federal legislature may do so only if there is a special need for uniform legislation. The Court saw no way to review federal legislation as to the existence of such a need. They regarded it as a purely political matter and withdrew from determining the meaning of the necessity clause. Hence, the mere fact that the federal legislature became active in this field was taken as proof of the need. After a number of years—together with a lot of amendments prompted by the unification—this clause was amended as well, making it completely clear that the question whether there was need for uniform legislation should ultimately be decided by the Constitutional Court.

Robert BADINTER: Your case presents an example in which the Court interpreted its own power restrictively or negatively and the Constitution was modified to require it to take action. It is not a case in which the Court began by interpreting its own power broadly and then retreated. Nor was it the Court that required the turn-around. The Court refused to do it, and then the legislature forced it to do so. But did the Court first act and then say that it lacked the authority to do so? A step forward, and then a step backward?

Dieter GRIMM: The Court began by interpreting the clause restrictively. Then the clause was modified.

Stephen BREYER: There are examples. The example I gave is part of a trilogy of cases in which the Court held that courts could not create procedures, which agencies must follow, beyond those already listed in a statute. In the civil rights area, the Court held that "discrimination" included only actions that flowed from a discriminatory "purpose"; the constitutional prohibition did not include actions that, without discriminatory purpose, nonetheless created, say, a racially discriminatory "effect." This holding took considerable power away from the courts (which had previously thought that the law, to the contrary, encompassed discriminatory effect).

One can argue that more conservative governments in the United States have tried to appoint judges who would share a restrictive view of what courts should decide—who would hold a judicial philosophy that would lead them to oppose expansions of court jurisdiction.

Antonio CASSESE: I think that we all agree that there is much opportunity for courts to be innovative and to create new law, as long as, of course, one offers convincing reasoning, one relies upon general principles, and one applies or, if you prefer, one manipulates those principles in a proper and well-balanced way.

However, and this may be of some interest from the perspective of jurisprudence, I think that there is one area where you have to face a huge hurdle, a sort of stumbling block, namely, the area of criminal law. In that field, no court can disregard the right of the accused to know the charge against him, the facts on which the charge is based, and the law supporting the charge. That is why, I think, for instance, in international law, we cannot apply what is normally applied to some extent to Germany, no doubt in France and in Italy— the so-called principle *jura novit curia*. The court is master of the law and can reclassify a crime. So, what if the prosecutor said, "This is theft," and the high court says, "No, no, you are wrong. At the end of the day, I say this is robbery"? Both in common law countries and in international courts, you cannot reclassify the fact because otherwise you impinge upon the basic right of the accused to be fully aware of the legal ingredients of the crime of which he stands accused and to prepare his defense. Therefore, in criminal law, the scope of the court's creativity is limited to a very notable extent.

Let me just give you a very quick example. In the statute of the Yugoslavia Tribunal, there is a very short sentence saying that crimes against humanity are prohibited; it then gives a sort of illustrative list of, say, rape, massive killing of civilians, and so on. But this provision does not specify some of the objective elements of the crime, in particular, the fact that rape as such is a war crime, but becomes a crime against humanity if it is part of a widespread or systematic practice. Nor is the *mens rea* specified, namely, the fact that the accused must be aware not only that he was raping and intended to rape a woman, but also that actually there were a lot of people elsewhere belonging to his own ethnic group raping enemy women. Now, the Court could then specify that, although this was not in the Statute of the Tribunal, it was an important element. This element would play into the hands of the accused, as it places a huge burden on the prosecutor to prove not only that the accused raped a woman, but also that there was a practice in the same area—say, a particular region of Bosnia of, say, all Serbs raping Muslim women.

Ronald DWORKIN: And he knew about it.

Antonio CASSESE: Yes, and that the accused knew about that. Therefore, at one point, the Court could say to the prosecutor, "Look, be careful! The burden of the proof is on you." Now, if this had been against the accused, we could not have done anything, I believe, unless this was done right away, as soon as the trial started.

This is something that is totally extraneous to us in Spain and France and Italy, because in Italy, in France, and in Spain, we have criminal codes with detailed definitions of the crime and of the subjective and objective elements of the crime. As a consequence, it is very easy for a judge to say, "I have the power to reclassify the crime. I do not care if the prosecutor was totally wrong. You should have known that this crime was not probably simply a theft, but was, say, robbery," which is more serious, of course.

Dieter GRIMM: In my understanding, a legal norm consists of three elements, all of which must be taken into account when it comes to interpreting the meaning of a provision vis-à-vis a particular problem. The first element is the text of the norm. The text usually allows more than one interpretation, but not just any interpretation. The text is, however, only the more or less accurate expression of a legislative purpose. The purpose is the second element of the norm. It reduces the number of interpretations compatible with the text. The legislature formulates the norm in light of a certain situation, a given social reality where the norm shall take effect. It is impossible to understand a norm without taking into account the situation that the legislature had in mind when it enacted a law. The segment of social reality in which the norm is to take effect, therefore, constitutes the third element of the norm. The goal of interpretation is to give the purpose of the norm the utmost effect under given conditions of the segment of social reality at which it aims, but only within the limits that the text draws. The text is not at the disposal of the law applicant. It can be changed only by the lawmaker, or, in the case of a constitutional norm, by the constitution maker. Neither is the purpose of the norm at the disposal of the law applicant. Purpose, as well as text, can be modified only by the lawmaker. But unlike the text, which is given, the purpose has to be determined by the law applicant, and this may be a more or less difficult task, which often gives some leeway to the law applicant. The segment of social reality at which the norm is directed is under nobody's control. It is subject to social change, mostly induced by scientific and technological progress and its commercial use. But it can also be a change in value orientation within society. Now, I think that an expansive or creative interpretation is legitimate if, due to social change in the segment of reality addressed by the norm, the traditional interpretation would fail to give the utmost effect to the purpose of the norm. It is also legitimate if, should the interpretation remain the same, the norm would not reach its purpose as effectively as possible or would not reach its purpose at all or would even create dysfunctional results. In this case, it is not only the right but also the duty of the law applicant to give the norm a different—in most cases an enlarged—meaning. Not the law applicant who sticks to a once-found interpretation shows fidelity to the norm, but the one who is willing to adapt the meaning to changing conditions under which the purpose takes effect.

Ronald DWORKIN: What do you mean by the "purpose"? Do you have in mind a psychological fact?

Dieter GRIMM: The purpose is the goal that the legislature pursued by enacting the rule.

Ronald DWORKIN: There is no such fact, is there, typically? There is no fact of the matter about what the legislature's motive is, for a dozen reasons. First, you are not talking about one person, you are talking about hundreds of people. Second, you are talking about a political process in which any one person's motives are several, intertwined, and maybe even contradictory: to win the next election, to curry favor with some constituents, to advance some personal political agenda, to respect some overriding abstract principle of justice, to help cure some immediate technical or commercial problem, and so forth. Third, these different motives are at different levels of abstraction. An individual legislator might want to combat all forms of unjust discrimination, for example, but also not realize that some kinds of discrimination generally accepted in his community—such as discrimination against homosexuals—are actually indefensible. If he votes for a law that condemns unjust discrimination generally, shall we assign him a motive that includes protecting homosexuals from discrimination, even though he did not realize that his overall purpose had that consequence? It is a question of which level of abstraction we choose to formulate his purpose, and there is nothing in his psychological state that decides that for us. A legislative purpose is not a fact waiting to be discovered, but as much a matter of judicial creation as the adaptation to social reality that you want to contrast it with. So, though your suggestion is immensely appealing, I do not think that it is finally helpful, because it depends on there being very hard facts about legislative purpose that can act as independent checks on judges.

Dieter GRIMM: I must admit that the subjective purpose of the authors of the law is almost impossible to determine in a parliamentary democracy. Rather it is the objective purpose of the law that the law applicant tries to determine, and he may take the legislative history into account. In this sense, an element of judicial construction is involved. But I do not think that it is completely impossible to determine the purpose in an objective manner.

Ronald DWORKIN: Yes, but your idea that, when social reality changes, the underlying purpose remains the same suggests that you have a way of discovering the motive that is independent of an assessment about the contemporary needs of the society. And that presupposes a psychological historical fact that you are trying to discover, which seems to me an illusion. Do you see what I mean? If legislative motive is itself a construction, if we must choose one among the myriad possible motives that we can assign to the legislature, can we do that without being guided, in that choice, by our own sense of what the legislature ought to have done? I don't think so.

Dieter GRIMM: I agree. Still, I see a progress of methodology in the way that I described: Formalistic, positivistic methods relied on text only. More illuminated methods, coming up at the turn of the nineteenth to the twentieth century, added purpose. Present methodology takes the segment of reality in which the norm shall take effect as its third element and it allows a fuller understanding of the norm, certainly under conditions of accelerated social change.

Stephen BREYER: I agree. But why does a focus on purpose, which may lead you to consider social conditions, necessarily lead to an expansion of court jurisdiction? Would it not sometimes lead to a contraction?

Dieter GRIMM: This is possible, but usually the opposite happens.

Stephen BREYER: Our Court is currently arguing about "federalism," and that may lead to "contraction."

Dieter GRIMM: Yes. Expansion is not that important for me. My concern is rather: When are changes in interpretation legitimate or even necessary? May I give two examples? I have the idea, although I am not completely sure about it, that, whenever social change appears in the form of technical, scientific, or economic development, it is up to the law applicant to determine the consequences. When it is a value change in society, it is instead up to the legislature to draw the consequences. Here are two examples from the German Constitutional Court:

One is the invention of electronic data processing, a technical innovation with important consequences for the fundamental right, the admittedly very broad fundamental right, of free development of one's personality. People cannot develop their personality freely if the state may know everything about them while they themselves do not know what the state knows. That is it in very brief terms. So, the interpretation of Article 2, Section 1 of the Basic Law amounted to an invention of a new fundamental right, the so-called informational self-determination. Of course, it was derived from this very broad fundamental right, but it amounted to a new fundamental right. Nevertheless, I think that this was legitimate. On the other hand, we now have the draft of a law allowing homosexual couples a sort of legalized partnership that comes close to marriage.

Robert BADINTER: What does "close to marriage" mean?

Dieter GRIMM: There is a public register, where they can register as a recognized partnership that is not called "marriage." They enjoy social security rights, they enjoy inheritance rights and tax privileges similar to those married couples have.

Robert BADINTER: Is it registration by declaration or by contract?

Dieter GRIMM: As far as I know, it is by declaration, and there are some requirements, such as the length of the relationship and the seriousness of relationship. If the requirements are fulfilled, the partnership is recognized in a register like the register for marriages.

Robert BADINTER: And this has legal consequences?

Dieter GRIMM: Yes. Even more than I mentioned. For instance, with regard to children from a previous traditional marriage . . .

Robert BADINTER: Pension rights also?

Dieter GRIMM: I am not quite sure. The bill was introduced only recently.

Robert BADINTER: We have had problems in France with the contractual agreement for homosexuals that is registered. In my opinion, the principle was right, but the legal techniques were bad ones. That is why I wanted to know. The two people go, make a declaration, and they have certain rights under the law.

Dieter GRIMM: My knowledge of the draft stems from the newspapers, so I would not rely on it. But it was introduced in the Parliament.

Robert BADINTER: And passed?

Dieter GRIMM: No, it is pending. The Parliament is now in its summer recess and will discuss the draft soon.

Robert BADINTER: Was it presented by the government or by a member of the Bundestag?

Dieter GRIMM: By the government. Enacting such a law has been part of the coalition agreement between the Social Democrats and the Greens.

Ronald DWORKIN: Suppose a constitutional document has two clauses. The first is a general command for equality, like the Equal Protection Clause of the American Constitution. The second is a clause declaring that marriage enjoys the special protection of the state. Then the question arises, because of some statute like the German legislation you describe, whether the legislature may or even must make distinctions between the kind of legal relationships that are available to heterosexual and homosexual couples. We know, as a matter of historical fact, that, when the clause about the special status of marriage was adopted, most of the people involved in adopting it and the public at large had only heterosexual marriage in mind. We cannot say that, if they had thought about the possibility of homosexual marriage, they would probably have thought of that as a marriage as well. We can say something like that in some cases. We might assume that the drafters of an old statute regulating broadcasting, before television was developed, would have included television if they had known of it. But we cannot say anything parallel about homosexual marriage. So, we need an account of how judges can come to see homosexual marriage as at least consistent with the "special protection" clause that does not depend on any such fiction.

Stephen BREYER: I suspect that your example, referring back to legislative or constitutional purpose, suffers from the levels-of-abstraction problem that you mentioned. One might ask why marriage is given a special status under the law. Suppose the word "marriage" in the Constitution was written at a time when every marriage was a conventional heterosexual union blessed by the Church. Suppose later that civil ceremonies become widespread. Suppose later still that couples live together in what they consider a special relationship—including some of the same sex. Do we want to say that the point of the Constitution's protection is to recognize the religious wedding, the union for the purpose of procreation and the raising of children, and/or the special relationship that the community regards as involving a special long-term commitment? Marriage can be any or all of the above. But how we characterize the "purpose" of the constitutional provision—at what level of abstraction we define it—can affect the outcome.

Dieter GRIMM: I admit that what I said about the level of abstraction also applies to defining the purpose.

Stephen BREYER: We do impute purposes to institutions. We talk about a basketball team's defensive game, which refers to the purpose of the team, not the individual players. We can use the same term about an army and about a legislature. I agree with Ronnie that judges have developed a set of conventions for determining legislative purpose. I can use those conventions to decide whether Congress intended the word "he" in an old jury statute to include women today (even though women, then, did not serve on juries).

Now, I suddenly come to the Constitution. And why it is so difficult is because the conventions that govern how judges resolve the very kind of problem that Dieter is raising are so much less certain and so much more obviously the subject for debate. I can easily, as Ronnie talks, imagine a world in which marriage is as obviously applicable to homosexuals as "he" is to "she." But that is not this world at the moment. I might then ask, what kinds of changes would occur before I thought that? Those changes would not be changes in deciding what the writers meant, as they would be changes in what Dieter has called the social conditions. But where what you are saying becomes so interesting is in trying to determine in that case what the conventions are. That is what I find fascinating in what you are saying. What are the conventions? I am relying on a set of complicated, but rather specific, conventions. They are hard to tease out, but still the nerve of the judicial function is interpretation and the conventions that govern it.

Robert BADINTER: Yes, but then the distinction you have drawn—that it is easier to interpret a statute than the Constitution—seems to me not a technical distinction, but a distinction about the limits of the "sacred." Statutes are contingent. They can easily be changed. But the Constitution in the United States is almost a sacred document. It embodies the birth of the United States. It is the expression of the United States.

The same is not so in our own case. We have gone through 14 constitutions in the two centuries during which you have used only one. Thus, ours is not a sacred document. That is why its interpretation is easier than when one approaches the tablets of the Ten Commandments. I might add that the eighteenth-century constitution has an abstract quality that lends itself to an interpretation that is creative but does not seem to reshape the intentions of those who wrote it. Today, statutes are much more technical and precise. One can adapt them, for one is only changing technical dispositions.

I have an observation about method. We have returned to the problem of judicial interpretation and of jurisprudential creativity. But the agenda for today consists of the question of the judge confronting himself, the judge's responsibility for his own actions. And I would not want us, at the end of the record, to seem to avoid the question that so often is posed to judges: "Very well. You do your work. You are perfectly happy with what you do. But suppose you make a mistake? To whom are you responsible? And for what?"

Gil Carlos RODRIGUEZ IGLESIAS: In my view, the problem of responsibility is tied to that of independence, in that independence limits the possibilities for holding judges responsible. Independence is thought to be a *sine qua non* of judicial activity. But the problem is that the need for judicial independence is hard to reconcile with the creation of a system for assuring responsibility. What kind of responsibility is one to impose upon judges? I refer to Mario Cappelletti's typology, which I mentioned in my paper: political responsibility; social or public responsibility; the state's juridical responsibility for damages caused by judicial actions; and, finally, the judge's personal responsibility of a criminal, civil, or disciplinary nature. It is clear that the judge's personal responsibility should be determined only by a judicial body. And that demand, which seems to me undeniable, is perceived (and I refer particularly to the perception of Spanish public opinion) as creating a kind of responsibility that is, in fact, in practice, limited by the judiciary's "corporate solidarity." Hence, it is a responsibility subject to the criticism of a kind of corporatism, like the kind of ethical responsibility demanded by professional corporations.

In respect to constitutional judges, I believe that the kind of personal responsibility that is required is of a political kind, and more political than that of an ordinary career judge. That personal responsibility is political in the sense that the machinery for determining that responsibility must decide at the end of the day whether a judge's behavior is, or is not, compatible with his continuing to exercise his judicial function. Putting this kind of political responsibility into effect can produce exceptional cases. I believe that this occurred once in the United States. There was a judge who was impeached, wasn't there?

Stephen BREYER: In the early years of the Republic, President Jefferson thought that he could have a Supreme Court Justice impeached on grounds of disagreement with the judge's ideas. The procedure failed. The judge was not convicted.

Robert BADINTER: That is the only example.

Stephen BREYER: That is an important example because it established a precedent that judges could not be impeached on the basis of ideological disagreement.

Robert BADINTER: Are there other examples where the disagreement concerned not ideas, but behavior? Say, for example, he was a drunk.

Stephen BREYER: Yes, but they did not involve Supreme Court Justices. There are other examples of impeachment of federal judges. If a judge is accused of a crime, for example, he is also subject to impeachment, so that he cannot remain a judge.

Gil Carlos RODRIGUEZ IGLESIAS: Thus, I mean that that is the path toward political control. The other possibility is to leave it to the court itself to determine the circumstances. In the one case, there is the risk of an attack on judicial independence through a biased political supervision. In the other case, there is the risk of corporate solidarity. In my paper, I provide the example of the ECJ system. Article 6 of the Statute says that neither judges nor advocates general can be relieved of their duties nor deprived of their rights or other benefits except through a unanimous decision of the Court's judges and advocates general (excluding, naturally, the vote of the interested person). Happily, it has never been necessary to apply this system in practice. It simply provides an example showing how the protection of judicial independence makes it difficult to put in place an effective system of responsibility. That is because the protection of independence involves a certain risk of corporate solidarity.

Robert BADINTER: But suppose it were a majority. How would that change the effect on independence? Now, one can smell corporatism, or so it could be said. It is quite serious. Suppose it were a three-fifths, or two-thirds, majority? Now, one might say it is not independence; it is self-protection. It is more than independence. It is something else besides.

Stephen BREYER: There is a difference between the lower courts and the Supreme Court. We have two disciplinary systems for the lower courts. There is an external system, which is through impeachment. And there is an internal system, involving judicial councils. In respect to the Supreme Court, there is only the external system. And the values of judicial independence prevail. Even when the Justices discuss ethical problems among themselves, no judge would say how another should act—though the latter might ask his colleague's advice. The result is that within the Court one feels very independent. That independence reflects tradition. It is a matter of the Court's customs or habits. If there is a system that perfectly balances the values of independence and responsibility, I am not aware of it.

Gil Carlos RODRIGUEZ IGLESIAS: Thus, in my view, the problem of responsibility is a problem that has not been resolved.

Dieter GRIMM: We require a two-thirds majority in the Constitutional Court in order to impeach a judge.

Gil Carlos RODRIGUEZ IGLESIAS: In respect to the personal responsibility of a constitutional or supreme court judge, I do not see any good solution that could reconcile independence and responsibility. To give political bodies the authority to supervise judicial responsibility threatens independence. And the prevailing system, which gives the judges themselves sole power to supervise, places corporate solidarity in the balance over and against responsibility.

The problem obviously is different in respect to lower court judges. There, the general direction taken in our countries has been to remove disciplinary power—the power to supervise—from the executive, from the Ministry of Justice, in order to give it to bodies that are independent of executive power, such as the Conseil Supérieur de la Magistrature. That amounts to considerable progress.

Apart from situations that call for criminal or political responsibility, I believe that the kind of responsibility more effective in supervising judicial activity, particularly that of constitutional courts, is what is called public or social responsibility (in Cappelletti's typology). These courts, in order to carry out their functions, must have *Akzeptanz*, as they say in German. They must enjoy social acceptance. They must have a credibility without which they cannot survive. And I believe that insistence that courts give reasons for their decisions, along with criticism of their decisions, arising both in judicial circles and also political, economic, and social circles, provides an important method for supervising and for insisting upon a certain public or social responsibility.

Before concluding, I should like to mention the composition of the Spanish General Council of the Judiciary. It has broad jurisdictional authority, not only in disciplinary matters, but also in respect to training, judicial nomination, selection, promotion, and other matters. According to the Constitution (and it is a body for which the Constitution provides), the Council is composed of 20 members, who then elect the President. That President is, at the same time, President of the Supreme Court, serving a term of five years. According to the Constitution, 12 members will be selected from among the judiciary; 8 members will be selected from among those jurists with 15 years of professional experience who have been elected by the two chambers of Parliament. The first organic statute for the judiciary provided that the 12 judges would be elected by the judges themselves—a practice that has taken on considerable importance for Spanish judicial organizations.

This system began to operate in 1979. Then, in 1985, the organic statute was changed to provide that the Parliament would henceforth elect all the members. Twelve must be judges, but elected by the Parliament with a three-fifths majority. This modification was challenged before the Constitutional Court. Those who claimed that the law was unconstitutional argued that electing the 12 magistrates through the vote of their peers guaranteed judicial independence, the representative nature of those who governed, and, hence, self-government by the judiciary. The Constitutional Court did not accept this argument. The Court decided that the statute was in conformity with the Constitution. It was consistent with the text (12 members must be elected from "among" the judges, not "by" the judges). The Constitutional Court also believed that judicial independence is not independence of a corporate body of judges. It is the independence of courts and of each judge when that judge exercises judicial jurisdiction. It is not a form of corporate independence.

Robert BADINTER: Judicial independence is independence of the judge, not of a corporate body. That is very interesting.

Gil Carlos RODRIGUEZ IGLESIAS: The Court also said that the 12 judges are meant to be members of the Council, not in order to represent judges, but so that the Council would be composed in part of 12 people who, because of their professional experience as magistrates, could help the Council reach proper decisions. It added that it was not a matter of assuring judicial self-government, but of assuring that the governmental judicial body would be independent of the other governmental authorities. That could be done through other guarantees, without insisting that the body represent the judges' corps.

I believe that was the essence of the holding. But there were quite a few nuances. The Constitutional Court also said that it would be unconstitutional to apply the system in a way that simply reproduced, within the Council of the Judiciary, the balance of forces within the Parliament.

Stephen BREYER: Is there a tradition that conservative parliamentarians will try to elect conservative judges?

Gil Carlos RODRIGUEZ IGLESIAS: The connection with parliamentary forces is reflected in the political bent (if I can call it that) of the majority and the minority within the General Judicial Council. And that Council selects the judges. But I do not think that that has any consequence in respect to the actual selection of judges, which is not at all a politicized process.

Robert BADINTER: By "selection," do you mean promotion or initial nomination?

Gil Carlos RODRIGUEZ IGLESIAS: Initial nomination.

Stephen BREYER: Promotion is important. But in our federal system, there is almost no promotion.

Robert BADINTER: There is no promotion? That is to say that a trial court judge will not become an appellate court judge?

Stephen BREYER: Exactly so.

Robert BADINTER: Why?

Stephen BREYER: Because when you leave a lawyer's career to become a judge (at the age of between 40 and 50), you enter at a particular level and do not expect to be promoted.

Robert BADINTER: Thus, at the beginning, one is a candidate for a certain judicial function. Subsequently, you do not change. You do not advance.

Stephen BREYER: Except in certain exceptional cases.

Robert BADINTER: But all the Supreme Court Justices were judges before.

Stephen BREYER: Yes, but you cannot expect to be appointed to the Supreme Court. That kind of nomination is like a stroke of lightning. And it would not only be inappropriate, but also futile for a judge to work toward it, *i.e.*, decide cases with an eye toward being appointed to that Court.

Judges are appointed to federal trial courts at the age of 40 to 50 years old. State court systems of selection vary among the states. There are quite a few that provide for direct election of judges by the voters. There are others where the governor appoints a judge subject to confirmation by the voters. There are also systems in which voters reconfirm a judge every seven years. Systems like this can bring politics into the selection process and threaten judicial independence.

Gil Carlos RODRIGUEZ IGLESIAS: As I told you, I believe that, in Spain, a judicial appointment has nothing to do with politics. I also believe that promotions are based upon professional criteria, perhaps placing a little too much weight upon seniority. It is also my impression (though I stress that I am an outside observer, for I have never been a judge in Spain) that, when appointments to high posts, important posts (such as presidents of Superior Regional Courts of autonomous regions and Supreme Court Justices), are at issue, considerations related to a candidate's political profile sometimes play an important role. That does not happen systematically, but it happens.

Robert BADINTER: That strikes me as a dangerous system. That is because the Parliament is, of all bodies, the one where appointments will have the most political character. That is how parliaments work. They do not make gifts. The majority never gives the minority a gift. A three-fifths majority requirement may help create a balance.

Originally, the selection process for the Italian High Council of the Judiciary involved parliamentary appointment by a weighted majority. It took a long time to fill the positions because the Parliament could not agree. Eventually, negotiations took place in the corridors. The Right would vote for a judge presented by the Socialists on the condition that the Socialists would vote for a judge presented by the Right. What was done took place through negotiation in the corridors. And, whatever might be the intent, the judges eventually appointed are seen by the public, in the High Council of the Judiciary, as, one, a judge from the Left and, the other, a judge from the Right. Hence, political bent viewed from the outside is striking. That is very bad.

Stephen BREYER: In France?

Robert BADINTER: In France, we are in the midst of an evolution. In 1993, there was a reform, which created a body composed of a majority of elective judges, with the remainder being personalities named by the President of the Republic, by the President of the Senate, and by the President of the National Assembly. But that was not sufficient, and, now, we are going further.

We are trying to re-equilibrate. We speak of independence, yes, but on the condition that it does not lead to corporate solidarity. Hence, the powers of the High Council of the Judiciary have grown, but, inside the Council, the number of judge-members will be one less than the number of non-judge-members. The latter will be appointed in various ways. Some will be designated by the President of the Senate, others designated by the President of the National Assembly, others by the President of the Republic, still others are designated by agreement among the presidents of the three major jurisdictions, the Cour de Cassation, etc. It has become a cocktail. But that has happened through trying to avoid both corporatism and politicization. We hope that it will work. We think it particularly important that, as we increase the judiciary's independence from political bodies, we avoid corporatism.

Dieter GRIMM: In Germany, it differs from state to state, and between the *Länder* and the federation. The first two instances of the judiciary are state courts, the third instance is a federal court. On the federal level, that is to say, for the courts of last resort, a council is established, which is composed of the Federal Minister of Justice, 16 state Ministers of Justice, and an equal number of parliamentarians. But the court has a great say in it. The court to which the appointment is to be made gives its opinion. If the court regards a candidate as not sufficiently qualified, the committee is unlikely to elect the person. On the state level, some states have similar councils, others do not. Appointments are then the responsibility of the Minister of Justice. The Constitutional Court is under a different regime. One-half of the judges is elected by one house of Parliament, the other by the other house, always with a two-thirds majority. The quorum makes an agreement among the major political parties necessary. The practice is not that one party lets the candidate of the other pass and vice versa. But both sides try to find a common solution. This excludes strong partisan members and favors mainstream members with a good professional record who are acceptable for both sides.

Stephen BREYER: What stops the judiciary from becoming overly political if the promotion of judges is in the hands of the committee that includes parliamentarians?

Robert BADINTER: No, in France, there are no members who are parliamentarians.

Dieter GRIMM: The quorum plays an important role. It prevents the majority party from putting its candidates through. The majority has to find an agreement with the minority. This necessity works in favor of professional criteria and against political criteria. But it would be false to deny that a political element is involved.

Stephen BREYER: In France, you are thinking of changing the High Council of the Judiciary. But in what direction? Would you give more power, or less power, to the politicians?

Robert BADINTER: Less self-government to the judges.

Stephen BREYER: With respect to promotions?

Robert BADINTER: Decisions about promotions today are made in practice by the High Council of the Judiciary.

Stephen BREYER: And after the changes take place?

Robert BADINTER: The revision will increase the High Council's power in respect to prosecutors (*le parquet*). Currently sitting judges (*le siège*) are appointed by the High Council directly. The Council proposes candidates for top positions to the President of the Republic, but, in fact, it is the Council that decides.

Prosecutors are a different matter. The chief prosecutors (the *procureurs généraux*) are named in the Council of Ministers. That means that the President of the Republic and the Prime Minister must agree upon the Justice Minister's proposal. The national prosecutors (*procureurs de la république*) are named by the Minister with the consultative advice of the High Council of the Judiciary. In the beginning, between 1993 and 1995, the Minister followed that advice when appointing prosecutors. From 1995 to 1997, the Minister did not follow that advice when it did not suit her. She even decided contrary to that advice, which produced quite a few tales. But now, the Minister of Justice scrupulously follows the High Council's advice, even if she thinks that the advice is bad. Why? In order to show that judging is an independent career. How does it happen that sometimes the advice is bad? Because the choice of judges by judges reflects a certain union struggle within the judicial corps. And the system for electing the members of the High Council of the Judiciary favors the majority centrist union within the judiciary.

Dieter GRIMM: This is very interesting—whether the judges are organized in unions or not. In Germany, we have a professional organization of judges, and many judges are members. But this organization does not have the status and the function of a union. There is no special union for members of the judiciary. Judges have the right to become members of a more general union, the union for the civil service, for instance. But only very few make use of this right.

Robert BADINTER: In France, judges' unions play a very important role. In Italy too. I do not know if that is so in Spain.

Gil Carlos RODRIGUEZ IGLESIAS: In Spain, I believe that only a minority of judges are affiliated with an association. But the associations still play an important role.

Robert BADINTER: The unions play a role. But the risk is not one of selection for top jobs by the High Council. The true risk is that the members of the High Council simply express the views of the unions. There, we have pure corporatism with union leaders dominating the judiciary. I consider that worse than domination by politicians, for politicians are subject to the invective and criticism of the press and in the Parliament. But if you are president of the majority judges' union, then it is you who in reality determine a judge's career—without regard to criticism and without fear of losing your own job (given the way elections go within the judiciary). That is very, very serious. It amounts to power without responsibility. And it is one of the great dangers that we have mentioned during this discussion: We turn from the Charybdis of political supervision of the judge's career to the Scylla of corporatist control of the judge's career.

Dieter GRIMM: I believe that there is a decisive difference. In Germany, unions play no role in the selection or promotion of judges.

Robert BADINTER: I do not know what happens in Spain in respect to promotion or selection, but, in France, they are ardent.

Stephen BREYER: Before the revision, what was the composition of the Council?

Robert BADINTER: The Council was composed of a majority of elected judges, and completed with personalities designated—I do not know if it is two or three—by the President of the Republic, the President of the Senate, and the President of the National Assembly. It is the same in respect to the Conseil Constitutionnel. Because the selection system for the Conseil Constitutionnel worked well, it inspired the High Council selection system. Thus, there is no direct selection by assemblies or only by presidents.

Stephen BREYER: And after the revision, the judges are going to elect only a minority?

Robert BADINTER: Yes, a minority. They will not have a majority, but only by one vote. And the Conseil d'Etat will elect a representative to the High Council of the Judiciary.

Stephen BREYER: But there will still be less political influence because the Minister must listen to the Council and will lose the power to select someone else?

Robert BADINTER: No. The procedure must begin with the Council. And remember that, as far as the sitting judges, those who judge (*magistrats du siège*) are concerned, it is the Council who appoints them. They are consequently protected from complete control of nomination and selection by the Minister of Justice.

Stephen BREYER: Hence, both systems risk bad exterior influence, either political influence or the influence of judicial corporatism. But despite those risks, but for rare instances, judges decide cases without being affected by those influences—even in the United States in states with systems that elect judges. Why?

Robert BADINTER: I shall tell you. I very deeply believe that the reason is *esprit de corps*—the feeling that one is part of a body that has its ethic, its role, and where esteem and internal respect have major importance. Apart from a few careerists, that esteem, that *esprit de corps*, even if it has a corporatist aspect, has very great importance.

Dieter GRIMM: I would say professionalization and institutional self-interest. The institution of the judiciary can only be upheld in its importance if it shows that it is something different from politics. I think that this is well known, and these two considerations, which may be two sides of the coin—professionalization and institutional self-interest—are, in my view, the most important safeguards. But it can happen that a system declines so much that it is very difficult to get it back to the level it should have.

Stephen BREYER: Why? Certainly, we have a professional system, and we are all professionals—even where, as in the United States, a judge does not follow a judicial career throughout his life. There are professional customs, such as those opposed to media exposure. And the American judge who has made himself a star in the press will find himself scorned by other judges. What do people think in France about such a judge?

Robert BADINTER: They think that his behavior is narcissistic; he needs to be a star, to have his name in the newspaper, and to appear on television. And they sneer, they laugh, and they make disagreeable comments. But the temptation of media stardom may nonetheless be strong among the generation of young magistrates. They may have a taste for media glory and for celebrity that will prevail against the more corporatist considerations. I am not certain. But I think that the media temptation is very strong within the contemporary *magistrature.* When you become as famous as Judge Garzon, you become a world celebrity—because he succeeded in prosecuting Pinochet. He provides an example for young magistrates. He is a veritable celebrity both within and outside his own country. And that opens up many possibilities. That, in my view, is a new element.

If I may, I should like to make a distinction. The judges who decide cases, the *juges du siège,* are less sensitive to the temptations of stardom. Those temptations are strongest at the level of *juges d'instruction* or certain prosecutors. Because they, the investigators and prosecutors, represent good against evil, and because they represent the small individual against the powerful forces of evil, they appear in the media as those who render justice. They do so far more than the judges themselves. Consequently, this media temptation, the taste for stardom, is encountered more frequently at the prosecutorial level, the level of *juges d'instruction* and *procureur.*

Why? Because what interests the public is criminal cases. The element that fascinates the press is the search for the truth and, preferably, snatching away from the powerful their masks of hypocrisy and revealing their faults. The prosecutor loves the cameras. If I remember correctly, the judge in the *O. J. Simpson* case seemed ridiculous; it was the prosecuting attorney who became a star and sold her memoirs for several million dollars.

Stephen BREYER: Perhaps. But the professional reputation of a judge who seeks media stardom is not a good one. Still, our prosecutors, the equivalent of your *juges de parquet,* can become known in the media and begin a political career. Some say that that is a good reason to have a more thorough training system for prosecutors, such as you have in France with your system that is more inquisitorial than adversarial.

Robert BADINTER: Prosecutors everywhere launch prosecutions and carry them forward. But certain ones like others to know what they do. In Italy, everyone knows the story of Mr. Di Pietro, who became a national star and a political personality, and who thought seriously about the presidency of the Republic. In France, when the public opinion polls ask, "Who, among the outsiders, after Mr. Jospin and Mr. Chirac, would you like to see as President of the Republic?" the person who receives the most votes is Mme. Eva Joly, the prosecutor. It opens quite a few paths.

Dieter GRIMM: I could not name one German *procureur* by name.

Robert BADINTER: You couldn't name one?

Dieter GRIMM: No. I could name the *Generalbundesanwalt,* the chief prosecutor. I could name him. But nobody else. Prosecutors do not get much attention as individuals in Germany.

Stephen BREYER: Are they judges?

Dieter GRIMM: They are not judges, but they must be qualified to be judges. They have the same education and undergo the same exams. And very often there is a back and forth. Even in highly political cases like the Kohl investigation at present, one does not know who the prosecutor is who did that. And he does not, or she does not, appear in public. If someone appears in public, it is the press spokesman of the office. It is not the inquiring prosecutor in person. I think that it is astonishing that I, although I am an insider, could not tell you names.

Stephen BREYER: In the United States, you would know. To make the French or Spanish system more adversarial and less "inquisitorial" might not change the behavior of prosecutors. But it would lead the public to stop thinking of them as judges and it could lead to the development of other, adversarial-like, safeguards.

Dieter GRIMM: Take Bavaria, for instance. Bavaria has a rule that everyone who is appointed to be a judge first has to serve for some years in the prosecution office. Some like it so much that they stay, but most of them look forward to entering the judiciary as soon as possible. It may well have an impact on mentality when you want to become a judge, when you do not see prosecution as your ultimate goal.

Robert BADINTER: In my view, the temptation, the problem of the media star, is diabolical. That is because the journalists are interested not in the magistrate (the prosecutor), but in the case. Consequently, the magistrate, if he suffers from the star syndrome, will devote himself to those cases most likely to attract that kind of interest. It is more interesting to investigate a misappropriation of funds, even if very minor, carried out by a politician than a very important misappropriation of funds carried out in a company that interests no one. That is because there is a consequence called "stardom." It is all narcissism. And, unfortunately, I am convinced that it is a motive that is in play. I was scandalized and appalled by the presence of all the television cameras and all the photographers the day when the *juges d'instruction* went to question Roland Dumas.

Stephen BREYER: Our prosecutors also have been known to handcuff suspects where there is no need to do so, perhaps with an eye toward a picture in the press.

Robert BADINTER: We saw the cars of the major newspaper photographers arrive before the *juges d'instruction*. When Dumas left his house with those judges, there was a crowd of journalists there to photograph him, including the television cameras. There was not yet proof of wrongdoing. It is terrible. And it appeared in Paris on the eight o'clock evening news. That is political death. For a constitutional judge, it is worse still. And, of course, those judges proclaimed their good faith: "It was chance. Someone working with the police must have told the press. I do not know who it was." How can you prove who was responsible for that performance?

Stephen BREYER: Are there rules about what can be said to the press?

Robert BADINTER: Absolutely. Respect for professional secrets exists in our law. There is a charming nineteenth-century phrase to the effect that "discretion suits judges as virtue suits women." We are very far from those old principles.

Stephen BREYER: There seem to be three kinds of remedies. First, there is the judge's age. Age brings with it wisdom, tranquility, and maturity. Second, there are rules that limit what can be given to the media. Third, there are rules that take account of the fact that the media will learn everything anyway and try to protect defendants.

Robert BADINTER: Yes, but there is another also, which I personally consider very important. That is the judge's own ethics. That is why I called this session "The Judge Confronts Himself as Judge." It is necessary to inculcate in the young magistrates the conviction that it is not in the media that their fulfillment lies and that the court of public opinion is not the court that judges the merits of the magistracy. You are not a better judge because you are talked about. One must find one's satisfaction in the work itself and not in the narcissistic vanity that accompanies that work. It is not the kind of craft where you should become interested in the opinion that people hold of you. Otherwise you are lost.

Men and women who are politicians depend upon their image. But a judge? For what does a judge need to become a star and have his or her photograph in *Paris Match*? That in itself is a deviation. I believe that it is an error for a magistrate. The lawyers are worse. But inside the *magistrature*, certain ones think differently. The glory of appearing like a sheriff meting out justice provides a considerable narcissistic satisfaction, but it will not make you a good professional, let alone a decent professional.

Stephen BREYER: They look for glory in the press. But he who lives by the sword, dies by the sword.

Robert BADINTER: Yes, but the judge will not die. It is those whom he judges whom it may kill.

NOTES

1. Case 302/87, Rec. p. 5615.
2. Case C-70/88, Rec. p. I-2041.
3. Case C-2/88, Rec. p. 3365.
4. Aharon Barak, *Judicial Discretion,* Yale University Press, 1987, p. 121.
5. Ninian M. Stephen, "Judicial Independence—A Fragile Bastion," in *Judicial Independence: The Contemporary Debate,* Martinus Nijhoff, 1985, p. 529.

6. See, for example, the writings of P. Pescatore, the former judge of the Court of Justice of the European Community, most notably, "La protection judiciaire des droits individuels comme facteur de démocratie" ("Judicial Protection of Individual Rights as an Element of Democracy"), Centre Universitaire de Luxembourg, 1995.

7. BOE of August 13, 1986.

8. *In re Pinochet,* Jan. 15, 1999.

9. M. Cappelletti, "Who Watches the Watchmen? A Comparative Study on Judicial Responsibility," in *Judicial Independence: The Contemporary Debate,* Martinus Nijhoff, 1985, p. 550.

10. 470 U.S. 821 (1985).

About the Participants

Robert Badinter
Former president of the Constitutional Council of France
Former Minister of Justice of France

Stephen Breyer
Justice of the Supreme Court of the United States
Former Professor of Law, Harvard Law School

Antonio Cassese
Professor of Constitutional Law, University of Florence
Former President, Criminal Tribunal for the former Yugoslavia

Ronald Dworkin
Frank Henry Sommer Professor at NYU School of Law
Quain Professor of Jurisprudence at University College, London
H. L. A. Hart Professor of Jurisprudence Emeritus at Oxford University

Dieter Grimm
Professor of Constitutional Law, University of Berlin
Former Member, Federal Constitutional Court of Germany

Gil Carlos Rodriguez Iglesias
President, Court of Justice of the European Communities